The Pedagogy of
Violent Extremism

Violence Studies

Felix Ó Murchadha
General Editor

Vol. 4

This book is a volume in a Peter Lang monograph series.
Every volume is peer reviewed and meets
the highest quality standards for content and production.

PETER LANG
New York • Bern • Frankfurt • Berlin
Brussels • Vienna • Oxford • Warsaw

Ygnacio V. Flores

The Pedagogy of
Violent Extremism

PETER LANG
New York • Bern • Frankfurt • Berlin
Brussels • Vienna • Oxford • Warsaw

Library of Congress Cataloging-in-Publication Data
Names: Flores, Ygnacio V., author.
Title: The pedagogy of violent extremism / Ygnacio V. Flores.
Description: New York: Peter Lang, 2017.
Series: Violence studies vol. 4 | ISSN 2161-2668
Includes bibliographical references and index.
Identifiers: LCCN 2016031295 | ISBN 978-1-4331-3529-3 (hardcover: alk. paper)
ISBN 978-1-4539-1923-1 (ebook pdf) | ISBN 978-1-4331-3850-8 (epub)
ISBN 978-1-4331-3851-5 (mobi)
Subjects: LCSH: Radicalism—United States.
Political violence—United States. | Terrorism—United States.
Classification: LCC HN90.R3 F625 2017 | DDC 303.48/4—dc23
LC record available at https://lccn.loc.gov/2016031295
DOI: 10.3726/978-1-4539-1923-1

Bibliographic information published by **Die Deutsche Nationalbibliothek**.
Die Deutsche Nationalbibliothek lists this publication in the "Deutsche
Nationalbibliografie"; detailed bibliographic data are available
on the Internet at http://dnb.d-nb.de/.

The paper in this book meets the guidelines for permanence and durability
of the Committee on Production Guidelines for Book Longevity
of the Council of Library Resources.

I want to thank my colleagues and friends, Kurt Motamedi, Alexander Siedschlag, Don Mason, Tracy Rickman, Masis Sossikian, and Tarek Azmy, that provided me with valuable feedback and criticism on my draft manuscripts. I especially want to thank my wife, Kaori, and our children, Mitsumi, Kanami, and Yoshihisa, for providing me with the time to research and write this book—they let me stay in "the zone." Kaori and Mitsumi also served as my sounding board—particularly Mitsumi who challenged my ideas. He also created the illustration below after reading one of my draft manuscripts. It captures the essence of my message. I cannot say thank you enough.

Last, this is dedicated to my parents, Lydia and Ygnacio. They left this world too soon. Also, to my step-mother Lupe, who kindly shared with me, my father's time. I will especially miss my morning conversations with my father. His critical perspective of the world strengthened how I presented my ideas used in this book. I regret I did not finish this project sooner so he could comment on it.

Hegemonically Provoked Violent Extremism.
Source: Peach Munkey, Copyright 2015.

TABLE OF CONTENTS

Table of Figures   xi
Preface   xiii

Book 1: Pedagogy Reframed   1
  Paulo Freire's Critical Pedagogy   1
  Phenomenology of Violent Extremism   3
  Theory of Hegemonically Provoked
  Violent Extremism   4
  Hegemonic Oppression   10
      Banking Hegemony: Analysis of American Strategy on
      Preventing Violent Extremism   12
  Discovering how to Hate   15
      Banking American Hegemony: The Global Area   16
      Banking American Hegemony: The Domestic Area   20
      Violent Extremism Supports Regime Continuity   22
      Folktales, Heroes and Violence   24
      Min Erhabi?   28
  Evolution of the Terrorist Training Curriculum   31

Book 2: The Face of America's Third Civilization   63
    Mismanaging America's Demographic Shift and the
    Rise of Violent Extremism   63
        Overview   63
        Violent Extremism in Response to a Demographic Shift   66
        The Faces of American Civilizations   68
        Faith, Conversion, and Fundamentalism   70
        Diaspora and Tribalism   72
        Rise of Homegrown Violent Extremism in America   76
        Enriching America's Third Civilization   79
        The Internet and Violent Extremism   80
        Conclusions: The Calculus of Convergent Variables in
        Creating Homegrown Terrorism   82
Book 3: Homegrown Violent Extremism as an IED   91
    Part I—U.S. Immigration Policy   91
        Background   91
        Effects of Immigration   94
        Acculturation   95
        Failure to Assimilate   97
        Immigrant Power   98
    Part II—Anti-immigration Attitudes   100
        The Right: Anti-immigrationism   101
        The Left: Proimmigrationism   103
        Analysis of Threats Now and in the Future   105
        Inferences   106
    Part III—Immigration and Religious Intolerance   107
        Overview   107
        Homegrown Terrorism as Violent Extremism   107
        Islamic Extremists   109
        Christian Extremists   110
        Fearing Change   112
        The Decay of Religious Tolerance   113
        The Future of Extreme Violence   114

Book 4: Advance and Transfer   131
    Naval Shiphandling and Violent Extremism   131
    The Farsighted: Voices of Thunder   134
    Conclusions   135

References   139
Index   167

TABLE OF FIGURES

Figure 1.1: Hegemonically Provoked Violent Extremism.   6
Figure 1.2: Formula for Violent Extremism.   6
Figure 1.3: Violent Extremism Increasing Model.   7
Figure 1.4: Violent Extremism Decreasing Model.   8
Figure 1.5: Dictatorial Police State Model.   8
Figure 1.6: Anarchic Model.   8
Figure 1.7: Iceberg of Violent Extremism.   9
Figure 2.1: Demographic Shift in the United States, 1900–2000.   64
Figure 2.2: Refugee Arrivals in the United States, 2004–2013.   65
Figure 3.1: Immigration as IED Components.   92
Figure 4.1: Advance and Transfer Model.   133

PREFACE

First and foremost, let me be clear that I have spent twenty-seven years proudly serving in the U.S. Navy as an enlisted and commissioned officer, specializing in law enforcement, physical security, antiterrorism, and force protection. Following my military service are ten years of working in higher education, educating and training men and women to serve in law enforcement, fire and emergency medical services. I am a proud American who has put his life on the line many times, and would do so again without hesitation. While The Pedagogy of Violent Extremism introduces many controversial ideas, these viewpoints are not necessarily mine; however, they represent thematic perspectives of what I discovered through extensive research. While I introduce ideas intended for provoking thought, many discussions within this book create dialogue in sensitive areas, are poignant philosophies that strike a nerve—even in me, as I try to remain unbiased—nevertheless, the sentiments captured in my analysis do exist.

I have explored terrorism in its many constructs for over thirty years. Besides reading the books of the leading experts on terrorism like Brian Michael Jenkins (2010; 2011; 2014) and Bruce Hoffman (2006; 2007; 2013), I also sought out the voices of those who spoke for changes that countered mainstream Western society with violence. There was Carlos Marighella and his Minimanual of the Urban Guerrilla (1969/2008), William Powell's The

Anarchist Cookbook (1971), Che Guevara's *The Motorcycle Diaries* (1995/2003) and *Guerrilla Warfare* (1961/2012), and Andrew Macdonald's *The Turner Diaries* (1978/1996). Later, there was the *Al Qaeda Training Manual* (2000) and speeches of Usama bin Laden (Lawrence, 2005), Ayman al-Zawahiri (Mansfield, 2006), and Anwar al-Awlaki (Sloan & Al-Ashanti, 2011). Understanding the latest wave of terrorism caused a resurgence of reflection and a return to the writings of Seyyid Qutb (1953/2000; 1991; 2005), Thomas Edward Lawrence (1922/2011), David Galula (1964/2001), and Mao Tse Tung (2012).

Western academia kept pace with the changing nature of terrorism as Jessica Stern (2000), Mia Bloom (2005), Reza Aslan (2009), and Fareed Zakaria (2013) added to the knowledge domain of terrorism. New to contemporary terrorism was the introduction of a Middle Eastern voice through Al Jazeera. Perspectives on terrorism now had a serious opinion that was not supportive of the Western hegemony many terrorists were fighting. Protecting America within its borders became a priority that had tentacles reaching into every social, political, market, and religious practice around the world. This effort coined the term homeland security (9/11 Commission, 2004). While protecting America, on paper, at least, the idea of homeland security (Bush, 2007) and its global reach became a raison d'être for escalating the use of extreme violence in confronting America and its allies as the War on Terrorism entered a quagmire murkier than that of the Vietnam War. New to American planning was the idea of America being a theater of war. Learning how to protect the homeland entered the undefined space between defense and security. Law enforcement and the Department of Defense never worked as closely as they have since homeland security became a priority mission for America. Unfortunately, America learned too late that terrorism was to become part of the American landscape (9/11 Commission, 2004).

After the 1983 bombing of the Marine Barracks in Beirut, military leaders developed a Department of Defense wide system to protect its personnel and bases overseas. The protective structure became the force protection system. Other than forces stationed overseas, there was little attention given to force protection by civilians in America. During this period, the violence of terrorism was viewed as an "over there" phenomenon. This changed on September 11, 2001 when America experienced multiple attacks by Al Qaeda terrorists using passenger airplanes as the delivery system for violence.

Al Qaeda changed the paradigm on using extreme violence as part of terrorism (German, 2007). In response, the War on Terrorism (Carafano, Bucci & Zukerman, 2012) resulted in America invading Afghanistan and later Iraq.

The killing of Usama bin Laden in 2011 did not result in a victory over terrorism as Al Qaeda continued to attack their enemies (Habeck, 2012). As many in the Western world thought America was winning the War on Terrorism, a new threat rose in the Levant. Though American leaders initially disregarded the threat posed by Abu Bakr al-Baghdadi as he sought to establish an Islamic state in territory that spanned parts of Syria and Iraq, al-Baghdadi declared a caliphate in 2014 under the name of the Islamic State (Dassanayake, 2015).

The Islamic State, shunned by Al Qaeda for its extreme use of violence, set a new bar for violent extremism through its signature use of recording the beheadings of its victims, mass killings, and the execution of a Jordanian pilot by resurrecting the act of auto-da-fé as a punishment (Rose, 2014; Warrick, 2015). The idea of a quick victory over the Islamic State is an idea only a fool would still believe as al-Baghdadi manages to expand his territory, terror, and violence.

Along with the rise of violence introduced by Al Qaeda and perfected by the Islamic State, came the escalation of individual actors using violent extremism to support terrorist causes or make a distinct statement to their society (Rose, 2014; Didymus, 2015). Distinctive among those supporting terrorist causes, particularly those with Islamic-based extractions was the emigration of Westerners to the terrorist wars overseas (Straziuso, Forliti & Watson, 2012), especially those fighting for the Islamic State (Coughlin, 2014). The concept of Westerners fighting for the Islamic State became an inconceivable idea to leaders, parents, and friends in Europe and America (Zalikind, 2015).

Adding to the tapestry of violent extremism is the increase of what many (Jenkins; 2011; Jenkins, Liepman & Willis, 2014) have called the lone wolf actors—though not always associated with terrorism (Ziv, 2014; Blinder, 2016)—that orchestrate acts of extreme violence with plans to kill as many people as possible before being captured or killed themselves. This trend caused many in America to ask questions of why people like Nidal Hasan (Kenber, 2013), Aaron Alexis (Hermann & Marimow, 2013), Elliot Rodger (Wolf, 2015), James Holmes (Takeda, 2015), One Goh (Fraley, 2015), John Zawahiri (Serrano, Blankstein & Gerber, 2013), Adam Lanza (Ziv, 2014), Dylann Roof (Blinder, 2016), Chris Mercer (Healy & Lovett, 2015), and others chose to use extreme violence to relate a message to society.

Notable in the coverage of these killings is how the Islamic faith became a focal point as a cause of the violence while Christianity's role in the violence largely escaped attention as a casual factor. These mass killings also caused security professionals and academia to question the definition of terrorism as contemporary violent extremism did not fit the previous concepts of terror-ism (Burke, 2016). Terrorism, as the term du jour became pedestrian as many insignificant acts, like a child drawing a picture of a gun (Thompson, 2010) falls into the realm of terrorism—complete with arrests and judicial proceed-ings. Conversely, the tendency to align terrorism with Islam missed labeling many acts committed by Americans as criminal acts instead of terrorism (Sha-pira, 2010; Sonner 2014; Ziv, 2014). Therefore, I approach this book with the view that terrorism as defined by the end of the previous century, has outlived its past defining factors and been superseded by violent extremism—a concept that looks at the outcomes, or intended outcomes of acts committed.

A significant challenge I encountered while exploring violent extremism was how to approach a serious study of the phenomenon. Reiterating past per-spectives only adds to the numerous volumes on terrorism that do not explore the deep causal factors of violent extremism. While pundits on terrorism point to alienation, disenfranchisement, and cultural divides as causes of violence, their analysis does not go deep enough into the social foundations and con-structs that foster and nurture the ability of a person to commit acts of violent extremism. I recognized the call for an innovative approach to understanding violent extremism. The current construct of terrorism, as used in the West, has long nurtured hate against America since the end of the Second World War. While professing democratic growth in the Third World, we have seen the effects of a cradle to grave process in which American values have the unin-tended consequences of teaching people to hate Westernization—much like the West African terrorist group, Boko Haram, whose very name translates to a version of *Against Western Learning* (Sergie & Johnson, (2015). Therefore, I decided to reframe Paulo Freire's educational approach immortalized in his seminal book, *Pedagogy of the Oppressed* (1970/2000; Jackson, 2007), to show how the current challenges of violent extremism are the pedagogical product of—often unintentionally—America's foreign and domestic policies.

This book is the result of my purposeful focus on the relationship between violent extremism and the perceived mismanagement of the demographic shift in America. In 2014, I enrolled in the Masters in Professional Studies in Homeland Security program at Pennsylvania State University with the intent of exploring violent extremism in America. I had been studying terrorism and violence in various universities since at least 1995. Books 2 and 3 are the product of research I conducted as part of fulfilling the requirements for my master's degree. Yet, I was missing a framework to introduce the basic model I had in my mind concerning the similarity between the fire triangle and my theory of hegemonically provoked violent extremism. While working with my mentee, Marielena Hernandez, the subject of Paulo Freire came up. Through our dialogue on social justice, I knew that I had found a framework for completing my analysis of violent extremism. Freire's works led me to other works on critical thinking as well as revisiting the writings of revolutionary and freedom seeking authors long past. I found in their collective voice a warning for violent extremism if the hegemonic powers of their days continued to rule as imperialists. Unfortunately, their messages received little attention outside small circles of critical thinkers. Among my research, I also came upon Noam Chomsky (2003/2004; 2007), someone I had ignored while serving in the military. What surprised me was the ease of coupling the discoveries I made in my analysis with the warnings they have provided for over forty years.

Combining the conjectural approaches gained from holding advanced degrees in education, business, international relations, and homeland security, I use Freire's critical pedagogy (1970/2000) to go beyond the classroom learning environment (Roberts, 2007) to illuminate the deep roots of how people learn to use violent extremism in the larger classroom that is the world. Where *banking education* (Freire, 1970/2000) kept many oppressed people in a place where the oppressors could maintain control of their society by educating a population to learn their roles according to the oppressor established norms and mores (Zorn, 2001; Schroeter, 2013), I use the idea of *banking* to represent a systemic mechanism (Machiavelli, 2008) operating on a global scale to maintain hegemonic power. Banking hegemony, however, is failing to control unequivocally the global population as those resisting hegemonic authority are joining the Islamic State or committing acts of violent extremism against Western targets, including objectives in America. My intention is not to posit a one-size-fits-all approach to ending violent extremism; that is an unattainable goal for anyone. Though it is possible to kill an individual, it is impossible to kill an ideology. Much as Freire's educational reforms have not solved the issue of poor education (Gonzalez, 2013) or oppression, the *Pedagogy of Violent Extremism* will not solve the many forms of terrorism that exist in our complex world.

An issue I encountered while exploring violent extremism is many pundits take an, us against them perspective. In *Pedagogy of Violent Extremism*, it is not my intention to declare either side is right or wrong in its ideology, what I am illustrating are the factors leading to violent extremism, regardless of the motive. Framing violent extremism from a singular ideological perspective would not be responsible as it blinds the academic outcomes of research. Politically, policy blinded by unbending ideology runs the risk of regime extinction. This is why America has not been successful in its War on Terrorism. Currently, American leaders foresee its victory over terrorism by attaining a replica of their sovereignty throughout the developing world.

I expect my perspective on violent extremism to receive criticism or to be ignored by some pundits because my stance on the casual factors of violence is on the fringe of normally accepted literature on security studies, a viewpoint in which the metric for jus ad bellum favors American interests. I hold that researchers and professionals need to listen to and understand the voices and sentiments of all the actors involved in the phenomenon of violent extremism. My hope is that this book will spark in the reader the ability to think about violent extremism critically. Critical thinking among all the actors on the stage of violent extremism can serve as a starting point for developing change in a society that will reduce the use of violence in the future.

The Pedagogy of Violent Extremism is meant for a wide body of readers. I found this approach the best to discuss an important topic in a critical manner that draws from several disciplines; critical theory, human and security studies, anthropology, sociology, political science, international relations, and violence studies to name a few.

While conducting research I was not surprised to discover that my conclusions on the mismanagement of the demographic shift taking place in America, and throughout the world, was at the crux of violent extremism. I found intellectuals other than Freire (1970/2000) whose warnings failed, in my opinion, to gain notice over the years. They were Edward Said (1978/1994), like Freire (1970/2000), Frantz Fanon (1952/2008; 1961/2004), Noam Chomsky (2003), and Henry Giroux (2014)—all validated what I developed in my mind over the previous decades of working to keep the American public safe. I see the possibility of countering violent extremism, but the response must contain an unprejudiced consideration of all the factors that cause and prevent violent extremism.

References

9/11 Commission. (2004). The 9/11 commission report; Final report to the national commission on terrorist attacks upon the United States. Harrisonburg: W.W. Norton & Company.
Al Qaeda Terrorist Training Manual (AQTM). (2000). (UK/BM-2 Translation, May) Manchester: UK/BM2.

Aslan, R. (2009). *How to win a cosmic war: God, globalization and the end of the war on terror.* New York: Random House.

Blinder, A. (2016, May 24). Death penalty is sought for Dylann Roof in Charleston church killings. *The New York Times.* Retrieved from http://www.nytimes.com/2016/05/25/us/dylann-roof-will-face-federal-death-penalty-in-charleston-church-killings.html.

Bloom, M. (2005). *Dying to kill: The allure of suicide terror.* New York: Columbia University Press.

Burke, J. (2016, February 25). How the changing media is changing terrorism. *The Guardian.* Retrieved from https://www.theguardian.com/world/2016/feb/25/how-changing-media-changing-terrorism.

Bush, G. W. (2007). *National Strategy for Homeland Security (NSHS).* Washington, DC: Government Printing Office.

Carafano, J., Bucci, S., & Zukerman, J. (2012, April 25). *Fifty terror plots foiled since 9/11: The homegrown threat and the long war on terrorism.* The Heritage Foundation. Retrieved from http://www.heritage.org/research/reports/2012/04/fifty-terror-plots-foiled-since-9-11-the-homegrown-threat-and-the-long-war-on-terrorism.

Chomsky, N. (2003/2004). *Hegemony or survival: America's quest for global dominance.* New York: Henry Holt.

Chomsky, N. (2007). *Interventions.* San Francisco: City Lights Books.

Coughlin, C. (2014, November 5). How social media is helping Islamic State to spread its poison. *The Telegraph.* Retrieved from http://www.telegraph.co.uk/news/uknews/defence/11208796/How-social-media-is-helping-Islamic-State-to-spread-its-poison.html.

Dassanayake, D. (2015, February 13). Islamic State: What is IS and why are they so violent?. *Express.* Retrieved from http://www.express.co.uk/news/world/558078/Islamic-State-IS-what-is-ISIS-why-are-ISIL-so-violent.

Didymus, J. (2015, December 4). San Bernardino shooter Syed Farook clashed with Jewish co-worker Nicholas Thalasinos over religion, was teased about his long Islamic beard. *Inquisitor.* Retrieved from http://www.inquisitr.com/2608967/san-bernardino-shooter-syed-farook-clashed-with-jewish-co-worker-nicholas-thalasinos-over-religion-was-teased-about-his-long-islamic-beard/.

Fanon, F. (1952/2008). *Black skin: White masks: Get political.* London: Grove Press.

Fanon, F. (1961/2004). *The wretched of the earth.* (R. Philcox, Trans.). New York: Grove Press.

Fraley, M. (2015, October, 6). Accused Oikos University massacre shooter declared competent to stand trial. *The Mercury News.* Retrieved from http://www.mercurynews.com/crime-courts/ci_28924738/oakland-accused-oikos-massacre-shooter-declared-competent-stand.

Freire, P. (1970/2000). *Pedagogy of the oppressed.* New York: Bloomsbury.

Galula, D. (1964/2006) *Counterinsurgency warfare: Theory and practice.* Westport: Praeger Security International.

German, M. (2007). *Thinking like a terrorist: Insights of a former FBI undercover agent.* Washington, DC: Potomac Books.

Giroux, H. A. (2014). *The violence of organized forgetting: Thinking beyond America's disimagination machine.* San Francisco: City Lights Books.

Gonzalez, M. (2013, August 28). The new American divide. Opinion. *New York Post*. Retrieved from http://nypost.com/2013/08/28/the-new-great-american-divide/.

Guevara, E. C. (1995/2003). *The motorcycle diaries: Notes on a Latin American Journey*. Melbourne: Ocean Press.

Guevara, E. C. (1961/2012). *Guerrilla warfare*. Melbourne: Ocean Press.

Habeck, M. (2012, June 27). Can we declare the war on al Qaeda over? *Foreign Policy*. Retrieved from http://foreignpolicy.com/2012/06/27/can-we-declare-the-war-on-al-qaeda-over/.

Healy, J., & Lovett, I. (2015, October 2). Oregon killer described as man of few words, except on topic of guns. *The New York Times*. Retrieved from http://www.nytimes.com/2015/10/03/us/chris-harper-mercer-umpqua-community-college-shooting.html.

Hermann, P., & Marimow, A. E. (2013, September, 25). Navy yard shooter Aaron Alexis driven by delusions. *The Washington Post*. Retrieved from https://www.washingtonpost.com/local/crime/fbi-police-detail-shooting-navy-yard-shooting/2013/09/25/ee321abe-2600-11e3-b3e9-d97fb087acd6_story.html.

Hoffman, B. (2006). *Inside terrorism*. New York: Columbia University Press.

Hoffman, B. (2013, April 27). Answers to why people become terrorists. *The Daily Beast*. Retrieved from http://www.thedailybeast.com/articles/2013/04/27/answers-to-why-people-become-terrorists.html.

Hoffman, B., Rosenau, W., Curiel, A., & Zimmermann, D. (2007). *The radicalization of Diasporas and terrorism: A joint conference by RAND corporation and the Center for Security Studies, ETH Zurich*. Santa Monica: RAND.

Jackson, S. (2007). Freire re-viewed. *Educational Theory*. Vol. 57/2.

Jenkins, B. M. (2010). *Would-be warriors: Incidents of jihadist terrorist radicalization in the United States since September 11, 2001*. Santa Monica: RAND.

Jenkins, B. M. (2011). *Stray dogs and virtual armies: Radicalization and recruitment to jihadist terrorism in the United States since 9/11*. Santa Monica: RAND.

Jenkins, B. M., Liepman, A., & Willis, H. (2014). *Identifying enemies among us: Evolving terrorist threats and the continuing challenges of domestic intelligence collection and information sharing*. Santa Monica: RAND.

Jenkins, B. M. (2014, July 30). An evil wind. *The RAND Blog* at http://www.rand.org/blog/2014/07/an-evil-wind.html

Kenber, B. (2013, August 28). Nidal Hassan sentenced to death for Fort Hood shooting rampage. *The Washington Post*. Retrieved from http://www.washingtonpost.com/world/national-security/nidal-hasan-sentenced-to-death-for-fort-hood-shooting-rampage/2013/08/28/aad28de2-0ffa-11e3-bdf6-e4fc677d94a1_story.html.

Lawrence, B. (Ed.) (2005). *Messages to the world: The statements of Osama bin laden*. New York: Verso.

Lawrence, T. E. (2011). *Seven pillars of wisdom: A triumph*. Blacksburg: Wilder Publications.

Macdonald, A. (1978/1996). *The Turner diaries*. Fort Lee: Barricade Books.

Machiavelli, N. (2008). The Prince: And other writings. (W. K. Marriott Trans.). New York; Fall River Press.

Mansfield, L. (2006). *His own words: Translation and analysis of the writings of Dr. Ayman Al Zawahiri*. San Bernardino: TLG Publications.

Marighella, C. (1969/2008). *Minimanual of the urban guerrilla*. St. Petersburg: Red and Black Publishers.

Powell, W. (1971). *The anarchist cookbook*. Fort Lee: Barricade Books.

Qutb. S. (1953/2000). *Social justice in Islam*. (J. B. Hardie, & H. Algar Trans.). Oneonta: Islamic Publications International.

Qutb, S. (1991). *The Islamic concept and its characteristics*. (Mohammed Moinuddin Siddiqui Trans.). Plainfield: American Trust Publications.

Qutb, S. (2005) *Milestones*. (2nd Ed). Damascus: Dar al-Ilm.

Rose, S. (2014, October 7). The ISIS propaganda war: A hi-tech media jihad. *The Guardian*. Retrieved from http://www.theguardian.com/world/2014/oct/07/isis-media-machine-pro paganda-war.

Said, E. W. (1978/1994). *Orientalism*. New York: Vintage Books.

Serrano, R. Blankstein, A., & Gerber, M. (2013, June 8). Santa Monica shooting suspect, possible motive identified, officials say. *Los Angeles Times*. Retrieved from http://articles.latimes.com/2013/jun/08/local/la-me-ln-santa-monica-gunman-identified-john-zawahri-20130608.

Schroeter, S. (2013). "The way it works" doesn't: Theatre of the oppressed as critical pedagogy and counternarrative. *Canadian Journal of Education*. Vol. 36/4, pp. 394–415.

Sergie, M. A., & Johnson, T. (2015, March 5). Boko Haram. *Council on Foreign Relations*. Retrieved from http://www.cfr.org/nigeria/boko-haram/p25739.

Shapira, I. (2010, March 7). Pentagon shooter's spiral from early promise to madness. *The Washington Post*. Retrieved from http://www.washingtonpost.com/wp-dyn/content/arti cle/2010/03/06/AR2010030602537.html.

Sloan, A. A. A., & Al-Ashanti, A. (2011). *A critique of the methodology of Anwar Al-Awlaki and his errors in the Fiqh of Jihad*. Leyton: Jamiah Media

Sonner, S. (2014, July 10). Report shows how Cliven Bundy has emboldened right-wing extremists. *Huffington Post*. Retrieved from http://www.huffingtonpost.com/2014/07/10/cliven-bundy-report_n_5574512.html.

Stern, J. (2000). *The ultimate terrorists*. Boston: Harvard University Press.

Straziuso, J., Forliti, A., & Watson, J. (2012, January 14). Al Shabaab's American recruits in Somalia. *Huffington Post*. Retrieved from http://www.huffingtonpost.com/2012/01/14/americans-al-shabaab_n_1206279.html.

Takeda, A. (2015, July 16). Colorado theater shooter James Holmes found guilty of first-degree murder. *US Weekly*. Retrieved from http://www.usmagazine.com/celebrity-news/news/col orado-theater-shooting-verdict-james-holmes-found-guilty-of-murder-2015167.

Thompson, P. (2010). Autistic child charged with terrorism over school drawing. *The Telegraph*, May 16. Retrieved from http://www.telegraph.co.uk/news/worldnews/northamerica/usa/7731513/Autistic-boy-charged-with-terrorist-offence.html.

Tse-tung, M. (2012). *On guerrilla warfare*. San Bernardino: Import Books.

Warrick, J. (2015). *Black flags: The rise of ISIS*. New York: Doubleday.

Wolf, N. (2015, February 20). Chilling report details how Elliot Rodger executed murderous rampage. *The Guardian*. Retrieved from https://www.theguardian.com/us-news/2015/feb/20/mass-shooter-elliot-rodger-isla-vista-killings-report.

Zakaria, F. (2013, January/February). Can America be fixed? The new crisis of democracy. *Foreign Affairs*.

Zalikind, S. (2015, June 22). How ISIS's 'Attack America' plan is working. *The Daily Beast*. Retrieved from http://www.thedailybeast.com/articles/2015/06/22/how-isis-s-attack-america-plan-is-working.html.

Ziv, S. (2014, November 25). Report details Adam Lanza's life before Sandy Hook. *US Newsweek*. Retrieved from http://www.newsweek.com/report-details-adam-lanzas-life-sandy-hook-shootings-286867.

Zorn, J. (2001). Henry Giroux's pedagogy of the oppressed. *Academic Questions*. New York: Fall River Press.

· 1 ·

PEDAGOGY REFRAMED

Paulo Freire's Critical Pedagogy

In 1970, Paulo Freire's *Pedagogy of the Oppressed* (1970/2000) turned education upside down by calling for educators to approach pedagogy from a reciprocal interaction between the teacher and student in which both actors learned from the relationship (Moran, 2015). Concentrating on the plight of oppressed people in Brazil, Freire held that critical pedagogy was a method to teach the oppressed to learn about the value of their humanness (Lewis, 2009; 2010; 2012; Corman, 2011). Perpetrating the power of oppression is the concept of banking education. Banking education is a practice that impairs greater society by ensuring the oppressed, maintain a social framework that teaches the oppressed to be under the control of the oppressor. Banking is the use of an educational system to reinforce and continue the idea of oppression in a society.

Banking education exists in a realm that is often unrecognized by the social structure it supports. Moreover, banking does not support the discovery of progressiveness within a society. The most harm caused by banking education is that banking excludes an opportunity for critical thinking to better humanity. Countering the consequences of banking education is problem-posing education/pedagogy. By having the oppressed solve problems unique to themselves, the oppressed can become aware of their own humanness and how it fits into bettering society as a whole. Thus, Freire (1970/2000) holds that meaningful pedagogy calls for the development of education in concert with the oppressed and not just for the oppressed (Hughes, 2005). When a person oppressed builds in him the courage he did not know existed, he can acknowledge that he is dependent on the oppressed; and through this action, becomes independent.

Freire's perception of education is still relevant as its precepts continue to draw attention in university curriculum around the world. This is because the current education system continues the practice of banking education. Though forty-five years have passed since the *Pedagogy of the Oppressed* was first printed, the concept of oppression has transformed as many in contemporary society can lay claim to oppression at one time or another in their life. What is still current is the oppression created and sustained through the structure of a school system that ignores the oppressed in favor of the oppressors. Consequently, ignoring what is important to the oppressed ensures the oppressors maintain their version of freedom and liberation.

Freire further explored the idea of institutionalized oppression in his subsequent books *Pedagogy of Freedom* in 1998 and *The Politics of Education* in 1985. The ground breaking approach of educating people to create freedom in their lives continues with the next generation of progressive academicians like Donaldo Macedo (Freire & Macedo, 1987) and Antonia Darder (1991/2012). Freire's contemporaries such as Noam Chomsky (2003/2004), Ivan Illich (1968; 2000), and Henry Giroux (2014) also gave life to critical thinking and social justice. Together these academicians, sought to identify and right systemic errors in identifying and championing freedom and liberation. They also saw education as the lynchpin of many of society's ills. The significance of their findings in a broken educational system is that education is the foundation of what a society will become in the succeeding generation of leaders.

Linking the lessons and wisdom of the past is where *The Pedagogy of Violent Extremism* reaches back to Freire and his contemporaries to explain and predict how violent extremists will find the curriculum that will nurture in them the capability to wield violence without malice. Just as many disciples of Freire have used his critical pedagogy to benefit many populations affected by oppression, including those labeled as oppressors (Allen & Rossatto, 2009); critical pedagogy is a double-edged sword providing a learning process (Leistyna, 2004) creating antisocial and sociopathic humans. Critical pedagogy uses the village approach to explore learning processes. This is true on a micro as well as macro level in developing knowledge, culture, identity, and social mores. The current use of violent extremism is the realization of Freire's fears of the oppressed having no other options than to turn to violence as a recourse for their oppression.

Since Freire first published *Pedagogy of the Oppressed* in 1970, many Westerners dismissed his advice and warnings because of his use of Marxist principles to support his message. Western aversion to communism and its ideology closed the eyes and ears of its critics as they clung to the mantra of opposing communism instead of thinking critically about Freire's message. While preparing drafts of this book, a search to replace Freire's employment of *oppressed*, to identify those not in an elite status within their respective societies was elusive. This task proved unfeasible as the replacement words all served to support an ideology of Marxist theory such as revolutionary, activist, burdened, and even terrorist.

Therefore, the search revealed no better term to describe the emotional perception a person controlled by a superior authority feels other than—that of *being oppressed*. With oppression comes powerful feelings of alienation, disenfranchisement, servitude, belittling, condescending treatment, patronization, humiliation, debasement, shame, disgrace, inferiority, and many more adjectives that remind the oppressed person that he is not 100% human in the world he lives. This broad term will serve as an identifier of those discussed in the remainder of the book. Remember, oppression is a feeling owned by the oppressed and not a label provided by the oppressor. The oppressor, systemically, is the hegemonic power exercising authority over the oppressed.

Phenomenology of Violent Extremism

Reality is what we make it. Consider how oppression has changed throughout the last hundred years. Frantz Fanon (1952/2008; 1961/2004), an influential critical theorist that studied postcolonial oppression saw revolutionary action against an oppressive authority as a romantic endeavor to write the wrongs of tyranny. For Fanon, violence was required to deal with the oppressive bearing of his French and Western overlords. In the Americas, Che Guevara (1961/2012; 1995/2003) added to the romanticism of revolution in pursuit of relieving oppression from an elite hegemonic class corrupting the Americas south of the United States border.

In the disputed Palestinian-Israeli debate, Leila Khaled (1973) fought for freedom that would be inclusive of all actors in Palestine-Israel as part of the ultimate solution for peace. Sadly, she recognized that violence bred more violence as each successive hegemonic authority used violence for control over and against a population. Usama bin Laden learned this while working with, and then against America (Lawrence, 2005). His goal was the establishment of an Islamic state that was absent many of the Western practices he saw as offensive to his culture, religion, and mores. Abu Bakr al-Baghdadi used violence to create his version of what an Islamic state should be as a caliphate—the result is the Islamic State continuing to grow in the Levant (Dassanayake, 2015).

Through the succinct chain of events aforementioned, we see how each generation has used its experiences to structure a consciousness that created a definition of acceptable violence to fight for or gain control over a society. Terrorism and its associated violence are subjective to a collective interpretation of what is right in the mind of the person creating a belief system he can support. Defining jus in bellum and jus ad bellum is as difficult as defining terrorism. This is why one person's terrorist is another's freedom fighter. Therefore, it is not surprising that the language associated with violent extremism is hostage to an individual's unique consciousness of his world as developed through an educational process that began in the high chair. Coupling this pedagogical structure with the fervor of a dominant political and faith system, violence is abhorrent when it is committed against that same person and, justified when used against another person to punish him for transgressions against the dominant belief system. This phenomenon is the dyadic relationship between a hegemonic authority and an oppressed individual or people. The dynamics of these relationships working against each other forms the mechanisms in the theory of hegemonically provoked violent extremism.

Theory of Hegemonically Provoked Violent Extremism

The theory of hegemonically provoked violent extremism hypothesizes that violent extremism is the result of three variables that come together to create a situation that inclines a person or people to use violent extremism to express their emotive ideology. The factors of hegemonically provoked violent extremism are the oppressor, the oppressed and resignation. Figure 1.1 illustrates the factors that form the core of violent extremism through provocation caused by oppression. Similar to the *fire triangle*, violent extremism occurs in an environment where the oppression from hegemonic authority is perceived as severe an unrelenting. When the oppressed see no other option to counter their oppression, resignation to use violence becomes their last resort to stop or shunt the oppression they are suffering. Resignation closes the violent extremism triangle opening up to the oppressed, a wide range of options that are only limited by imagination.

In understanding the working of oppression in this theory, the reader needs to broaden the meaning of oppression past the ideas usually associated with Marxism or socialism (Marx & Engles, 1948; Marx, 1983). Oppression is the prejudiced use of power, prestige, and privilege in a social environment. While oppression does reflect the relationships in a society based on class or pseudo-class systems, it also includes macro relationships such as country versus country or individual versus individual. A central factor in oppression is the understanding of the perceptions of the actors involved in the relationships. Actions need not necessarily be intentionally oppressive to be oppression in the eyes of the person feeling oppressed. An example of this interaction on a national level is in the implementation of the USA PATRIOT Act. On a larger macro level, it can be the treatment of refugees fleeing Syria to Western nations. Still, on a micro level, it can be the frustration of an individual ridiculed by the popular kids in school—a reason behind many mass shootings or attempted mass shootings (McIntyre, 2000). Oppression therefore, is like a kaleidoscope. The interactions between people are too dynamic to capture in one picture the entire phenomenon of violent extremism. It is possible for a person to be the oppressor as well as the oppressed at the same time, the differences being dependent on the construct of the interacting relationships within a society.

An issue when discussing the model in Figure 1.1 is that few people have the impartiality to recognize that the use of violent extremism is the consequence of closing the last leg of the violent extremism triangle. This realization is a perception that sometimes only the violent extremist can fully comprehend. Aggressive actions are not limited to the oppressed who have resigned their lot in life. The oppressor can also, in view of his resignation with losing control of authority over his perceived society, act out with extreme violence. Once resignation manifests itself as acknowledgment of a whirlpool of incapability to affect action to better the humanness of one's society, violent extremism is the recognized option to right the perceived wrongs. For the oppressor, his violence is committed in the name of regime continuity. For the oppressed, his violence is committed in the name of regime annihilation.

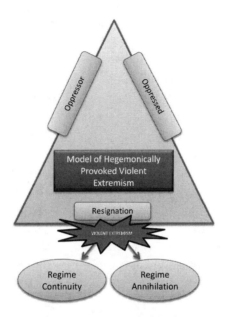

Figure 1.1: Hegemonically Provoked Violent Extremism.
Source: Author, Copyright 2015

One shortcoming of this model is that it does not fully consider the extreme violence created by a pure sociopath that hates most if not all in their society. Their violence does not have a solid foundation in religion or politics—that is measurable. A study to explore this type of person warrants research beyond the scope of this book to explain the distinctive development and use of extreme violence against society. As seen in Frank Robertz (2007) study of school shootings in *Scientific American*, fantasy has a role to play in using extreme violence as each shooter learns from previous violent acts. For the purposes of this book, the actions of active shooters fall within the acts of violent extremism since hate is a motivator in the expression of their violence. This hate is an emotive factor in the aggression of this theory.

Figure 1.2 shows the formula representing the theory of hegemonically provoked violent extremism. In this equation, violent extremism is—over time—the sum of the functions of hegemonic oppression, plus the functions of perceived oppression, multiplied by the functions of resignation.

$$VE = \int_0^T \Sigma f(HO) + f(pO) \cdot f(R)$$

Figure 1.2: Formula for Violent Extremism.
Source: Author, Copyright 2015

An important aspect of this formula is that it includes the consideration of a period over time to represent the indefinite integral (∫) of violent extremism. The emotive perceptions of the model, whether they support regime continuity or regime annihilation, possess in the corpus of experiences, perceptions that can span generations. The formula also uses the concept of functions of phenomena allowing the formulas to transit the various periods and perceptions of violence experienced throughout human history as well as into the future (Hill, Griffiths & Lim, 2011).

To illustrate how the formula for violent extremism represents the theoretical model of hegemonically provoked violent extremism shown in Figure 1.1, the four action models of violent extremism below represent the interaction between the hegemonic dyadic relations (HDR) in a society measured against the levels of resignation (R) a person or person has against hegemonic authority. The combined sum of the functions of hegemonic oppression and perceptions of oppression ($\Sigma f(HO) + f(pO)$) form the HDR on the vertical axis of the models. The multiplier of the functions of resignation ($f(R)$) represents activity on the horizontal axis of the action models (R).

The model in Figure 1.3 represents a rise in HDR along with a rise in R. The positive slope represents the current situation of violent extremism in America. This action model holds that the experiences of violent extremism will continue to rise if society maintains a status quo or increases oppressive activity in the American environment.

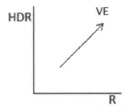

Figure 1.3: Violent Extremism Increasing Model.
Source: Author, Copyright 2015

Conversely, the negative slope shown in Figure 1.4 is the result of a decline in the HDR and R relational conflict. Even though this book concentrates on violent extremism in America, strategic planning needs to be coordinated across the globe to limit safe havens for people willing to use violent extremism.

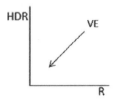

Figure 1.4: Violent Extremism Decreasing Model.
Source: Author, Copyright 2015

The third action model, shown in Figure 1.5, represents a rise in HDR and a decrease in R. This interaction results in a dictatorial police state. America needs to avoid this model as the nation develops legislation and cultural practices to keep America safe. As seen in Iraq and Afghanistan, the abrupt loss of dictatorial authority leads to the situation illustrated in the anarchic model given in Figure 1.6.

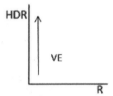

Figure 1.5: Dictatorial Police State Model.
Source: Author, Copyright 2015

The last model, shown in Figure 1.6, represents a low HDR and a high R. This interaction illustrates anarchy due to an ineffective government. The result is civil war, loss of a functioning government and uncontrolled violent extremism. The Islamic State took advantage of these conditions when they decided to claim territory for their fledgling statehood.

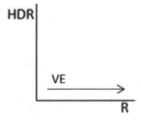

Figure 1.6: Anarchic Model.
Source: Author, Copyright 2015

Violent extremism is the result of cognitive development, either consciously or unconsciously. Central to a learning process is the village that creates a person's reality. On a macro level, a nation or region serves as the village. This systemic classroom nurtures, forms, and produces people as a product of that village. A product can be elite within that society or an oppressed within the same society. Since those outside the mainstream society often perpetrate violent extremism, it is safe to say they identify with oppression—at least in the mind of the extremist. An exploration of what creates the perception of oppression is recognizable by viewing it through a sober lens that is empathetic, tolerant and accepting.

Reinforcing the hegemonically provoked violent extremism model is the analogy of using an iceberg to illustrate the various factors that create violent extremism. Figure 1.7 shows that the visible part of violent extremism finds support through influences not normally considered as fueling violence. While most learn about violent extremism and terrorism from the media, there is a realization that much more contributes to the phenomenon of violent extremism.

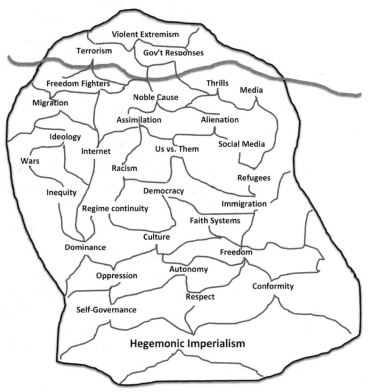

Figure 1.7: Iceberg of Violent Extremism.
Source: Author, Copyright 2015

Developing a solution to counter violent extremism requires knowing what lies below the waterline. One way to accomplish this is to lift the entire iceberg out of the water. This however, is almost impossible so the other solution is to delve deep under the waterline to identify and understand all the components of the iceberg. This is not an enviable task, but a task that requires attention nonetheless to understand and prevent violent extremism. By deconstructing the components causing violent extremism, it is easier to develop a strategy to address the more pressing issues causing violent extremism.

Violent extremism, as a term, must supersede anachronistic notions of terrorism. Consider how the December 2015 Attacks by Syed and Tashfeen Farook in San Bernardino initially concentrated on whether the violence committed was a matter of workplace violence (Didymus, 2015; Woodyard & Heath, 2015). Later the motivation for the violence became terrorism (Schmidt & Peres-Pena, 2015) while some analysts maintained it was a hybrid of both classifications (Didymus, 2015). The framing of the mass killings used antiquated ideas and terminology. The Farook actions were the result of violent extremism resulting from their resignation with Americana as well as with Syed's coworkers. The experiences of the Farooks multiplied the level of their combined resignation as evidenced by their killings. While the investigation is ongoing at the time of this writing, there is proof of radicalization as well as Syed being the subject of harassment based on his religion. Absent in many of the postevent analyses done in the media was the question of, how did the couple—or Syed, at least—become radicalized? Instead, there was a concentration on, when did Syed become radicalized? Knowing the *why* of the *how* can provide security professionals and academics with a deeper understanding of the phenomenon of violent extremism. The attacks have proven one thing: the paradigm for violent extremism has changed what most Americans think of terrorism.

Hegemonic Oppression

America is losing its sole place in the theater of political power as the last hegemonic power (Fukuyama, 2014). This has not prevented American leaders from the continued wielding of its hegemonic authority over the world as if their reign will continue for a thousand years (Chomsky, 2003/2004). While claiming not to be an empire, America practices its international relations like the empires of the past (Hopkirk, 1990/1994). Tribute has given way to acquiescence to American social values and mores, particularly in the global market and economy (Giroux, 2014). As an example, America encourages and demands democracy in its global dealings (Obama, 2015). Democracy though, must be of the American version of social control over society, a version of government that supports American hegemony (Chomsky, 2007). Adhering to American hegemony results in the benefits of Westernization as long as the foreign government is willing to act on the wishes of American leaders. Herein lays the problem of self-actualization for people desiring to maintain their cultural, social, and religious ways of life. Forcing the American way of life on another person denies that person true educational opportunities to develop a humanity that is based on self-consciousness. Sharing or losing hegemonic power on the local, national, and global stage creates a fear in the ruling elite of America. Questioning the American status quo threatens the current hegemonic normalcy at the cost of exploring new and progressive ideas.

Hegemonic normalcy in America drives a social structure that favors European-descendent, Christian supremacy (Adi, 2012). For people inside and outside of America's borders that do not fit this mold of supremacy, they learn not to belong. Inclusion in the hegemonic sphere of influence educates its citizens and followers to protect the dominant hegemonic society (Fanon, 1952/2008) that promises oppression for nonmembers as the hegemonic elite flaunt their superiority through the various institutions that tout equality, freedom, and security. Reflect on how a nonmember of the hegemonic elite may view success in such a society.

According to people exposed to oppression (Fanon 1952/2008; 1961/2004; Freire, 1970/2000), contemporary society ranks accomplishments by how much a person can benchmark their actions to those of the hegemonic leaders of the regime—a phenomenon Fanon (1952/2008) called becoming White. Thus, the perception held is, the more a person looks and acts like those in the dominant society, the more the hegemonic elite recognize their accomplishments. Feelings of this success quickly diminish with qualifying statements (Jimenez, 2010) linking a sub-human identity by receiving comments such as "you really did well," "you have helped people of color with your accomplishment," and "you are just like one of us." While uttered as praise, consciously or unconsciously, the message received is that, as a nonmember of the hegemonic elite there is an expectation a minority is not capable of the customary accomplishments of the dominant elites. Pejorative comments like these ignore the value of critical pedagogy that favors what a person discoverers as the highest form of achievement. Consequently, it is not surprising that perceptions of being an outsider denigrate anything outside the realm supporting the hegemonic monopoly over a society.

After September 11, 2001, America reinforced its hegemonic monopoly over the world by extending its reach in the name of security (Bush, 2002). Negative commentaries (Chomsky, 2007; Giroux, 2014) equate the result of these security measures with an economic imperialism that reaches down to every aspect in the global market place. Objectors to America's wide-ranging influence say if a person, company, or country wants to act in the global environment, he must adhere to American authority since the primary currency is monetarily and politically, American (Freeman, 2012).

History has taught us that hegemonic power is fleeting. No amount of preparation or size of army can prevent the cyclic certainty of power transferring from one dominant culture to another. There will always be a domineering group as oppressors, sustained by the subservient actions of those dominated, as the oppressed. The global political stage acquires institutional drive from the labor of the oppressed. Today, many ethnic and cultural minority groups claim the ideas of a White Christian-based elite dominates American hegemonic power (Greenman & Xie, 2008; Jimenez, 2010; Leong, 2013). Interestingly, the next hegemonic regime in America could be a different race or other singular identifying quality not yet recognized by contemporary society. Dyadic relationship based on the phenomenon of Us versus Them will determine the future hegemonic power. Likewise, a strong military will use the ideas of safety and security to maintain hegemonic supremacy over future societies.

Banking Hegemony: Analysis of American Strategy on Preventing Violent Extremism

This section discusses how America, as a hegemonic authority, creates oppression inside and outside of its borders by trying to maintain a fleeting status quo of democracy ala Americanism. Many American leaders have yet to recognize that American democracy is a significant source of its challenges with violent extremism (Office of the Inspector General, 2004; Obama, 2011b; Obeidallah, 2015). Understanding that the American way is not a culture envied by all peoples of the world is significant in identifying current security issues (Lawrence, 2005; Mansfield, 2006; Sloan & Al-Ashanti, 2011; Christian Broadcasting Network, 1990). Instead, detractors see American leaders using increased levels of violence to control global societies (Williams, 2007; Zakaria, 2013). Failing to receive notice in this scenario is the understanding that violence breeds more violence. That is, of course, unless the ulterior motive is to use violence as the means to justify the ends of increased hegemonic authority.

Noam Chomsky (2003/2004) and Henry Giroux (2014) are examples of critical theorists that claim the American version of democracy is unsustainable in a global environment because it relies on total control from Washington, DC—a practice diametrically opposed to the idea of democracy (Schubert, 2008). Effectively, this means American democracy, in its present form, equates to *constant war to keep the peace*. Democracy then becomes the opposite of the intensions of rule by the people. These claims point to an America that is morphing into an empire built on a massive war machine to spread democracy to foreign shores.

President Obama's White House Summit on Countering Violent Extremism in 2015, was a venue designed to prevent violent extremism (The White House, 2015). However, an analysis using an antihegemonic lens to explore the White House's plan on *Empowering Local Partners to Prevent Violent Extremism in the United States* (Obama, 2011b), the document driving the summit's design (The White House, 2015), reveals how out of touch America is with the root causes of violent extremism. Instead, the White House's plan is a categorical example of America concentrating on banking its hegemony at the expense of actually preventing violent extremism. The *Empowering Local Partners* plan views the problem of violent extremism through the lens of America maintaining its position of global dominance.

In calling out the hateful ideology of Al Qaeda, the plan does not inform the reader why Al Qaeda hates America. This is a significant omission in a systemic plan to protect the nation. Further, *Empowering Local Partners* concentrates on Muslim children being the target of extremists. Recent events like the arrest of Terrence McNeil in Ohio, a man arrested for soliciting support for ISIS, show how more than just the American children of Muslim faiths can become extremists. The 2016 shootings of police officers in Dallas, Texas (Achenbach, Wan, Berman & Balingit, 2016) and Baton Rouge, Louisiana (Jansen, 2016) reveal that the current management of America's society across a wide spectrum is causing people to commit acts of violent extremism for more than religious ideology.

What the plan should have concentrated on was a robust campaign to counter the rising fears of Islamophobia (Beck, 2015). A seen in the media (Christian Broadcasting Network, 1990) (Chumley, 2014; Coughlin, 2014), as well as making a presence in the presidential race, is the anxiety of incorporating Muslims into American society (Inserra, 2015; Johnson & Weigel, 2015). Islamophobia is the opposite end of the spectrum on violent extremism that supports violence in the name of regime continuity. Developing critical social change in an America that accepts Islam, as well as all non-Christian belief systems, will provide a positive perspective on being a citizen in this nation.

Additionally, critics, like the American Civil Liberties Union (ACLU, 2016) and American-Arab Anti-Discrimination Committee (ADC, 2015) say the plan's implication of reducing civil liberties in the name of security is a road that that only leads to an American police state. *Empowering Local Partners* (Obama, 2011b) concentrates on a network of communities working together to invest in a national system of intelligence gathering—a point these critics (ACLU, 2016; ADC, 2015) of the plan assert are not too far from what fascist states in the past century developed to secure their regimes. The criticism hints at the plan's mindset of a *Us* versus *Them* perception that feeds the paranoia making the average citizen willing to relinquish civil liberties in the name of safety (ACLU, 2016; ADC, 2015). Making *Them* into an evil of biblical proportions does little to prevent violent extremism. Instead, it encourages the use of violence to quell an imagined violent threat that produces violence as an outcome.

Welcoming immigrants to the fabric of America must recognize the value of absorbing different cultures into Americanism (Lazear, 2005; Vigdor, 2008; Myers & Pitkin 2010). Trying to make all immigrants into the image of a Europeanized people is not only impossible; it serves to divide American society based on cultural practices and beliefs. Remarkably, this is a point *Empowering Local Partners* (Obama, 2011b) misses in its strategy. Likewise, the plan does not recognize the possibility that some violent extremism is a self-created phenomenon resulting from the oppression of immigrant and disadvantaged populations.

Lastly, *Empowering Local Partners* (Obama, 2011b) needs to acknowledge that American democracy is not the model of government desired by all communities throughout the world. Achieving global homogeneity requires more than a one-size fits all model of government. Particularly when the governmental model imposed on other nations promotes foreign or unwanted concepts as the ultimate goal (Lawrence, 2005; Mansfield, 2006; Ross & Ferran, 2011). Subsequently, *Empowering Local Partners* supports the view by those afraid of America's expanding security mission, as an exercise in banking hegemony, as the warnings the plan purports is that America will use violence to support its way of life—an approach that has kept America at war against terrorism.

Discovering how to Hate

The pedagogy of learning has many interconnecting factors that enhance the experience of scholarship (Freire, 1970/2000; Zorn, 2011). One factor missed in many a contemporary curriculum is the power of discovery (Darder, 1991/2012). Discovery is different from the mindless memorization of facts required to pass a test. While media reports claim test scores are increasing throughout national testing efforts (Desliver, 2015; Soergel, 2015) there is no metric to see how well wisdom is developing in the nation. Gaining wisdom is a unique understanding of knowledge that gives intelligence an extra perception in how to employ that knowledge. In the fight against violent extremism, the extremists are learning more than the national efforts as seen in each new violent attack experienced. Learning to hate follows the same pattern of pedagogy (Kilner, 2003). When a person hates something to the point he is willing to use extreme violence, his hate becomes more dangerous by discovering how to translate hate into original acts of extreme violence rather than by simply repeating past actions.

A factor in developing wisdom is the application of discovery to pedagogy. This form of pedagogy is difficult to develop in curriculum since the act of discovery is dependent on the faculties each individual possesses. The epiphanic power a person realizes in the moment of discovery imbeds the experience deep in the learner's psyche. Learning through discovery, opens up new roads to pedagogy, as the learner seeks new and innovative ways to expand knowledge.

This is a dynamic seen in violent acts of extremism. As an example of the spectrum of learning from a violent act of extremism, we can look at two diametrically opposed responses to the use of extreme violence. Because of the many school shootings in America, many school administrators established procedures for guests checking in at the main office and locking exterior points of ingress. This procedure sounds effective but it is no more protective than the use of cosmetics to hide a blemish. The blemish is still there, and often visible. Likewise, cosmetic security measures provide a false sense of security to an unknowing population.

Contrasting this rote response to learning from crises is the discovery Adam Lanza (Ziv, 2014) had in defeating the enhanced security measures at Sandy Hook Elementary School by simply shooting out the glass panel next to the locked door. The investigation of the shooting revealed Lanza had studied previous school shootings in America, developing a score sheet on effectiveness of the extremists involved in previous shootings (Ziv, 2014). While Lanza's motive was never determined, it was clear that he discovered how best to defeat laws and security measures designed to prevent him from carrying out his plan.

Similar to Lanza discovering how to better on the last plan (Ziv, 2014), many violent extremists do the same (Mansfield, 2006). Reflect on the successful second terrorist attacks carried out in the failures of the first World Trade Center bombing (9/11 Commission, 2004), Operation Bojinka (Bonner & Weiser, 2006), and on the USS Sullivans (9/11 Commission, 2004). In comparison, most security measures in America plan to prevent the last incident and often do not look forward. This could be because security planners and politicians get more currency out of this nearsighted logic than they would by discovering what the extremists will do next.

Banking American Hegemony: The Global Area

Violent extremism is a product of hate. Hate is a product of experiencing unrelenting oppression. Oppression continues through the banking of hegemony. The level of identification with oppression creates in a person a classroom that never closes its doors as that person learns to hate what the oppressor represents. This pattern of learning to hate (Post, 2005) an oppressor forms the foundation of why many Muslims, hate the Westernization of their culture, religion, and social mores (Lawrence, 2005; Qutb, 2005; Sloan & Al-Ashanti, 2011; Serrano, Blankstein & Gerber, 2013). Currently, many Islamic fundamentalists carrying out the most heinous of their violent crimes in the name of seeking freedom are acting out on a vision of a return of a caliphate on the world stage (Dassanayake, 2015). Freedom is their answer to oppression. The Islamic State is proving to be the vanguard in a revolution to create a caliphate that Seyyid Qutb calls for in his *Milestones* (2005), a collection of his writings charging the Muslim Brotherhood to take action against jahili— uncivilized—governments.

There are other actors in the global arena that have acted out or called for violent extremism to further their cause for freedom from American rule (Lawrence, 2005; Qutb, 2005; Sloan & Al-Ashanti, 2011; Serrano, Blankstein & Gerber, 2013). In this section, the primary concentration is on the violence acted out in the name of Islam since this form of violence has monopolized the world stage. At the root of violent extremism is the use of violence to get the Western world to allow Muslims to rule their civilization, as they desire (Qutb, 1953/2000; 1991; 2005). Influential extremists (Fanon, 1952/2008; 1961/2004; Jansen, 1986/2013; Qutb, 2005) trace their struggle back to colonialism, an era when Western powers ruled Muslim counties with impunity. Under these conditions, oppression of humans eventually leads to a call to arms in pursuit of equality.

Frantz Fanon, a French intellectual, described this in his piercing work, *The Wretched of the Earth* (1961/2004). As a member of the Algerian National Liberation Front, he fought against his colonial motherland in the Algerian War of Independence from France. Seyyid Qutb (1953/2000; 1991; 2005), an Egyptian intellectual who studied in America, also realized that, as Fanon had (1961/2004), violence was the only method of resistance left to those oppressed by Western hegemonic powers. Fanon's *The Wretched of the Earth* (1961/2004) and Qutb's *Milestones* (2005) outlived the lives of their authors as revolutionaries around the world sought, and continue to seek, advice from the pages that only the oppressed could value.

This is where many security pundits in the West wrongfully analyze the characteristics of a terrorist (Nelson, 2010; Johnson, 2011; Huffman, 2011; Combs, 2013; Schmidt & Perez-Pena, 2015). These pundits characterize the terrorists as normal ordinary men and women who, for reasons not really understood, became extremists. The point missed is that these people are anything but normal or ordinary. For many (Lawrence, 2005; Qutb, 2005; Sloan & Al-Ashanti, 2011; Serrano, Blankstein & Gerber, 2013), oppression by a Western hegemonic authority is a state they can no longer live with. Within their good conscious, they discover the power of violence. This misrepresentation is not surprising since the ideas many Westerners have of people not of a European civilization, is that *they* are less than European people are (Said, 1978/1994). This deeply rooted idea of less-thanism, expertly captured in Edward Said's *Orientalism*, enlightened academic circles throughout the West in 1978. The idea of the West—Occidentals—being superior in all respects, to those the West colonized—the Orientals—is unquestionable. Those colonized could only be what their hegemonic masters told them they could be (Said, 1978/1994; 1993). This hereditary reasoning, understood by those oppressed, is why non-European cultures continue to confuse contemporary scholars and security pundits. This attitude is clear in T. E. Lawrence's *Seven Pillars of Wisdom* (2011). Lawrence's perspective of the Arab is clearly of a people bordering on the savage. Had the British not needed the Arabs to fight against the Ottoman Turks, the sands of Arabia would be without the benefit of Western advantages.

Fanon (1952/2008; 1961/2004) was able to encapsulate many oppressive practices in the paternalism of colonialism, or first worlds as compared to third world lifestyle. Principle among them is that humanism had a distinct definition based on identifying the Europeaness in a person's life. Indigenousness is a state requiring correction but not necessarily acceptance by the hegemonic elite (Fanon, 1952/2008). This concept is verbalized by the hegemonic elites that have a penchant for referring to the oppressed as animals instead of by their humanness (Fanon, 1952/2008; Freire, 1978/2000; 1988). Colonized people smell like pigs, form packs of wolves, and other zoological terms designed to strip people of their humanity. The animalization of oppressed is a trait recognized by Freire (1978/2004) as well as a tactic used by bin Laden and seen in the Al Qaeda training manual (2000). A majority of players in the arena of violent extremism have use animalization to justify the use of violence against those they fear and hate (Marighella, 1969; Fanon, 1952/2008; 1961/2004; AQTM, 2000: Lawrence, 2005).

Though the names of Fanon and Qutb have mostly faded into a footnote on terrorism, their lessons have not been lost on modern terrorists. People like Usama bin Laden (Lawrence, 2005), Ayman al Zawahiri (Mansfield, 2006), Anwar al-Awlaki (Ross & Ferran, 2011; Sloan & Al-Shanti, 2011), and Abu Bakr al-Baghdadi (Lister, 2014) have learned from Qutb as his words continue to drive the desire to establish a caliphate (Milestones, 2005). Adding to these classics of Muslim calls for freedom is Muhammad abd-al-Salam Faraj's pamphlet, *The Neglected Duty* (Jansen, 1986/2013). Faraj too, saw jihad as a means of freeing Islam from the corrupting shadow of Westernism.

Unlike Western assessments of these men being terrorists, these men have effectively created their own agency revealing the possibility of freedom through action in a world that long ignored them. Egyptian authorities executed Qutb and Faraj. Likewise, American forces assassinated bin Laden and al-Awlaki. America still offers a reward for the capture of Al Zawahiri. The killing of these men has shown that ideology lives longer than the men who had the original ideas of freedom, independence and violent extremism.

What is interesting is that al-Awlaki was an American (Ross & Ferran, 2011), while bin Laden and al Zawahiri had worked with Americans when Afghanistan was fighting the Soviet Union (Mansfield, 2006). Bin Laden saw that the American desire to aid Afghanistan was a tactic to become the new overlords of the country. This idea became more prevalent to him when American forces started basing military troops in Saudi Arabia (Lawrence,

2005). Democracy to these terrorists was in essence, a return to oppressive colonialism, a practice that made their culture and customs subservient to Westernization.

Missing from any dialogue on violent extremism, terrorism or revolution is why the idea of creating a caliphate is iniquitous. If the Western countries can bring back the state of Israel, why cannot they support the creation of a caliphate that can be a contributing member of the global world community? The Islamist answer to this is that Western powers fear the possibility of Islam spreading into and consuming Western ideas of Christianity. Facing this realization, the writings of Qutb (2005), Faraj (Jansen, 1986/2013), al Zawahiri (Mansfield, 2006), and al-Awlaki (Sloan & Al-Shanti, 2011) point to violence as the only recourse left to ensure the practice of their religion, as their culture dictates for them.

The plans of Al Qaeda concentrated their violence in attacks designed to break the American will (Lawrence, 2005). Besides their academic degrees, bin Laden and al Zawahiri were students of history as is seen in many of their statements (Lawrence, 2005; Mansfield, 2006). It is not extraordinary to think that targeting military targets was a way to show that size does not matter. Additionally, attacking the people is the best way to get a population to tire of a war. General Vo Nguyen Giap (Giap, 1976; Currey, 1997) knew this as he directed the North Vietnamese war machine in victories against both France and America. Attacks, as learned from Sun Tzu (1994), do not have to attack militarized units directly to win a battle. Therefore, the multiple attacks of 9/11 (9/11 Commission, 2004), the multiple attacks in France in 2015 and 2016 (Fantz & Brumfiled, 2015; Rubin, Blaise, Nossiter & Breeden, 2016), and the March 22, 2016 attacks in Brussels (Agence France-Presse, 2015) show that violent extremism can shake a nation to its core. A mighty military machine loses its luster when the average citizen is not safe in his neighborhood, at a theatre or in commuter conveyances.

Besides attacking the World Trade Center as a symbol of capitalism (9/11 Commission, 2004), there is the claimed attack on the financial sector via the internet that sent the Western world into frenzy (Freeman, 2012). The patterns of these attacks reveal that hate has more currency when directed toward the soft targets that the hegemonic governments are responsible for protecting— people included. A person who serves in the military knows there is risk of dying in fulfilling his duties to his nation. This is an unexpected risk for the normal civilian that has difficulty seeing himself as part of the cosmic battlefield.

Violent extremists are also following the lessons of Sun Tzu (1994) by choosing the places of battle. In choosing the places to wage their violence, the extremists are sure to catch their foes off guard, regardless of the security measures in place. Strengthening the extremists' approach of selecting the battlefield, bin Laden (9/11 Commission) has repeated what Mao Tse Tung (2012) learned in his revolution—time is an ally the West does not have. Efforts to combat violent extremism have the nonstrategic metric of being successful in one president's term at the least, two terms at the longest. The extremists have shown they are willing to wait as demonstrated by the repeat attacks on the World Trade Center, U. S. Navy ships in Aden and using commercial airplanes as missiles (9/11 Commission, 2004). A recognition of time as part of the strategy to combat violent extremism has to include an understanding that overrides contemporary political processes.

Banking American Hegemony: The Domestic Area

Studies, like David Roediger's book *Working Toward Whiteness* (2005) and Nancy Leong's (2013) Harvard Law Review's article *Racial Capitalism*, have shown the first wave of immigrants tolerates oppression in the hopes of assimilation to an American culture while the second and later generations come to realize assimilation is futile. After the later generations fail to assimilate to America's dominant culture, the immigrants slowly began to see violence as the preferred option to create change (Jenkins, 2010). If mismanaged, cultural change is potentially synonymous with a level of violence comparable to the changes taking place.

Understanding the emotions of the oppressed is challenging for members of America's hegemonic elite. Oppression is actually a word avoided in daily conversation as it rings of Marxist ideology and socialism, ideas that are anathema to American versions of democracy. While many may claim to possess empathy for the oppressed, or underprivileged in American argot—empathy is, something an elite person can rarely experience in the dominant American culture. Empathy is an emotion gained through experience, not by reading a book or watching a training video. True empathetic emotion has to be lived. More than once, a minority person has related to the author that tolerance trainers have spewed out textbook language on how they were supposed to feel about racism. What these nearsighted and presumptuous trainers never did, was ask the minority people how they actually felt. Instead, the trainers told the minority people how they should feel. The lesson being that minority people need to be more tolerant of racism along with the understanding that unconscious bias was an excusable offense in a democratic society. Is there really a question why some people want to change their society? Reports like these ring of Fanon's experiences with colonialism (1952/2008; 1961/2004).

Learning to hate is not restricted to people oppressed. The oppressors learn to hate too (Romano, 2005; Blinder, 2016; Mapping Police Violence, 2017). A crucial drive in their hate is their fear of losing hegemonic control over their society—or ideas of what their society should be. Andrew Macdonald (1978/1996) revealed a society in his *The Turner Diaries* that describes an America where White supremacists fight back against a nation losing its Whiteness. Turner's exploits are heroic as he helps develop the new order that rules America the way its religion had prophesied. Though *The Turner Diaries* is a fictional novel, it has served as doctrine for many White supremacists like Timothy McVeigh (Kifner, 1995). The book (Macdonald, 1978/1996) serves on par with Qutb's *Milestones* (2005) when the levels of influence it has on dedicated readers willing to carrying out violent extremism.

Literature supporting the banking of American hegemony also come from mainstream sources people often do not consider extremists, like leading academics such as Noam Chomsky (2003/2004), Henry Giroux (2014), Antonia Darder (2002; 1991/2012), and Donaldo Macedo (Freire & Macedo, 1987). Those that realize the dominance of a European-Christian-based hegemony is giving way to an Americanism that is inclusive of multiple cultures find a strong voice in many Fox productions. However, it does not take much insight to see the partiality of Fox's network. Serving as the high priests of Fox's ideology are notables like Bill O'Reilly, Glenn Beck, and Neil Cavuto. Countering the predisposed subjectivity of the Fox Network is CNN and its less influencing high priests, Wolf Blitzer and Brooke Baldwin, whose liberal viewpoints draw a commensurate amount of controversy. Though these pundits appear to battle each other from the political extremes of a two-party system, they show unification in promoting the banking of hegemonic authority for America.

From these pundits comes a book that adds to the banking of hegemony on a level that rouses in Americans a fear of the unknowns and misunderstood teachings of Islam. Glenn Beck's (2015) *It IS about Islam*, claims to uncover the true and ruinous intentions of Islam. Regrettably, opinions like Beck's do little to quell violent extremism. Instead, biased perspectives like this, add to the tendency for people to commit violent extremism as the pages create a fear of fellow Americans. Equally, *It IS about Islam* creates violence in Muslims who view the book as offensive and insulting.

Literature written in the same vein of hegemonic banking exists in many forms (Obama, 2011b; Beck, 2015; Christian Broadcasting Network, 1990). Besides championing the precepts of an apple pie Americana above all else, banking hegemony also sends a message to minorities, particularly non-Christian people that they can be accepted if they take their right place in the hierarchy of current Americanism (Said, 1978/1994; Sakuma, 2015). The primary target of contemporary hegemonic Americanism is an anti-Islamic rhetoric of noninclusion (Johnson & Weigel, 2015). Kids in playgrounds often repeat the phobia produced by educators, church leaders, and politicians as they get an "A" for learning to hate. Unfortunately, there is no discovery for many of these people because they only repeat what the hegemonic authorities expect them to believe (Chomsky, 2003/2004). The reported events of attacks against minorities of various extractions (Goldfarb, 2006; Beutel, 2007; Brown, 2011; Sanchez & Cano, 2014; Rice 2016; Mapping Police Violence, 2017) and places of worship (ACLU, 2016n.d.) validate the misdirected violence conducted in the name of preserving Americana.

Pedagogy in the name of regime continuity lacks the expansion of learning in the world as a classroom that Darder (1991/2012) discusses in *Culture and Power in the Classroom*. Limiting exposure to global knowledge increases the size of the blinders American society wears as the rest of the world learns to grow in response to the sociopolitical challenges of this century. Such restrictive behavior also reinforces the, *Us* versus *Them* mentality that increases the probability of violent extremism in America.

Violent Extremism Supports Regime Continuity

There needs to be more recognition that the call to use extreme violence is a tactic some White supremacists use in an effort to maintain the hegemonic control European-Americans have had in America for nearly 300 years (Kifner, 1995; Blinder, 2016). Dylann Roof (Blinder, 2016) and Timothy McVeigh (Kifner, 1995) demonstrate many of the mysteries of the psychology surrounding the phenomenon of violent extremism in supporting the continuing or correcting of their ideas of White supremacy. A factor in the use of violence used by Roof and McVeigh is that violence was necessary to promote their ideologies. For McVeigh (Kifner, 1995), he had hopes of starting a revolution that would overthrow the government in the hopes of forming a government according to that fanaticized in *The Turner Diaries*

(Macdonald, 1978/1996). Far from being crazy, these extremists demon-strated mental stability in how they used violence to send their governments a message of displeasure. This logical detachment allowed them to kill inno-cents in pursuit of their anti-governmental goals because of a just cause that echoes of the phenomenon in policing called noble cause corruption (Marti-nelli, 2006). Roof and McVeigh self-identified as warriors that were justified in the use of extreme violence for the pursuit of righteousness that exceeded the physical and normative boundaries of their secular lives.

Andrew Macdonald (1978/1996) and Seyyid Qutb (2005) both envi-sioned extremely violent acts against the hegemonic authorities they saw as enemies of their ideologies in order to wake the common people. It was their belief that the commoners—oppressed—would fill the ranks of a revolution-ary force that would defeat corrupt governments. Their envisioned violence (Jurgensmeyer, 2000) was called for in the name of freedom. Freedom for McVeigh and Roof was logically, viewed through the lens of their respective religious beliefs.

This is what Mark Jurgensmeyer (2003) referred to in *Terror in the Mind of God*, as terrorism taking on a cosmic element in how violence becomes a practice of religious duty. This definition aligns with the idea of terrorists as crusaders. Crusading is a concept learned in the Eurocentric histories taught in Western schools and houses of religion. These two crusaders could not see anything wrong in their extreme violence, as the victims of their acts were extensions of the wayward governments they were fighting. Such behavior constitutes violence as a normality in the causes they saw overriding the con-cerns of the mainstream society. Violence therefore, to them, is acceptable regardless of the extremeness of the savagery used.

Roof and McVeigh are similar in that they, as Americans, choose to fight against their parent government. An interesting similarity in Roof and McVeigh is that they are images of *normal* Americans. McVeigh, a veteran of Operation Desert Storm, turned against the country he had once served (Kifner, 1995). Similar in the changing of the psychology and ideology of these two men was the aversion they held for the federal government. Roof and McVeigh viewed the preemptive use of violence as a way to strike a more powerful enemy as well as serve as an example for future extremists (Kifner, 1995; Blinder, 2016). Violence, to these two men was a sound tactic based on their perceptions of righting a wrong against a larger and more powerful society.

Supporters of White supremacy movements perceive their war being against a weak government that coddles liberals, foreigners, and un-American ideas (Kifner, 1995; Blinder, 2016). The use of violence, in the example of Roof and McVeigh materializes the practice of dehumanization as a form of justifying revolutionary actions using extreme violence. These two men drew power from the act of dehumanization as they indiscriminately killed innocent people through activities that were, to them, no different from going to the corner store to buy milk. Even though the public continues to feign shock by the extreme violence Roof and McVeigh used, a sterile analysis of these violent extremists reveal they operated like normal people; making the violence they employed a new normal for America. Operating on this psychological level disturbs the normal American who does not see violent extremism as part of and a result of the changing American lifestyle.

Folktales, Heroes and Violence

A good way to measure what motivates a person is to know who their heroes were as they grew up. Learning whom the heroes were in the folktales told in family gatherings can tell a lot about what a person considers as noble actions. Heroism as an observable metric is included in this book to provide a comparison of West and East differences in interpreting the study of heroic motivation in the use of violent extremism. Interestingly, though not surprising is that the discussion of heroes became a topic point in the national media in 2015 when Fox pundits criticized the creation of a black Captain America (Leon, 2015). In addition to breaking the color scheme of American heroes, black Captain America faced villains in the form of racist vigilantes. Can such an argument be anything other than the fight to maintain the perspectives of an American hegemony practiced over the last few hundred years, here and abroad? Is the issue that a black person cannot be Captain America or that racists cannot be enemies of the state? Why cannot black people be American heroes? This question goes back to Second World War when an investigation into the awarding of the nation's highest medal for valor revealed that seven black soldiers and another twenty-three Hispanic and Jewish soldiers' actions received less consideration for the nation's highest medal. A second review for their actions reconsidered the award of receiving the Medal of Honor because they originally lacked the cultural and ethnic identity of being an American War hero ("Medal of Honor," 2015). This review took place in 1993, nearly forty-eight years after these brave soldiers committed acts of heroism.

Can banking hegemony be clearer than denying an American the chance to become a hero?

Contemporaries may claim that many athletes are American heroes. However, the recent treatment of black students at the University of Missouri show that the athletes are more of work horses in the university's golden egg machine then they are accepted as heroes (Dowling, 2015). At least racism took a backseat to the university's concerns about losing up to $1 million per game the black students did not play. Contrast this with a similar movement by black students at Occidental College in Los Angeles a few days later (Watanabe, 2015). The protesters called for the president to resign as they took over the main administrative offices of the college. When the demands of the protestors went unmet, the protest ended in a lesson that spoke more to the power of economics than racial equality. Where the football players received accolades for their heroism, the Occidental protestors lacked an economic impact to the college's revenue stream. Which model of racial remonstrating will the next protest use?

Heroes in American folklore are limited to America being a young nation compared to other civilizations around the world. Currently, the heroes are limited to a few presidents, military personnel, athletes, and corporate giants. What is noteworthy is the characteristics of a hero changed over the years. What Americans find worthy of imitation were initially political leaders like George Washington, Benjamin Franklin, and Abraham Lincoln. Then we see military leaders of the World Wars as heroes. Modernity recognized athletes and corporate leaders as heroes. The principle demarcation to be a hero relies on individual accomplishments more than on the behavior they exhibited. This is why contemporary heroism struggles with the personal behavior of heroes gone wild (Schoch, 2012). There is also the fashionable practice of calling too many people heroes for acts that are becoming normal responses to societal woes. Setting the standard for many acts of heroism is an expectation by a majority of the population that looks to reality television as a form of reality worth imitating. What is amusing in this growing trend of hero worship is that reality television is far from being real (Jones, 2014).

Going back to the understanding of comic book heroes, what drives people to create fictional heroes? What is their purpose? Invented to fill the void people have in recognizing their personal limitations, comic book heroes illustrate the power wielded by the ancient Greek and Roman gods. Due to the current political climate, many comic book heroes have now taken on the role of not only protecting America from villains, they also protect the complete hegemonic way of American life (Aucoin, 2014). What image do young children conjure in their mind when imagining what it is like to be a super hero? Other than fighting for the American way of life, what makes a hero's actions unique? Heroism requires an enemy, a villain to subdue to keep the people safe. This is a distinction in American heroes. Keeping the civilian population safe, especially the weak and poor of society is heroic.

Since the end of the Cold War, the identifiable enemy has been terrorists (9/11 Commission). The problem with terrorism is that many terrorists are stateless. The Taliban, who supported terrorism, quickly left the seat of government because of America's superior military force. Not seen in the invasions of Afghanistan and Iraq were any sustainable heroes representing America. This could be due to the proclaimed victories not really being victories (Resnick, 2015), since America left the countries in a worse condition than they were under despotic rule.

The Islamic State is changing this perspective. Even though the Islamic State lacks recognition by the West as a nation state, their global reach is causing the West to react to Islamic State's threats with actions, normally seen in the relationships between warring nations (Rose, 2014; Zalikind, 2015). America lacks a hero to face the Islamic State. With a lame duck president in the office, the White House is wary of bequeathing another lengthy war to the new president. Both political parties have failed at creating democratic and peaceful nations in the Middle East. Is it possible the new and possibly untried president will be the hero America is looking for? On the other hand, will he or she be another link in a long chain of failures at imposing American democracy in the Middle East?

The Middle East has a longer history than America. As such, the history of folktales and heroes is richer (Bushnaq, 1986). Though Islam is the primary religion in the Pan-Islamic world, there are folk stories including other religions. A review of Arabic folktales is not much different than those America adapted from its European roots (Mardrus & Mathers, 1964/1987; Bushnaq, 1986; Lyles, 2012). Where European folktales concentrated on doing the right thing to benefit humankind (Wright, 1916; Tiger, 1999), Pan-Islamic folktales concentrate on doing the right thing because living the Muslim faith is the most heroic action a person can demonstrate (Mardrus & Mathers, 1964/1987; Bushnaq, 1986; Lyles, 2012). This element is a distinction in tales of the Pan-Islamic heroes. Instead of keeping civilians safe, recognition of heroic deeds measures how well a person lives a righteous life according to the Quran and sharia law. Following a devout, Muslim life, leads to heroic outcomes.

Another feature in Pan-Islamic heroism is the craftiness of the protagonist. For hundreds of years, stories told before putting kids to bed centered on the wiles of a Muslim outsmarting the evils of jinn, ghouls, afreets, and unbelievers (Lyles, 2012). Trickery and deception over evil are positive characteristics for a hero of the Pan-Islamic world. While wealth is a reward in many a European folktale, wealth is not the driver of Pan-Islamic folklore. Instead, wealth forms part of the outcomes for being a devout Muslim. Like Christianity, greed is disgraceful in Islam. Likewise, those that cheat and test the teachings of Islam find as their reward pain, suffering, and often a horrible death.

Most likely, the most famous hero of Islam known to the West is the real and mythical figure of Harun al-Rashid. Al-Rashid's popularity in the West comes mainly from stories told of his deeds in *The Book of One Thousand and One Nights* (Mardrus & Mathers, 1964/1987). As a caliph in the Golden Age of Islam, al-Rashid ruled with wisdom and justice. His position as caliph meant he was the primary protector of the faith. The linking of deeds to faith is an unbreakable bond in Islamic heroism. Dating back to the Prophet Muhammad, distinguished caliphs have advanced knowledge, won wars, expanded the faith, and most importantly defended Islam (Goldschmidt & Davidson, 2009).

A reflection of the contemporary heroes in Islam includes many Islamists. The Islamists, like bin Laden, al Zawahiri, al-Awlaki, and al-Baghdadi demonstrate a professed life of fighting for Islam against a power that is larger than they are (Lawrence, 2005; Mansfield, 2006; Sloan & Al-Ashanti, 2011). Much like Inea Bushnaq's (1986) version of, Hasan in the folktale, *A Tale within a Tale*, these men used their wiles to win victories against America, who they considered the far Satan. Their victories resulted in the attacks against the USS Cole, of 9/11 on American soil, as well as the recruitment of many Americans to join their jihad (9/11 Commission; Kenber, 2013). Their deaths rewarded their heroic deeds by making them martyrs in the eyes of many Muslims.

Al-Baghdadi, as a hero, holds claim to the creation of the first caliphate since the fall of the Ottoman Empire in First World War (Warrick, 2015). Linking al-Baghdadi to the heroic notions of the Abbasid caliph, Harun al-Rashid, is that al-Baghdadi made the city of Raqqah his capital—the same city where al-Rashid ruled from during his caliphate (Goldschmidt & Davidson, 2009).

Many Islamists preach the return of another golden age for Islam under the rule of a caliph (Qutb, 2005; Goldschmidt & Davidson, 2009). There could be no better location to validate the seat of a new caliphate than the ancient city of Raqqah. The city itself, in an anthropomorphic way, is heroic as its streets echo with greatness and prominence.

Despite the unmatched technology of America and its allies, al Zawahiri and al-Baghdadi remain wanted men by America. For al-Baghdadi, his elusiveness from capture validates his caliphate in a heroic umbrella that attracts followers to his regime (Warrick, 2015). The craft of deception these men maintain has successfully outsmarted America's brainpower. Even the deaths of bin Laden and al-Awlaki took years and the continued war on terrorism cost untold sums of money to accomplish (Amadeo, 2016). Celebrations by American leaders of these deaths were also celebrated by Islamists, who saw their emirs as heroes of their faith (Burch, 2011; Sloan & Al-Shanti, 2011). The violent deaths of their emirs are cause to return, in folktale fashion, extreme violence to the America, at a time of the Islamists' choosing. Islamists have contemporary heroes to spare. As the Islamic State and other Islamists causes continue to grow, they fear little from the evil world of jinn, ghouls, afreets, and unbelievers.

What is clear in the phenomenon of violent extremism is that the majority of the actors in the global arena seem to have more success in developing the concept of the enemy as an altar-hero. Bestowed on America, as well as those America calls terrorists, are a superhuman tendency that requires annihilation in the name of righteous (Warrick, 2015). This phenomenon is a peculiarity that fits the classic comic books heroes. The evil fiend is as important as the hero is in the larger volume of an ongoing story of good versus evil. Without an enemy, there is no need for heroes.

Min Erhabi?

Min erhabi? The Arabic question for *who is the terrorist* is an interrogative long debated by both sides of the terrorist spectrum. Understanding the depths of this question often disregard the perceptions of those referred to as terrorists. Labeling a person, a terrorist is a political way to reidentify oppressed people in order to fulfill other political purposes. In this sense, inclusive in the term terrorist is a derogatory sentiment with the purpose of overshadowing recognition of the rights a terrorist, as an oppressed person, may have. If oppression serves as the curriculum and a poor environment serves as the classroom, what is the likelihood a person will hold resentment toward the hegemonic authority that creates the conditions of cultural confinement?

Illustrating how people learn to develop pictures of the players in the question, min erhabi, two music videos provide examples of how people question their identity as possible terrorists. Those in the hegemonic power-wielding arena have referred to the artists analyzed as terrorists, gangsters, and other derogatory monikers of a criminal element. Through their music videos, these artists show how they perceive themselves within the phenomenon of terrorism. Violence, as a weapon supports hegemonic banking in subliminal campaigns that use selected emotive language to tip the scales of humanity. While each video has its carefully orchestrated scenes portraying a biased message, there is little doubt the suffering experienced by those oppressed is genuine. In the midst of those portrayed as suffering, the authority of the hegemonic governments continues to impose unquestioned domination in their world environments.

Public Enemy's video, *By the Time I get to Arizona* (1991), presents a perceived social breaking point in racial and social discrimination in America at the end of the twentieth century. Centered on Arizona's failure to recognize Martian Luther King's national holiday, Public Enemy presents imagery that bridges the institutional racism of the 1960s to that of contemporary America in the 1990s. The projected resolution to the xenophobia by Arizona's governor is armed resistance because peaceful means at ridding the nation of injustice over the decades failed to deliver equality across the nation. The character of this violent resolution is commensurate with contemporary definitions of homegrown violent extremism. Using rap videos to deliver a message to present oppression is not limited to America and its social problems.

Contrasting *By the Time I get to Arizona* (Public Enemy, 1991) to another ethnic struggle emphasizes how institutional oppression leads to violence as the means to deliver a message as well as a means to attain a goal. The Palestinian struggle as illustrated through the Da Arabian MCs (DAM) music videos, *Min Erhabi? (Who is the Terrorist)* (2006) and *Born Here* (2008), mirror the core implications of Public Enemy's message in 1991. Prominently pictured in the videos of Public Enemy and DAM (2006) are armed police controlling the oppressed populations, using excessive force as the acceptable method of enforcement. Whether it is an unarmed man bitten by a police dog as seen in Public Enemy's video or a boy throwing rocks at tank in DAM's 2006 video, unnecessary levels of violence should find no warrant in a civilized society. Overpowering in both videos are images of state officers beating on helpless victims. Further similarities in the videos show images of the substandard living conditions the oppressed live in, not by choice but through hegemonic cultural practices. Highlighted in the videos are messages of governments enforcing laws that facilitate ethnic cleansing while restricting the freedom of the oppressed to be vested citizens of their own societies. The music artists beg the tautological question, what options do victims of state terrorism have, except violence in kind.

Viewing, *By the Time I get to Arizona* (Public Enemy, 1991) through the lens of people collectively referred to as terrorists by many, adds credence to the message Public Enemy presents in its music video. Operating from the fringes of politically based music videos, Public Enemy (1991) and DAM (2006; 2008) find a foundation in calling for their respective societies to wake up and understand how institutionalized violence is a form of state sponsored terrorism. State sponsored terrorism has the advantage of a prejudiced use of violence that forces violent extremism from its targeted population. Public Enemy recognizes this dynamic in its music video by *gunning up* as a means of protecting a cultural identity and adding to their own humanness. The deeper message of the music videos is not to promote violence but to call for peaceful societies where equality is equal. This message is important to the youth that use music as a venue to explain inequality in their lives (Ardizzone, 2003) A fitting punctuation to Public Enemy's *By the Time I get to Arizona* (1991) is the title of DAM's (2006) video questioning the label of terrorism: Min Erhabi—Who is the Terrorist?

In opposition to Public Enemy and DAM being voices of the oppressed, their music videos serve as veiled threats against their respective hegemonic societies. Also considered in the analysis of the music videos is how the lyrics and choreography of the various scenes calling out for equality actually nurture in listeners a quiet call to rebel against hegemonic oppression by creating a human identity. The purposeful focus on the differences Public Enemy and DAM have from the mainstream identity of the dominant society calls humanism into question on many levels. In these videos, the responsibility for the societal inequality points to the practices of those that created the parameters of the oppression portrayed.

Evolution of the Terrorist Training Curriculum

The curriculum of the terrorist has progressed from teaching as a secret to teaching through open source. The *Al Qaeda Training Manual* found in the apartment of a suspected Al Qaeda member in Manchester, England, in May 2000 shed light on the development of its fighters. Though the *Training Manual* (AQTM, 2000) is over fifteen years old, and outdated in the training concepts it provides, it nonetheless offers insight into the pedagogy of the terrorist training organizations of Al Qaeda. Organized into eighteen lessons, the *Training Manual* is less than half of the lessons of the seminal work of Carlos Marighella's 1969 version of the *Minimanual of the Urban Guerrilla* that reigned supreme as the *how to* book of revolutionaries from the previous wave of insurgent terrorism that swept the world during the preceding century. Conspicuously different in these two works are the primary objectives of the authors. Where the *Minimanual* (Marighella, 1969) was primarily concerned with a regime change in Brazil, the *Training Manual* has a global perspective that supports the prosecution of a war of annihilation against Seyyid Qutb's (1953/2000; 1991; 2005) ideas of jahilia—non-Muslim—powers in support of creating a greater Pan-Islamic society.

The premise of the *Training Manual* is to train soldiers to fight in a global jihad spearheaded by Al Qaeda. The power of religious fervor present in a cosmic war was absent in the *Minimanual* that sought to liberate oppressed people from a tyrannical government based on the promises of Marx's (1983) socialism as a better way of life. Consequently, the *Training Manual* has little if any compunction about the requirement to kill non-combatants, women and children included if they are outside the definition of Al Qaeda's Islamism. The battle space of the manuals is apparent in the scope of the lessons that concentrate on using an urban environment to harass the government in the *Minimanual* as opposed to planning terrorism from an all-environment approach of the *Training Manual*. The *Training Manual* also has the provision for a member to kill their fellow members if the greater purpose requires it—a tactic that Marighella most likely would have considered outside the realm of his form of violence.

Interesting in the *Minimanual* is that Marighella worked within the framework of recognizing an international legal structure by not wanting to be a person operating outside of common law practices for precipitating unreasonable violent activity. The *Minimanual* is narrow in its targeting of the enemy while the *Training Manual*, through its lessons, definitely does not consider its purpose subject to international norms concerning people or places off limits to violent attacks. Killing was a means to securing additional weapons for the urban guerrilla whereas the *Training Manual* saw the killing as a way to create fear in their enemies as a way of furthering their religious ideology. Fear is a weapon Al Qaeda recognized as a powerful weapon to use against Western societies and civilian populations. They knew they could not meet the military strength of the West head on, therefore they targeted the will of the people.

Similarly, dissimilar in the tactics espoused by the training manuals was how fuel formed a terrorist resource. Where the *Minimanual* posits that destroying a train of fuel denies the government a valuable resource, Al Qaeda saw a fuel-laden vehicle as a weapon of mass destruction and extreme violence. Terrorism to Marighella was the creation of a destructive force that was parallel to the tactics of the urban guerilla; however, the *Training Manual* views terrorism as the creation of fear as a weapon that is larger than the actual weapon employed during an attack. Fear of violence, they realized, affected a society as much as an actual attack. The psychological impact of fear creates long-term damage in the psyche of the American citizenry.

Both training manuals mutually see value in learning techniques from the enemy military forces. Through deception, the terrorists can learn from the military training their agents receive from standardized military training and then return to their respective organizations to teach other terrorists the valuable lessons learned while serving in the armed forces of the enemy. Another striking similarity in the training manuals is how they dehumanized the enemy by linking them to animals. By using the animalification of the enemy, the terrorist links the authority of the government to images of brutish stupidity—gorillas in the *Minimanual* and the unclean savagery of dogs in the *Training Manual*. These impressions reinforce in the trainee the idea of killing the enemy is no more than killing an animal that is nothing more than a nuisance to their version of society.

Serving time in a prison is a reality terrorists have acknowledged across the centuries (Khaled, 1973/2008). Prison time is an eventuality used to reinforce the core of the terrorist's ideology among like members or brothers in a religion (Office of the Inspector General, 2004). Much like American prisons that serve as finishing schools for traditional street-based gangs, prisons to Al Qaeda (AQTM, 2000) and Marighella (1969/2008) become a venue to reinforce loyalty in their respective organizations as well as a place to impart ideological and technical knowledge to its members.

In discussing the assassinating of enemy targets, the *Minimanual* maintained its narrow focus on targeting a limited portion of the population that represented the abuses of paternalism. The *Training Manual* had similar goals in killing, except that the tactic of assassination targeted a wider group of the population. The *Training Manual* added value throughout its many lessons in the use of objective examples from history that directly related to how a descriptive lesson related to the real world. This is reminiscent of the classical tomes on strategy like Sun Tzu's (1994) or Antoine-Henri Jomini's (1862/2011) respective treatises similarly titled *The Art of War*.

Without a doubt, the greatest form of improvement on terrorist tactics is the idea of total war. A totality that even Carl von Clausewitz had not seen in his epoch-making work, *On War* (1976/2008). None of these classical military strategists seriously considered the aspects of cosmic war that the Al Qaeda network brought to the events of 9/11 Events that changed the security posture of the world forever (9/11 Commission, 2004). Instead of wanting the support of the local population in the direct locale of the terrorist attacks of the *Minimanual*, the *Training Manual* seeks to create global fear in non-Muslims while stirring up support from those Muslims that have yet to join in Al Qaeda's cause.

The most significant sea changes in the pedagogy of violent extremism came with the internet. Besides the pedestrian use of the internet, the dark or deep web provides access to its users not indexed by normal search engines and provider services. In this section of the web, criminal activity can take place almost unnoticed. The internet was quickly grasped by the Islamic State as a universal classroom that challenged the success of the best MOOKS—that is—massive open online courses (Rose, 2014). The Islamic State's use of the internet and social media has schooled many Westerners into joining their state, either in deed or through emigration to the Levant. This feat is an astonishing feat of pedagogy missed by Westerns nations in the early part of the phenomenon (Jenkins, 2011). While the debate continues of why a young adult would leave the supposed safety and security of Westernization, the efforts to stop the Islamic State from using web-based programs is dismal at best (Kaleem, 2014; List, 2014). What requires further exploration is how the Islamic State is deschooling the Western youth and reeducating them to serve a new hegemonic power that provides promises in their curriculum's outcomes that most Western people cannot fathom.

Western leaders continue to view the issue of violent extremism through a hegemonic lens that does not consider the deep anthropologic ties people have to their society, culture, and linguistics. Whereas Western leaders call the Islamic State terrorists, they fail to comprehend that the Islamic State leadership is providing a praxis revealing the dream of leaders like Qutb, bin Laden, and Ayman Al Zawahiri, which prognosticated the creation of an Islamic state (Lister, 2014). Despite the labels the above men have regarding their role as world citizens, the caliphate created by the Islamic State provides proof of the lesson that hard work attains planned outcomes (Warrick, 2015). The tangibility of Islamic State's caliphate is an unquestionable truth. It is providing an arena where young Muslims can take part in the creation of a prophetic state more real than the search for Shangri-La. The caliphate, to its followers is real and it is accessible. With this accomplishment in Islamic State's emerging historical textbooks, the West needs to concentrate on a caliphate that can join the world community. To do this, Western leaders need to look beyond parochial hegemonic banking that insists the Middle East is a collection of nation states created by a red pen during the Sykes–Picot Agreement—an agreement that carved the last caliphate into economic market areas for Europe to exploit (Goldschmidt & Davidson, 2009). This lesson is lost to many Western leaders.

American know-how, and use of the internet, resulted in the success Al-Awlaki had as a global spokesperson for Al Qaeda (Sloan & Al-Shanti, 2011). An American imam who joined Al Qaeda used recorded lectures and distributed them on VCR tapes, CDs, and the internet. His lectures primarily carried the message of Qutbism as he called for Muslims to fight against the West. While he attracted many followers, Nidal Hassan (Chumley, 2014), the Fort Hood shooter amongst them, many Islamic scholars declared him a charlatan that misunderstood the purpose of jihad. The critique of Al-Awlaki's teachings by Abu Ameenah 'AbdurRahman Sloan and 'AbdulHaq al-Ashanti (2009) point out how Al-Awlaki manipulated Islamic scholarship to feed on the fears many noninformed Muslims had about jihad. Much like Andrew Macdonald's (1978/1996), *The Turner Diaries*, Al-Awlaki's teachings blended enough truth with a misdirected message to fuel apprehension in Muslims. Reinforcing Al-Awlaki's teachings is the growing Islamophobia in the West (Beck, 2015). He also used his status as an American who was willing to stand against the power of America. Known as the *Bin Laden of the internet* by the Saudi news station, Al Arabia, Al-Awlaki broke new ground in spreading his version of jihad to a limitless virtual world (Sloan & Al-Shanti, 2011; Ross & Ferran, 2011; Savage, 2014). Even with his assassination by America forces in September 2011, his teachings continue to drive jihadi causes

(Sloan & Al-Shanti, 2011). Not surprising, is that America's foxhunt for Al-Awlaki, including being the first American on the CIA's targeted hit list, actually serves as reason, and continues to do so, to portray Al-Awlaki as a hero of the jihad (Johnston & Shane, 2009).

Since Al-Awlaki's death, the Islamic State leaders became the professor in residence for continuing the jihad against the West (Warrick, 2015). Using its status as a caliphate to authenticate many of the fears Muslims have about Western hegemony, its messages are accessible on the internet, free of tuition, to support self-discovery in young adults that will become the next wave of the caliphate's subjects. Adding to the allure of learning about the Islamic State is the use of video and testimonials that prove more productive in gaining the attention of young adults as well as serving as a source of constructive retention in applying pedagogy. The result is a learned willingness to act out with violent extremism in the name of their ideology.

The pedagogical methodology used in spreading jihadism is like a street hawker peddling a questionable product mix to passersby. The Islamic State provides enough of a glimmer in their messages to attract attention (Ross, 2014). The discovery phase is up to the *shopper*. Allowing discovery is a formidable variable in pedagogy. Discovery provides for embedded knowledge in the learner. Unlike teaching to the test, the dynamics of discovery center on the learner and not the teacher as the provider of understanding. Likewise, this practice provides the learner with ownership for retaining and using their new domain of knowledge. The learning progression of discovery is hard to counter without a similar experience to challenge the information in question. Unfortunately, many in the West have not figured this out. Efforts to profile and block the internet activities of targeted Western youth is a tactic that does not consider that learning can be done through various sources and various formats.

References

9/11 Commission. (2004). The 9/11 commission report; Final report to the national commission on terrorist attacks upon the United States. Harrisonburg: W.W. Norton & Company.

"A post-colonial France: A chronicle of years of fire, France's relationship with its Arab population is defined by hatred and hurt." (2014, March 1). *The Economist*.

Achenbach, J. Wan, W., Berman, M., & Balingit, M. (2016, July 8). Five dallas police officers Were killed by a lone attacker; authorities say. *The Washington Post*. Retrieved from https://

www.washingtonpost.com/news/morning-mix/wp/2016/07/08/like-a-little-war-snipers-shoot-11-police-officers-during-dallas-protest-march-killing-five/.

Adi. (2012, September 19). Characteristics Inherent to the Occidental and Oriental Races: A Comparative Study. *Faith & Heritage*. Retrieved from http://faithandheritage.com/2012/09/characteristics-inherent-to-the-occidental-and-oriental-races-a-comparative-study/.

Admin. (2014, November 4). '350 million Muslims secretly live as Christian converts.' *Muslim World Press, Statistics*. Retrieved from https://muslimstatistics.wordpress.com/2014/11/04/350-million-muslims-are-secretly-living-lives-as-christian-converts/comment-page-1/.

Agence France-Presse. (2016, June 17). Brussels bombing suspect Youssef EA formally charged by Belgian authorities. *The Guardian*. Retrieved from https://www.theguardian.com/world/2016/jun/18/brussels-bombing-suspect-youssef-ea-formally-charged-by-belgian-authorities.

Aguila, E., & Godges, J. (2013). *Heavy lift: Truly comprehensive immigration reform would span the migrant labor lifecycle*. Rand Review, pp. 18–26.

Akers, S. (2013, October 2). Muslim man wakes from coma, converts to Christianity. *Charisma News*. Retrieved from http://www.charismanews.com/culture/41212-muslim-man-wakes-from-coma-converts-to-christianity.

Al Jazeera America. (2013, September 12). Somalia's al-Shabaab kills US fighter: Omar Hammami, known as al-Amriki or the American, killed in an ambush after falling out with group's leader. *Al Jazeera America*. Retrieved from http://www.aljazeera.com/news/africa/2013/09/201391293315761506.html.

Algemeiner. (2014, January 27). Hate-filled protest in France attracts thousands: Crowd chants 'Jew, France is not for you!' *The Algemeiner*. Retrieved from http://www.algemeiner.com/2014/01/27/hate-filled-protest-in-france-attracts-thousands-crowd-chants-jew-france-is-not-for-you-video/.

Ali-Shaykh, S. S. b. A. A. (2008). *A warning against extremism*. Dar Ibn Rajab: Madeenah.

Allen, R. L. (2004). Whiteness and critical pedagogy. *Educational Philosophy and Theory*. Vol. 36/2.

Allen, R. L., & Rossatto, C. A. (2009). Does critical pedagogy work with privileged students? *Teacher Education Quarterly*. Winter, p. 163–180.

"Almost 100 hate crime killings linked to one website: Report." (2014, April 18). *The Guardian*. Retrieved from the Huffington post at http://www.huffingtonpost.com/2014/04/08/hate-crimes-linked-to-website_n_5173944.html?icid=maing-grid7 | main5 | dl7 | sec1_inl2%26pLid%3D466548.

Al-Misri, A. I. N. (1991/1994). *Reliance of the traveler: A classical manual of Islamic sacred law*. Beltsville: Maryland: Amana Publications.

Al Qaeda Terrorist Training Manual (AQTM). (2000). (UK/BM-2 Translation, May) Manchester: UK/BM2.

Alter, C. (2013, September 24). Born in the USA: 5 American terrorists: If Americans were among the Kenya mall attackers as claimed, they'll join a growing list of home-grown terrorism. *Time*. Retrieved from http://world.time.com/2013/09/24/born-in-the-usa-5-american-terrorists/.

Amadeo, K. (2016, February 23). War on terror: Facts, costs, timeline. *About Money*. Retrieved from http://useconomy.about.com/od/usfederalbudget/f/War_on_Terror_Facts.htm.

American-Arab Anti-Discrimination Committee (ADC). (2015.). Countering violent extremism (CVE) programs. Retrieved from the ADC website at http://www.adc.org/countering-violent-extremism-cve/.

American Civil Liberties Union (ACLU). (2016, February 4) ACLU briefing paper; What is wrong with the government's "Countering Violent Extremism programs. Retrieved from https://theintercept.com/wp-uploads/sites/1/2016/02/CVE-Briefing-Paper-Feb-2016.pdf.

American Civil Liberties Union (ACLU). (2016, December). nationwide ant-Muslim activity. *ACLU Webpage*. Retrieved on July 17, 2016 from https://www.aclu.org/map/nationwide-anti-mosque-activity.

Anonymous. (2012, September 14). Converting to Islam: "I'm a 17-year-old Latin-American girl who switched from Christianity to Islam. *Huffington Post*. Retrieved from http://www.huffingtonpost.com/2012/09/12/converting-to-islam_n_1877655.html.

Ansolabehers, S., Persily, N., & Stewart, C. III. (2010, April). Race, region, and vote choice in the 2008 election: Implications for the future of Voting Rights Act. *Harvard Law Review*, Vol. 123, No. 6, pp. 1386–1436.

"Anti-immigration groups." (2001). *Southern Poverty Law Center*. Retrieved from http://www.splcenter.org/get-informed/intelligence-report/browse-all-issues/2001/spring/blood-on-the-border/anti-immigration-.

Ardizzone, L. (2003). Generating peace: A study of nonformal youth organizations. *Peace & Change*. Vol. 28, No. 3, pp. 420–445.

Aristotle. (1953/2004). *The Nicomachean ethics*. (J. A. K. Thompson, Trans.) New York: Penguin Classics.

Artsinger, A., & Roberts, R. (2007, January 2007). But it's Thomas Jefferson's Koran! *The Washington Post*. Retrieved from http://www.washingtonpost.com/wp-dyn/content/article/2007/01/03/AR2007010300075.html.

Aurelius, M. (1862/1997). *Meditations* (George Long, Trans.). Chesapeake: Dover Publications.

Arango, T., & Yeginsu, C. (2016, July 16). Turkey detains thousands in military in bid to regain control. *The New York Times*. Retrieved from http://www.nytimes.com/2016/07/17/world/europe/turkey-attempted-coup-erdogan.html.

Aslan, R. (2009). *How to win a cosmic war: God, globalization and the end of the war on terror*. New York: Random House.

Associated Press. (2012, February 16). Interracial marriages in the U.S. hit all-time high 4.8 million: 1 in 12 involved in interracial union, rise pegged to steadily flow of Asian and Hispanic immigrants. *Daily News*. Retrieved from http://www.nydailynews.com/life-style/interracial-marriages-u-s-hit-all-time-high-4-8-million-article-1.1023643.

Aucoin, J. (2014, October 24). The superhero diversity problem. *Harvard Political Review*. Retrieved from http://harvardpolitics.com/books-arts/superhero-diversity-problem/.

"Authorities say hate motivated Kansa shooting." (2014, April 14). *Associated Press*. Retrieved from http://www.aol.com/article/2014/04/14/suspect-in-killings-at-kansas-jewish-centers-has-hate-filled-his/20868805/?icid=maing-grid7 | main5 | dl6 | sec1_lnk2%26plid%3D464554.

Aydinli, O. & Ersel, U. (2003). Winning a low intensity conflict: Drawing lessons from the Turkish case, pp. 101–118. In Efraim, I. (Ed.) *Democracies and small wars*. Portland: Frank Crass.

Balko, R. (2016, July 6). Alton Sterling's death appears to be another police shooting that was both legal and preventable. *The Washington Post*. Retrieved from https://www.washington post.com/news/the-watch/wp/2016/07/06/alton-sterlings-death-appears-to-be-another-police-shooting-that-was-both-legal-and-preventable/.

Basit, T. N. (2009). White British; dual heritages; British Muslim: young Britons' conceptualization of identity and citizenship. *British Educational Research Journal*. October, Vol. 35/5, pp. 723–743.

Beaubien, J. (2011, July 7). Drug cartels prey on migrants crossing Mexico. *National Public Radio*. Retrieved from http://www.npr.org/2011/07/07/137626383/drug-cartels-prey-on-migrants-crossing-mexico.

Becerra, D., Androff, D. K., Ayon, C., & Castillo, J. T. (2012). Fear vs. facts: Examining the economic impact of undocumented immigrants in the U.S. *Journal of Sociology & Social Welfare*, December, Vol. 39, No. 4, pp. 111–135. Retrieved from http://www.google.com/url?sa=t&rct= j&q=&esrc=s&source=web&cd=2&ved=0CCcQFjAB&url=http%3A%2F%2Fwww. wmich.edu%2Fhhs%2Fnewsletters_journals%2Fjssw_institutional%2Finstitutional_sub scribers%2F39.4.Becerra.pdf&ei=m2y3U_GXN9TboATn1oKAAQ&usg=AFQjCNH0iexe GuoXJbQQ7yyVFdYImbOsUQ.

Beck, G. (2015). *It is about Islam: Exploring the truth about ISIS, Al Qaeda, and the Caliphate*. Mercury Radio Arts: New York.

Beutel, A. J. (2007). Radicalization and homegrown terrorism in western Muslim communities: lessons learned for America. *Minaret of Freedom Institute: Calling the faithful to Freedom*. Retrieved from http://www.google.com/url?sa=t&rct=j&q=&esrc=s&source=web&cd= 5&ved=0CDsQFjAE&url=http%3A%2F%2Fwww.minaret.org%2FMPAC%2520Back grounder.pdf&ei=6mC4U77oMoffoAT004CQDA&usg=AFQjCNF1D79j_vew_ HEP3EFDzZYxdzfdqA.

Berrebi, C., & Ostwald, J. (2013, February). *Terrorism and the Labor Force: Evidence of an effect on female labor force participation and the labor gender gap*. RAND Working Paper, Santa Monica: RAND.

Blake, A. (2015, January 6). The GOP's major 2016 problem—in 3 maps. *The Washington Post*. Retrieved from http://www.washingtonpost.com/news/the-fix/wp/2015/01/06/the-gops-2016-problem-in-3-maps/.

Blake, J. (2011, September 11). Four ways 9/11 changed America's attitude toward religion. *CNN*. Retrieved from http://religion.blogs.cnn.com/2011/09/03/four-ways-911-changed-ameri cas-attitude-toward-religion/.

Blinder, A. (2016, May 24). Death penalty is sought for Dylann Roof in Charleston church killings. *The New York Times*. Retrieved from http://www.nytimes.com/2016/05/25/us/dylann-roof-will-face-federal-death-penalty-in-charleston-church-killings.html.

Bloom, M. (2005). *Dying to kill: The allure of suicide terror*. New York: Columbia University Press.

Bocanegra, M. (n.d.). Homegrown terrorism in the United States. *Michael Bocanegra: Political And Social Issues*. Retrieved from http://mikebocanegra.hubpages.com/hub/Homegrown-Terrorism-in-the-United-States.

Boffey, D. (2013, January 12). Immigration is British society's biggest problem, shows survey to public. *The Guardian*. Retrieved from http://www.theguardian.com/uk/2013/jan/13/immigration-british-society-biggest-problem.

Bonner, R., & Weiser, B. (2006, August 11). Echoes of early design to use chemicals to blow up airliners—Asia—Pacific—International Herald Tribune. *The New York Times*. Retrieved from http://www.nytimes.com/2006/08/11/world/asia/11iht-web.0811manila.2447764.html.

Boozeman, J. (2014). Immigration reform & border security. On John Boozman US Senator for Arkansas website. Retrieved from http://www.boozman.senate.gov/public/index.cfm/immigration-reform-border-security.

Bothelho, G., & Sciutto, J. (2014, August 27). Slain ISIS jihadi among more than 100 Americans fighting with militants in Syria. *CNN*. Retrieved from http://www.cnn.com/2014/08/26/world/meast/syria-american-killed/.

Bovsun, M. (2013, June 15). 750 sickened in Oregon restaurants as cult known as the Rajneeshees spread salmonella in the town of The Dalles. *Daily News*. Retrieved from http://www.nydailynews.com/news/justice-story/guru-poison-bioterrorrists-spread-salmonella-oregon-article-1.1373864.

Braukis, H. (2014, April 14). Europe, U.S. immigration issues are worlds apart. *AZ Central*. Retrieved from http://www.azcentral.com/story/opinion/op-ed/2014/04/13/europe-us-immigration-issues-different/7685611/.

Brooks, R. A. (2011). Muslim 'homegrown' terrorism in the United States: How serious is the threat? *International Security*. Vol. 36, No. 2 (Fall), pp. 7–47.

Brown, M. (2011, December 6). Do American Muslims want to take over our country? *Town Hall.com*. Retrieved from http://townhall.com/columnists/michaelbrown/2011/12/06/do_american_muslims_want_to_take_over_our_country/page/full.

Burch, J. (2011, May 2). Afghans describe bin Laden as al Qaeda's "No 1 Martyr." *Reuters*. Retrieved from http://www.reuters.com/article/us-binladen-afghanistan-reaction-idUS-TRE74120A20110502.

Burke, J. How the changing media is changing terrorism. *The Guardian*. (2016, February 25). Retrieved from https://www.theguardian.com/world/2016/feb/25/how-changing-media-changing-terrorism.

Bush, G. W. (2002, September). *The national security strategy of the United States of America*. Washington, DC: GPO.

Bush, G. W. (2007). *National Strategy for Homeland Security (NSHS)*. Washington, DC: Government Printing Office.

Bushnaq, I. (1986). *Arab folktales*. (Inea Bushnaq, Ed. And, Trans.). New York; Pantheon Books.

Camarota, S. A. (2004). The high cost of cheap labor: Illegal immigration and the federal budget. *Center for Immigration Studies*. Retrieved from http://cis.org/High-Cost-of-Cheap-Labor.

Camarota, A. A., Poston, D. l. Jr., & Baumle, A. K. (2003, October). Remaking the political landscape: The impact of illegal and legal immigration on Congressional apportionment.

Center for Immigration Studies. Retrieved from http://cis.org/ImmigrationEffectCongressio
nalApportionment.

Canble Network News (CNN). (2010, January 6). Study: Threat of Muslim-American terrorism in U.S. exaggerated. *CNN*. Retrieved from http://edition.cnn.com/2010/US/01/06/
muslim.radicalization.study/.

Carafano, J., Bucci, S., & Zukerman, J. (2012, April 25). *Fifty terror plots foiled since 9/11: The
homegrown threat and the long war on terrorism*. The Heritage Foundation. Retrieved from
http://www.heritage.org/research/reports/2012/04/fifty-terror-plots-foiled-since-9-11-the-
homegrown-threat-and-the-long-war-on-terrorism.

Casey, N. (2014, July 30). U.N. blames Israel for shelter attack. *The Wall Street Journal*.
Retrieved from http://online.wsj.com/articles/gaza-health-ministry-explosions-at-school-
kill-15-1406705906?mod=wsj_india_main.

Castagnera, J. O. (2009, June). America's homegrown terrorists of the 21st Century: The disgruntled, the obsessed, and the mad ... three types, one challenge? *Homeland Security Review*.
Vol. 3, No. 2.

Carter, S. (2014a, Jun 16). 'They keep coming': The 'rehearsed' answers illegal immigrants
are using at the border to gain entry into the U.S. *The Blaze*. Retrieved from http://www.
theblaze.com/stories/2014/06/16/they-keep-coming-the-rehearsed-answers-illegal-immi
grants-are-using-at-the-border-to-gain-entry-into-the-u-s/.

Carter, S. (2014b, June 24). 'Potential for a public health disaster': Illegal immigrant surge
leaves officials with 'no idea' which diseases are coming across. *The Blaze*. Retrieved from
http://www.theblaze.com/stories/2014/06/24/potential-for-a-public-health-disaster-illegal-
immigrant-surge-leaves-officials-with-no-idea-which-diseases-are-coming-across/.

Caulderwood, K. (2014, June 17). Different ends same means: Research shows what terrorists
and crime syndicates have in common. *International Business Times*. Retrieved from http://
www.ibtimes.com/different-ends-same-means-research-shows-what-terrorists-crime-syn
dicates-have-common-1603628.

Center for Disease Control (CDC). (2015, February 20). Measles Outbreak—California
December 2014–February 2015. *Center for Disease Control*. Retrieved from https://www.
cdc.gov/mmwr/preview/mmwrhtml/mm6406a5.htm.

Center for Immigration Studies (CIS). (2015, February, 9). Vaccination rates among immigrants are a legitimate concern. *Center for Immigration Studies*. Retrieved from http://cis.
org/cis/vaccination-rates-among-immigrants-are-legitimate-concern.

Chang, A. (2014, July 11). Morning Edition: Administration officials defend funding request
to stem border crisis. *National Public Radio*. Sound recording available at http://www.npr.
org/2014/07/11/330631664/administration-officials-defend-funding-request-to-stem-bor
der-crisis.

Chomsky, N. (2003/2004). *Hegemony or survival: America's quest for global dominance*. New York:
Henry Holt.

Chomsky, N. (2007). *Interventions*. San Francisco: City Lights Books.

Chomsky, N. (2016, May 10). The US 'war on terror' is playing right into ISIS' hands. *The
Nation*. Retrieved from https://www.thenation.com/article/the-us-war-on-terror-is-playing-
right-into-isiss-hands/.

Confucius. (1993/2000). *Analects* (Raymond Dawson, Trans.) New York: Oxford University Press.

Christian Apologetics & Research Ministry (CARM). (2014). CARM, retrieved on August 3, 2014. Retrieved from http://carm.org/more-stuff/features/religious-tolerance-america.

Christian Broadcasting Network. (1990). Q & A: Why are so many westerners converting to Islam? Retrieved from http://www.cbn.com/spirituallife/onlinediscipleship/understandin gislam/why_are_westerners_converting.aspx.

Chumley, C. K. (2014, August 29). Fort Hood shooter Nidal Hasan petitions to be 'citizen' of Islamic State. *The Washington Times*. Retrieved from http://www.washingtontimes.com/news/2014/aug/29/fort-hood-shooter-nidal-hasan-petitions-be-citizen/.

Churchill, R. P. (2006). *Human rights and global diversity*. Upper Saddle River: Pearson Education.

Citizenship in the Balance: How anti-immigration activists twist the facts, ignore history, and flout the Constitution. (2011, February). *People for the American Way*. Retrieved on July 5, 2014 from http://www.pfaw.org/rww-in-focus/citizenship-the-balance-how-an ti-immigrant-activists-twist-the-facts-ignore-history-and.

Cohen, L. (2013, October 14). Shutdown power play: Stroking racism, fear of culture change to push anti-government agenda. *Forbes*. Retrieved from http://www.forbes.com/sites/rob waters/2013/10/14/shutdown-power-play-stoking-racism-fear-of-culture-change-to-push-anti-government-agenda/.

College Board. (2014). *Major profile, American Indian Studies* webpage at https://bigfuture.col legeboard.org/majors/area-ethnic-cultural-gender-studies-ethnic-cultural-minority-gen der-group-studies-american-indian-studies.

Combs, C. C. (2013). *Terrorism in the twenty-first century* (7th Ed.). Boston: Pearson.

Condon, S. (2011). Americans split on American exceptionalism, poll shows. CBS *news* Online, November 18. Retrieved from http://www.cbsnews.com/news/americans-split-on-ameri can-exceptionalism-poll-shows/.

Considine, C. (2013, May 26). Honoring Muslim American veterans on memorial Day. *The Huffington Post*. Retrieved from http://www.huffingtonpost.com/craig-considine/lets-hon or-muslim-america_b_3339838.html.

Cooper, C., & Block, R. (2006). *Disaster: Hurricane Katrina and the failure of Homeland Security*. New York: Henry Holt and Company, LLC.

Cortes, J. (2014, June 25). Honduran kids flee terror at home, hope for opportunity in U.S. *Reuters*. Retrieved from http://uk.reuters.com/article/2014/06/25/uk-usa-immigration-mexi co-idUKKBN0F00CS20140625.

Coughlin, C. (2014, November 5). How social media is helping Islamic State to spread its poison. *The Telegraph*. Retrieved from http://www.telegraph.co.uk/news/uknews/defence/11208796/How-social-media-is-helping-Islamic-State-to-spread-its-poison.html.

Corasanti, N., Perez-Pena, R., & Alvarez, L. (2015, June 18). Church massacre suspect held as Charleston grieves. *The New York Times*. Retrieved from http://www.nytimes.com/2015/06/19/us/charleston-church-shooting.html?_r=0.

Corman, L. (2011). Impossible subjects: The figure of the animal in Paulo Freire's *Pedagogy of the Oppressed*. *Canadian Journal of Environmental Education*. Vol. 16, pp. 29–45.

Cox, J. D. (2014, July 10). The unsung heroes in the immigration crises. *National Border Patrol Council Local 2554*. Retrieved from http://www.nbpc2554.org/.

Crenshaw, M. (1998). Logic of terrorism: Terrorist behavior as a product of strategic choice. *Origins of terrorism*. (Reich, Walter, ed.). Baltimore: John Hopkins University, pp. 7–17.

Crenshaw, R. (1974). *Naval Shiphandling* (4th Ed.) Newport: Naval Institute Press.

Cronin, A. K. (2006, Summer). How al-Qaeda end: The decline and demise of terrorist groups. *International Security*, Vol. 31, No. 1, pp. 7–48.

Cullors, P., Tometi, O., & Garza, A. (2016). Black lives matter. Official Website. Retrieved from http://blacklivesmatter.com/about/.

Currey, C. B. (1997). *Victory at any cost: The genius of Viet Nam's Gen. Vo Nguyen Giap*. Dulles: Potomac Books.

Dade, C. (2012, December 24). Obama administration deported record 1.5 million people. *National Public Radio (NPR)*. Retrieved from http://www.npr.org/blogs/itsallpolitics/2012/12/24/167970002/obama-administration-deported-record-1-5-million-people.

DAM (Da Arab Mcs.). (2006). *Who's the terrorist?* (Min Erhabi?). Video available at http://vimeo.com/7163495. Lyrics available at http://www.damrap.com/album/whos-terrorist-%D9%85%D9%8A%D9%86-%D8%A5%D8%B1%D9%87%D8%A7%D8%A8%D9%8A/116.

DAM (Da Arab Mcs.). (2008). *Born here*. Video available at DAM.com at http://www.damrap.com/media/clip/dam-born-here-hebrewarabic-english-subtitles/35

Darder, A. (1991/2012). *Culture and power in the classroom*. Boulder: Paradigm Publishers.

Darder, A. (2002). *Reinventing Paulo Freire: A pedagogy of love*. Cambridge: Westview Press.

Dassanayake, D. (2015, February 13). Islamic State: What is IS and why are they so violent? *Express*. Retrieved from http://www.express.co.uk/news/world/558078/Islamic-State-IS-what-is-ISIS-why-are-ISIL-so-violent.

Davidson, A. (2013, February 12). Do illegal immigrants actually hurt the U.S. economy? *The New York Times*. Retrieved from http://www.nytimes.com/2013/02/17/magazine/do-illegal-immigrants-actually-hurt-the-us-economy.html?pagewanted=all&_r=0.

Dawsey, J., Perez, E., & Barrett, D. (2013, May 8). Manhunt ends with capture of Boston bombing suspect. *The Wall Street Journal*. Retrieved from http://online.wsj.com/news/articles/SB10001424127887324493704578432030609754740.

Desilver, D. (2015, February 2). U.S. students improving—slowly—in math and science, but still lagging internationally. *Pew Research Center*. Retrieved from http://www.pewresearch.org/fact-tank/2015/02/02/u-s-students-improving-slowly-in-math-and-science-but-still-lagging-internationally/.

De Vries, H. (2002). *Religion and violence: Philosophical perspectives from Kant to Derrida*. Baltimore: The John Hopkins University Press.

Dickson, C. (2014, June 23). How Mexico's cartels are behind the border kid crises. *The Daily Beast*. Retrieved from http://www.thedailybeast.com/articles/2014/06/23/how-mexico-s-cartels-are-behind-the-border-kid-crisis.html.

Didymus, J. (2015, December 4). San Bernardino shooter Syed Farook clashed with Jewish co-worker Nicholas Thalasinos over religion, was teased about his long Islamic beard. *Inquisitor*. Retrieved from http://www.inquisitr.com/2608967/san-bernardino-shooter-sy

ed-farook-clashed-with-jewish-co-worker-nicholas-thalasinos-over-religion-was-teased-about-his-long-islamic-beard/.

Dienst, J., Valiquette, J., Nious, K., & Millman, J. (2015, April 3). 2 Queens women accused of plotting to plant bombs in U.S. talked suicide attacks, had propane tanks: Complaint. *NBC New York*. Retrieved from http://www.nbcnewyork.com/news/local/Terror-Arrest-New-York-FBI-NYPD-Police-297422441.html.

Dinan, S. (2013a, February 5). Top democrat warns against using the term 'illegal immigrants.' *The Washington Times*. Retrieved from http://www.washingtontimes.com/blog/inside-poli tics/2013/feb/5/top-democrat-warns-against-using-term-illegal-immi/.

Dinan, S. (2013b, August 23). Obama adds to list of illegal immigrants not to deport: Parents. *The Washington Times*. Retrieved from http://www.washingtontimes.com/news/2013/aug/23/new-obama-policy-warns-agents-not-detain-illegal-i/?page=all.

Dowling, T. (2015, November 27). One month later, what's next for the University of Missouri protesters? *USA Today*. Retrieved from http://college.usatoday.com/2015/11/27/whats-next-university-of-missouri/.

Dumalaon, J., Korolyov, A., & Jones-berry, S. (2014, March 31). Immigration backlash is on the rise in Europe. *USA Today*. Retrieved from http://www.usatoday.com/story/news/world/2014/03/31/europe-anti-immigration/5706575/.

Dyloco, P. (2012, January 6). What are Japanese averse to immigration? *Japan Today*. Retrieved from http://www.japantoday.com/category/opinions/view/why-are-japanese-averse-to-im migration.

Dynon, N. (2014, March 5). Kunming: A new phase of terrorism in China. *The Diplomat*. Retrieved from http://thediplomat.com/2014/03/kunming-a-new-phase-of-terrorism-in-china/.

Epstein, R. (2014, June). National council of La Raza leader calls Barak Obama 'deporter-in-chief.' Politico. Retrieved from http://www.politico.com/story/2014/03/national-council-of-la-raza-janet-murguia-barack-obama-deporter-in-chief-immigration-104217.html.

Esposito, J. L. (2010). *The future of Islam*. New York: Oxford Press.

Executive Office of the President. (2013). *The economic benefits of fixing our broken immigration system*. Washington, DC: Government Printing Office.

Fanon, F. (1952/2008). *Black skin: White masks: Get political*. London: Grove Press.

Fanon, F. (1961/2004). *The wretched of the earth*. (R. Philcox, Trans.). New York: Grove Press.

Fantz, A., & Brumfield, B. (2015, November 19). More than half the nation's governors say Syrian refugees not welcome. *CNN*. Retrieved from http://www.cnn.com/2015/11/16/world/paris-attacks-syrian-refugees-backlash/.

Fernandez, M., Perez-Pena, R., & Bromwich, J. (2016, July 8). Five Dallas officers were killed as payback, police chief says. *The New York Times*. Retrieved from http://www.nytimes.com/2016/07/09/us/dallas-police-shooting.html.

Ferran, L. (2014, July 31). 'Troubling': Suicide bomber hung out in US after terror training. *ABC News*. Retrieved from http://abcnews.go.com/Blotter/troubling-suicide-bomber-hung-us-terror-training/story?id=24790407.

Ferrechio, S. (2014). House republicans hit wall on immigration reform. *Washington Examiner*, February 6, as linked to "GOP leaders face wave of Opposition on immigration reform" on the Tea Party website at http://www.teaparty.org/gop-leaders-face-wave-opposition-immigration-reform-34247/.

Fife, G. (2004). *The terror: The shadow of the guillotine: France 1792–1794*. New York: St. Martin's Press.

Fischer, A. (2007, January 3). News from the Library of Congress. *Library of Congress*. Retrieved from http://www.loc.gov/today/pr/2007/07-001.html.

Fontanella-Khan, A. (2016, July 16). Fetullah Gulen: Turkey coup may have been 'staged' by Erdogan regime. *The Guardian*. Retrieved from https://www.theguardian.com/world/2016/jul/16/fethullah-gulen-turkey-coup-erdogan.

Fraley, M. (2015, October, 6). Accused Oikos University massacre shooter declared competent to stand trial. *The Mercury News*. Retrieved from http://www.mercurynews.com/crime-courts/ci_28924738/oakland-accused-oikos-massacre-shooter-declared-competent-stand.

Freeman, K. D. (2012). *Secret weapon: How economic terrorism brought down the U.S. stock market and why it can happen again*. Washington, DC: Regnery Publishing.

Freire, P. (1970/2000). *Pedagogy of the oppressed*. New York: Bloomsbury.

Freire, P. (1985). *The politics of education: Culture power and liberation*. (D. Macedo, Trans.). Westport: Bergin & Garvey.

Freire, P. (1988). *Pedagogy of freedom: Ethics, democracy, and civic courage*. (P. Clarke, Trans.). Lanham: Rowman & Littlefield Publishers.

Freire, P., & Macedo, D. (1987). *Literacy: Reading the word and the world*. Westport: Bergin & Garvey.

Freudenrich, C. (2015). How IEDs work. *How Stuff works*. Retrieved from http://science.howstuffworks.com/ied1.htm.

Friedersdorf, C. (2012, August 8). Why the reaction is different when the terrorist is white. *The Atlantic*. Retrieved from http://www.theatlantic.com/politics/archive/2012/08/why-the-reaction-is-different-when-the-terrorist-is-white/260849/.

Fuchs, P. (1995, June). Jumping to Conclusions in Oklahoma City? *American Journalism Review*. Retrieved from http://ajrarchive.org/article.asp?id=1980.

Fukuyama, F. (2014, March 10). American power is waning because Washington won't stop quarreling. *New Republic*. Retrieved from https://newrepublic.com/article/116953/american-power-decline-due-partisanship-washington.

Galula, D. (1964/2006). *Counterinsurgency warfare: Theory and practice*. Westport: Praeger Security International.

German, M. (2007). *Thinking like a terrorist: Insights of a former FBI undercover agent*. Washington, DC: Potomac Books.

Giap, V. N. (1976). *How we won the war*. Philadelphia: Recon Publishers.

Gibbons-Neff, T. (2015, December 4). The striking militarization of the San Bernardino shooters. *The Washington Post*. Retrieved from https://www.washingtonpost.com/news/checkpoint/wp/2015/12/04/the-weapons-used-by-the-san-bernardino-shooters-were-strikingly-militarized/.

Gibson, G. (2013, July 24). Steve King doubles down on 'drug mules' comment. *Politico*. Retrieved from http://www.kfiam640.com/media/podcast-handel-on-demand-BillHandel/immigration-crisis-7a-0703-24985857/.

Gimpel, J. G. (2014, April 24). Immigration's impact on republican prospects, 1980 to 2012. *Center for Immigration Studies.* Retrieved from http://cis.org/immigration-impacts-on-republican-prospects-1980-2012.

Giroux, H. A. (2014). *The violence of organized forgetting: Thinking beyond America's disimagination machine.* San Francisco: City Lights Books.

Glanz, J. Rotella, S., & Sanger, D. E. (2014, December 21). In 2008 Mumbai Attacks, Piles of Spy Data, but an Uncompleted Puzzle. *The New York Times.* Retrieved from http://www.nytimes.com/2014/12/22/world/asia/in-2008-mumbai-attacks-piles-of-spy-data-but-an-uncompleted-puzzle.html?_r=0.

Gohmert: US will become 'third world nation' if feds cont. enforce immigration laws. (2014, July 1). *CBS, DC.* Retrieved from http://washington.cbslocal.com/2014/07/01/gohmert-us-will-become-third-world-nation-if-feds-dont-enforce-immigration-laws/.

Goldberg, D., & Griffey, T. (Eds.) (2010). *Black power at work: Community control, affirmative action, and the construction industry.* Ithaca: Cornell University Press.

Goldfarb, Z. (2006, December 21). Va. Lawmaker's remarks on Muslims criticized. *The Washington Post.* Retrieved from http://www.washingtonpost.com/wp-dyn/content/article/2006/12/20/AR2006122001318.html.

Goldschmidt, A. Jr., & Davidson, L. (2009). *A concise history of the middle east* (9th Ed.). Boulder: Westview Press.

Gonzalez, M. (2013, August 28). The new American divide. Opinion. *New York Post.* Retrieved from http://nypost.com/2013/08/28/the-new-great-american-divide/.

Greenman, E., & Xie, Y. (2008, March). Is assimilation theory dead? The effect of assimilation on adolescent well-being. *Social Science Research,* 31 (1), pp. 100–113. Retrieved from http://www.ncbi.nlm.nih.gov/pmc/articles/PMC2390825/.

Grimes, W. (2005, September 2). Legion of the lost: The true experience of an American in the French Foreign Legion. *The New York Times.* Retrieved from http://www.nytimes.com/2005/09/01/arts/01iht-bookfri.html?_r=0.

Griswold, D. (2002, February 8). Immigrants have enriched American culture and enhanced our influence in the world. CATO Institute, originally appeared in *Insight* magazine. Retrieved from http://www.cato.org/publications/commentary/immigrants-have-enriched-american-culture-enhanced-our-influence-world.

Guevara, E. C. (1995/2003). *The motorcycle diaries: Notes on a Latin American Journey.* Melbourne: Ocean Press.

Guevara, E. C. (1961/2012). *Guerrilla warfare.* Melbourne: Ocean Press.

Habeck, M. (2012, June 27). Can we declare the war on al Qaeda over? *Foreign Policy.* Retrieved from http://foreignpolicy.com/2012/06/27/can-we-declare-the-war-on-al-qaeda-over/.

Hagerty, B. B. (2010, March 18). Is the Bible more violent than the Quran? *National Public Radio, All things Considered.* Retrieved from http://www.npr.org/templates/story/story.php?storyId=124494788.

Handel, B. (2014, July 3). Immigration crises 7A. *KFI AM Radio,* podcast available at http://www.kfiam640.com/media/podcast-handel-on-demand-BillHandel/immigration-crisis-7a-0703-24985857/.

Haughney, C. (2013, April 23). The Times shifts on "illegal immigrant," but doesn't ban the use. *The New York Times*. Retrieved from http://www.nytimes.com/2013/04/24/business/media/the-times-shifts-on-illegal-immigrant-but-doesnt-ban-the-use.html?pagewanted=all.

Healy, J., & Lovett, I. (2015, October 2). Oregon killer described as man of few words, except on topic of guns. *The New York Times*. Retrieved from http://www.nytimes.com/2015/10/03/us/chris-harper-mercer-umpqua-community-college-shooting.html.

Hennessy-Fiske, M., Bennett, B., & Carcamo, C. (2014, June 20). Obama administration acts to ease immigration legal crunch at border. *Los Angeles Times*. Retrieved from http://www.latimes.com/nation/nationnow/la-na-nn-border-migrants-white-house-20140620-story.html#page=1.

Hermann, P., & Marimow, A. E. (2013, September, 25). Navy yard shooter Aaron Alexis driven by delusions. *The Washington Post*. Retrieved from https://www.washingtonpost.com/local/crime/fbi-police-detail-shooting-navy-yard-shooting/2013/09/25/ee321abe-2600-11e3-b3e9-d97fb087acd6_story.html.

Heyes, J. D. (2014, July 2). Mexican drug cartels using illegal immigration flood as cover to smuggle operatives and hard drugs into the U.S. *Natural News*. Retrieved from http://www.naturalnews.com/045822_illegal_immigration_Mexican_cartels_drug_smuggling.html.

Hill, R. C., Griffiths, W. E., & Lim, G C. (2011). *Principles of econometrics* (4th Ed.). Hoboken: John Wiley & Sons.

Hobbs, F., & Stoops, N. (2002). *Demographic trends in the 20th Century*. Washington, DC: U.S. Census Bureau.

Hoffman, B. (2006). *Inside terrorism*. New York: Columbia University Press.

Hoffman, B. (2013, April 27). Answers to why people become terrorists. *The Daily Beast*. Retrieved from http://www.thedailybeast.com/articles/2013/04/27/answers-to-why-people-become-terrorists.html.

Hoffman, B., Rosenau, W., Curiel, A., & Zimmermann, D. (2007). *The radicalization of Diasporas and terrorism*: A joint conference by RAND corporation and the Center for Security Studies, ETH Zurich. Santa Monica: RAND.

Holmes, D. L. (2006). The faiths of the Founding Fathers. New York: Oxford University Press.

Homeland Secretary: Agency that removes immigrants will be out of money by mid-September at 'current burn rate.' (2014, July 11). *CBS Local*. Retrieved from http://washington.cbslocal.com/2014/07/11/homeland-secretary-agency-that-removes-immigrants-will-be-out-of-money-by-mid-september-at-current-burn-rate/.

Hopkirk, P. (1990/1994). *The great game: The struggle for Empire in Central Asia*. New York: Kodansha.

House of Commons. (2005). *Report of the official account of the bombings in London on 7th July 2005*. London: The Stationary Office.

Houston, J. W., & Houston, J. D. (1973/2007). *Farwell to Manzanar*. Boston: Houghton Mifflin Company.

"How cartels use tunnels to send drugs into US." *New York Post*, Associated Press. Retrieved from http://nypost.com/2014/01/14/how-smuggling-tunnels-are-built-used-along-us-border/.

Hsu, H. (2009, January 1). The end of white America? *The Atlantic*. Retrieved from http://www.theatlantic.com/magazine/archive/2009/01/the-end-of-white-america/307208/.

Huffman, A. O. (2011). *Homegrown terrorism in the United States: Comparing radicalization trajectories in Britain and America* (Master's thesis). Retrieved from http://respository.library. georgetown.edu/bitstream/handle/10822/553516/huffmanAlexia.pdf?sequence=1.

Hughes, D. M., Chon, K. Y., & Ellerman, D. P. (2007, September) Modern-day comfort women: The U.S. military, transnational crime, and the trafficking of women. *The University of Rhode Island.* Retrieved from http://www.google.com/url?sa=t&rct=j&q=&esrc=s&source=web&cd=8&ved=0CFIQFjAH&url=http%3A%2F%2Fwww.cops.usdoj. gov%2Fhtml%2Fcd_rom%2Fsolution_gang_crime%2Fpubs%2FDreamsGangsandGuns TheInterplayBetweenAdolescent.pdf&ei=DJ24U4mMCJCgogTmz4LYBg&usg=AFQ jCNHLNY5ET9OFEDvqEBMFl48J90EJAg&bvm=bv.70138588,d.cGU.

Hughes, S. (2005). Theorizing oppressed family pedagogy: Critical lessons from rural family in the post-Brown south. *Educational Foundations.* Summer-Fall, pp. 45–72.

Human Rights Watch (HRW). (1999, October 1). Anti-Christian violence on the rise in India: New report details behind extremist Hindu attacks. *Human Rights Watch.* Retrieved from http://www.hrw.org/en/news/1999/09/29/anti-christian-violence-rise-india.

Huntington, S. P. (1996). *The clash of civilizations and the remaking of world order.* New York: Touchstone.

Huxley, A. (2013, January 25). It's official: "Terrorist" is the most inappropriately over-used word in American English. *Forming the Thread.* Retrieved from http://formingthethread.wordpress. com/2013/01/25/its-official-terrorist-is-the-most-inappropriately-over-used-word-in-american-english/.

Husain, E. (2013, September). A global venture to counter violent extremism. *Council on Foreign Relations.* Retrieved from http://www.cfr.org/radicalization-and-extremism/global-venture-counter-violent-extremism/p30494.

Ibrahim, R. (2012, May 15). Mexican jihad. *Front Page Mag.* Retrieved from http://www.frontpagemag.com/2012/raymond-ibrahim/mexican-jihad/.

"Illegal immigrants cause public school crisis." (2008, March 11). *The Judicial Watch.* Retrieved from http://www.judicialwatch.org/blog/2008/03/illegal-immigrants-cause-public-school-crisis/.

Illich, I. (1968, April 28). *To hell with good intentions.* Address presented to the Conference on Inter-American Student Projects (CIASP) in Cuernavaca, Mexico. Retrieved from http://www.swaraj.org/illich_hell.htm.

Illiach, I. (2000). *Deschooling society.* London: Marion Boyers Publishers.

"Immigration facts: Immigration and terrorism polls." (2009) *Federation for American Immigration Reform.* Retrieved from http://www.fairus.org/facts/immigration-and-terrorism-polls.

Immigration Watch Canada. (2014). Homepage at http://www.immigrationwatchcanada.org/.

Inserra, D. (2015, June 8). 69th Islamist Terrorist Plot: Ongoing Spike in Terrorism Should Force Congress to Finally Confront the Terrorist Threat. *The Heritage Foundation.* Retrieved from http://www.heritage.org/research/reports/2015/06/69th-islamist-terrorist-plot-ongoing-spike-in-terrorism-should-force-congress-to-finally-confront-the-terrorist-threat.

Jackson, S. (2007). Freire re-viewed. *Educational Theory.* Vol. 57/2.

Jansen, B. (2016, July 17). 3 police officers shot dead in Baton Rouge. *USA Today.* Retrieved from http://www.usatoday.com/story/news/2016/07/17/reports-baton-rouge-police-officers-shot/87218884/.

Jansen, J. J. G. (1986/2013). *The neglected duty: The creed of Sadat's assassins.* New York: RVP Publishers, pp. 199–213.

Jeffers, G. Jr., Scoggin, A., & Solis, D. (2014, June 28). Clay Jenkins wants Dallas County to house children. *Dallas News.* Retrieved from http://www.desertsun.com/story/news/local/2014/07/04/murrieta-california-border-patrol-immigration-protests-undocumented-immigrants-july-fourth/12217279/.

Jenkins, B. M. (2010). *Would-be warriors: Incidents of jihadist terrorist radicalization in the United States since September 11, 2001.* Santa Monica: RAND.

Jenkins, B. M. (2011). *Stray dogs and virtual armies: Radicalization and recruitment to jihadist terrorism in the United States since 9/11.* Santa Monica: RAND.

Jenkins, B. M., Liepman, A., & Willis, H. (2014). *Identifying enemies among us: Evolving terrorist threats and the continuing challenges of domestic intelligence collection and information sharing.* Santa Monica: RAND.

Jenkins, B. M. (2014, July 30). An evil wind. *The RAND Blog* at http://www.rand.org/blog/2014/07/an-evil-wind.html.

Jillson, C. (2009). *American Government: Political Development and Institutional Change* (5th ed.). New York: Taylor & Francis.

Jimenez, T. R. (2010). *Replenished ethnicity: Mexican Americans, immigration, and identity.* Berkley: University of California Press.

Johnson, J. (2014). *Quadrennial Homeland Security Review Report (QHSR).* Washington, DC: Government Printing Office.

Johnson, T. (2011, September 30). *Threat of homegrown Islamist terrorism.* Council on Foreign Relations. Retrieved from http://www.cfr.org/terrorism/threat-homegrown-islamist-terrorism/p11509.

Johnson, J., & Weigel, D. (2015, December 8). Donald trump calls for 'total' ban on Muslims entering United States. *The Washington Post.* Retrieved from https://www.washingtonpost.com/politics/2015/12/07/e56266f6-9d2b-11e5-8728-1af6af208198_story.html.

Johnston, D., & Shane, S. (2009, November 9). U.S. Knew of Suspect's Tie to Radical Cleric. *The New York Times.* Retrieved from http://www.nytimes.com/2009/11/10/us/10inquire.html.

Jomini, A.-H. (1862/2011). *The art of war.* (G. H. Mendell & W. P. Craighill, Trans.). Memphis: Bottom of the Hill Publishing.

Jones, A. (2011, May 11). 18 facts prove illegal immigration is absolute nightmare for U.S. economy. *Infowars.* Retrieved from http://www.infowars.com/18-facts-prove-illegal-immigration-is-absolute-nightmare-for-u-s-economy/.

Jones, L. (2014, February 28). Too many celebrities, not enough heroes. *The Washington Post.* Retrieved from https://www.washingtonpost.com/opinions/too-many-celebrities-not-enough-heroes/2014/02/28/dbfc3f5c-98e0-11e3-80ac-63a8ba7f7942_story.html.

Jurgensmeyer, M. (2000). *The global rise of religious violence.* Berkeley: University of California Press.

Juergensmeyer, M. (2003). *Terror in the mind of god.* (3rd ed.) New York: University of California Press.

Kaleem, J. (2014, October 6). Here's why these Muslims are refusing to criticize ISIS. *Huffington Post*. Retrieved from http://www.huffingtonpost.com/2014/10/06/muslims-condemn-isis-de bate_n_5927772.html.

Kaplan, A., & Phillip, A. (2015, September 16). They thought it was a bomb: 9th grader arrested after bringing a home-built clock to school. *The Washington Post*. Retrieved from http://www.washingtonpost.com/news/morning-mix/wp/2015/09/16/they-thought-it-was-a-bomb-ahmed-mohamed-texas-9th-grader-arrested-after-bringing-a-home-built-clock-to-school/.

Kaplan, E. (2009, January 8). Terrorists and the internet. *Council on Foreign Relations*. Retrieved from http://www.cfr.org/terrorism-and-technology/terrorists-internet/p10005.

Kettl, D. (2014). *System under stress: The challenge to 21st century governance*. Los Angeles: Sage.

Kenber, B. (2013, August 28). Nidal Hassan sentenced to death for Fort Hood shooting rampage. *The Washington Post*. Retrieved from http://www.washingtonpost.com/world/national-security/nidal-hasan-sentenced-to-death-for-fort-hood-shooting-rampage/2013/08/28/aad28de2-0ffa-11e3-bdf6-e4fc677d94a1_story.html.

Kilner, J. (2003). The pedagogy of terrorism. *Education Links*, Vol. 66/67, pp. 5–11.

Khaled, L. (1973/2008). *My people shall live: The autobiography of a revolutionary*. O. Sandberg, Digital Edition. Retrieved from https://archive.org/stream/MyPeopleShallLive/My%20People%20Shall%20Live%20by%20Leila%20Khaled#page/n1/mode/2up.

Khan, Y. (2008). *The great partition: The making of India and Pakistan*. New Haven: Yale University Press.

Kifner, J. (1995, December 31). McVeigh's mind: A special report; Oklahoma bombing suspect: Unraveling of a frayed life. *The New York Times*. Retrieved from http://www.nytimes.com/1995/12/31/us/mcveigh-s-mind-special-report-oklahoma-bombing-suspect-unraveling-frayed-life.html.

Killerman, S. (2014). 30+ examples of Christian privilege. Its Pronounced Metrosexual. Retrieved from http://itspronouncedmetrosexual.com/2012/05/list-of-examples-of-christian-privileg/.

Kirby, S. M. (2015, April 19). Congressman Ellison and Jefferson's Koran: What does Ellison know about the Koran he used for his ceremonial swearing-in? *Front Page Magazine*. Retrieved from http://www.frontpagemag.com/fpm/255250/congressman-ellison-and-jeffersons-koran-dr-stephen-m-kirby

Kotkin, J. (2010, August). The changing demographics of America: The United States population will expand by 100 million over the next 40 years. Is this a reason to worry? *Smithsonian Magazine*. Retrieved from http://www.smithsonianmag.com/40th-anniversary/the-changing-demographics-of-america-538284/.

Kumamoto, R. (2006). *The historical origins of terrorism in America: 1644–1880*. New York: Rutledge.

Krukenberg, K. A. (2008, April). *Multi-hued America: The case for the civil rights movement's embrace of multiethnic identity*. From the selected works of Kamaria A. Kruckenberg. Retrieved from http://works.bepress.com/cgi/viewcontent.cgi?article=1000&context=kamaria_kruckenberg.

Lake, E. (2013, September 12). Americans join Syrian jihad, sparking U.S. intelligence fears. *The Daily Beast*. Retrieved from http://www.thedailybeast.com/articles/2013/09/12/americans-join-syrian-jihad-sparking-u-s-intelligence-fears.html.

Lampen, C. (2016, July 18). Can you spot the reason people are upset about Paul Ryan's latest Instagram post? *AOL News*. Retrieved from http://www.aol.com/article/2016/07/18/can-you-spot-the-reason-people-are-upset-about-paul-ryans-lates/21433945/.

Lance, P. (2013, February 26). The blind sheikh: A flashpoint for terror 20 years after the World Trade Center bombing: Just how dangerous is the blind sheikh? *Alternet*. Retrieved from http://www.alternet.org/blind-sheikh-flashpoint-terror-20-years-after-world-trade-center-bombing.

Lawrence, B. (Ed.) (2005). *Messages to the world: The statements of Osama bin laden*. New York: Verso.

Lawrence, T. E. (2011). *Seven pillars of wisdom: A triumph*. Blacksburg: Wilder Publications.

Lazear, E. P. (2005, March). *Mexican assimilation in the United States*. Research report for the Hoover Institute and Graduate School of Business, Stanford University.

LeBaron, G. Jr. (1995). Mormon fundamentalism and violence: A historical analysis. *ExMormon*. Retrieved from http://www.exmormon.org/violence.htm.

Lee-Ashley, M. (2016, March 24). Congress should confront the rise of violent extremism on America's public lands. *Center for American Progress*. Retrieved from https://www.americanprogress.org/issues/green/report/2016/03/24/133730/congress-should-confront-the-rise-of-violent-extremism-on-americas-public-lands/.

Lehrer, J. (2007, June 18). Churches providing sanctuary for illegal immigrants. *Public Broadcasting System*, podcast transcript available at http://www.pbs.org/newshour/bb/social_issues-jan-june07-sanctuary_06-18/.

Leistyna, P. (2004). Presence of mind in the process of learning and knowing: A dialogue with Paulo Freire. *Teacher Education Quarterly*. Winter, pp. 17–29.

Lengall, S. (2014, February 12). Supreme Court Justice Clarence Thomas: racism worse now than era segregated South. *Washington Examiner*. Retrieved from http://washingtonexaminer.com/supreme-court-justice-clarence-thomas-racism-worse-now-than-era-of-segregated-south/article/2543918#null.

Leon, M. (2015, October 31). 'Captain America' writer slams Fox News for sympathizing with his xenophobic villains. *The Daily Beast*. Retrieved from http://www.thedailybeast.com/articles/2015/11/01/captain-america-writer-slams-fox-news-for-calling-his-xenophobic-villains-ordinary-americans.html.

Leong, N. (2013, June). Racial capitalism. *Harvard Law Review*, Vol. 126, No. 8, pp. 2152–2226.

Lerche, C. O. III. (1998). The conflicts of globalization. *The International Journal of Peace Studies*. Vol. 3, No, 1. Retrieved from http://www.gmu.edu/programs/icar/ijps/vol3_1/learch.htm.

Levy, G. (2016, March 10). Immigration dominates democratic debate. *U.S. News & World Report*. Retrieved from http://www.usnews.com/news/articles/2016-03-10/immigration-dominates-democratic-debate.

Lewis, T. E. (2009). Education in the realm of the senses: Understanding Paulo Freire's aesthetic unconscious through Jacques Ranciere. *Journal of Philosophy of Education*. Vol. 43/2, pp. 285–299.

Lewis, T. E. (2010). Paulo Freire's last laugh: Rethinking critical pedagogy's funny bone through Jacques Ranciere. *Educational Philosophy & Theory*. Vol. 42/5–6, pp. 635–648.

Lewis, T. E. (2012). Exopedagogy: On pirates, shorelines, and the educational commonwealth. *Educational Philosophy & Theory*. Vol. 44, No. 8, pp. 845–861.

Lewiston mayor reacts to immigrants' protest. (2014, July 2). *Lewiston-Auburn Sun Journal*. Retrieved from http://www.sunjournal.com/news/lewiston-auburn/2014/07/02/lewiston-mayor-reacts-immigrants-protest/1556623#.

Lind, D. (2014, May 9). What do pro-enforcement groups want out of the deportation review? *Vox*. Retrieved from http://www.vox.com/2014/5/9/5699288/what-do-pro-enforcement-groups-want-out-of-the-deportation-review.

Lipovsky, I. P. (2012). *Early Israelites: Two peoples, one history: Rediscovery of the origins of Biblical Israel*. Igor P. Lipovsky.

Lister, T. (2014, June 13). ISIS: The first terror group to build an Islamic state? *CNN*. Retrieved from http://edition.cnn.com/2014/06/12/world/meast/who-is-the-isis/.

Lovett, I., & Montgomery, D. (2014, July 21). For two slain Americans, commitment came early. *The New York Times*. Retrieved from http://www.nytimes.com/2014/07/22/world/middleeast/2-americans-among-israeli-soldiers-killed-in-gaza.html?_r=0.

Lowe, L. (1996). *Immigrant Acts: On Asian American cultural politics*. Durham: Duke University Press.

Lublin, J. S. (2014, January 9). Bringing hidden biases into light: Big businesses teach staffers how 'unconscious bias' impacts decisions. *The Wall Street Journal*. Retrieved from http://online.wsj.com/news/articles/SB10001424052702303754404579308562690896896.

Lucassen, J. (2009). The mobility transition revisited, 1500–1900: What the case of Europe can offer to global history. *Journal of Global History*, Issue 3.

Lyles, M. C. (2012). *The man of wiles in popular Arabic literature: A study of a medieval Arab Hero*. Edinburgh: Edinburgh University Press.

Macdonald, A. (1978/1996). *The Turner diaries*. Fort Lee: Barricade Books.

Mapping Police Violence. (2017, January 1). Unarmed black people were killed by police at 5X the rate of unarmed whites in 2015. *Mapping Police Violence*. Retrieved from http://mappingpoliceviolence.org/unarmed/.

Mardrus, J. C., & Mathers, P. (1964/1987). *The book of the thousand nights and one night*. (J. C. Mardrus & Powys Mathers, Trans.). New York: Dorset Press.

Machiavelli, N. (2008). The Prince: And other writings. (W. K. Marriott, Trans.). Fall River Press.

Mansfield, L. (2006). *His own words: Translation and analysis of the writings of Dr. Ayman Al Zawahiri*. San Bernardino: TLG Publications.

Marighella, C. (1969/2008) *Minimanual of the urban guerrilla*. St. Petersburg: Red and Black Publishers.

Martinelli, T. (2006, October 10). Unconstitutional policing: The ethical challenges in dealing with noble cause corruption. *The Police Chief*, Vol. 73, No. 10. Retrieved from http://www.policechiefmagazine.org/magazine/index.cfm?fuseaction=display&article_id=1025&issue_id=102006.

Marszal, A. (2014, June 6). Sword fight at India's Golden temple on raid anniversary. *The Telegraph*. Retrieved from http://www.telegraph.co.uk/news/worldnews/asia/india/10880015/Sword-fight-at-Indias-Golden-Temple-on-raid-anniversary.html.

Marx, K., & Engles, F. (1948). *Manifesto of the communist party*. New York: International Publishers.

Marx, K. (1983). *The portable Karl Marx*. (Eugene Kamenka, ed.). New York: Penguin Books.

Marzulli, J. (2013). Adis medunjanin, terrorist foiled in 2009 bomb plot on New York subway, to serve life sentence in notorious Colo. Prison: 'Cleaner version of hell.' *Daily News*, May, 27. Retrieved from http://www.nydailynews.com/news/national/foiled-terrorist-serve-life-noto rious-colo-prison-article-1.1355289.

Mascaro, L., & Bennett, B. (2014, June 29). Obama's bid to deport children complicates immigration reform effort. *Los Angeles Times*. Retrieved from http://www.latimes.com/nation/la-na-obama-immigration-reform-20140630-story.html#page=1.

Mateu-Gelabert, P. (2002). Dreams, gangs, and guns: The interplay between adolescent violence and immigration in a New York City neighborhood. *Vera Institute of Justice*. Retrieved from http://www.google.com/url?sa=t&rct=j&q=&esrc=s&source=web&cd= 8&ved=0CFIQFjAH&url=http%3A%2F%2Fwww.cops.usdoj.gov%2Fhtml%2Fcd_ rom%2Fsolution_gang_crime%2Fpubs%2FDreamsGangsandGunsTheInterplayBe tweenAdolescent.pdf&ei=DJ24U4mMCJCgogTmz4LYBg&usg=AFQjCNHLNY5E T9OFEDvqEBMFl48J90EJAg&bvm=bv.70138588,d.cGU.

Matthews, C. (2015, June 5). Edward Snowden: Privacy remains 'under threat.' *Fortune*. Retrieved from http://fortune.com/2015/06/05/edward-snowden-privacy-oped/.

McCartney, C. (2013, August 26). Mob of 1,000 Buddhists burns down Muslim homes and shops in Myanmar. *The Global Post*. Retrieved from http://www.globalpost.com/dispatches/global post-blogs/belief/mob-1000-buddhist-burn-down-muslim-homes-and-shops-myanmar.

McIntyre, A. (2000). Constructing meaning about violence, school, and community: Participatory action research with urban youth. *The Urban Review*. Vol. 32, No. 2, pp. 123–154.

McKinley, J. C. Jr. (2005, January 6). A Mexican manual for illegal migrants upsets some in U.S. *The New York Times*. Retrieved from http://www.nytimes.com/2005/01/06/international/americas/06mexico.html?_r=0.

Mears, B. (2014, February 12). Analysis: Justice Thomas comments spark fresh debate on race. *CNN Politics*. Retrieved from http://www.cnn.com/2014/02/12/politics/clarence-thomas-racism/.

"Measuring America: The decennial census from 1790 to 2000." (2015). *U.S. Census Bureau*. Decennial Census data. Retrieved from https://www.census.gov/history/www/programs/demographic/decennial_census.html.

"Medal of Honor Recipients: African American World War II Medal of Honor Recipients." (2015). *U.S. Army*. Retrieved from http://www.history.army.mil/moh/mohb.html.

Mehta, J. (2013, May/June). Why American education fails: And how lessons from abroad could improve it. *Foreign Affairs*. Vol. 92, No. 3.

Menon, R., & Fuller, G. E. (2000, March/April). Russia's ruinous Chechen war. *Foreign Affairs*. Retrieved from http://www.foreignaffairs.com/articles/55844/rajan-menon-and-graham-e-fuller/russias-ruinous-chechen-war.

"Mobility measured: America is no less socially mobile than it was a generation ago." (2014, February 1). *The Economist*.

Moeller, S. (2004, March 18). Think again: Bush's war on terror. *Center for American Progress*. Retrieved from https://www.americanprogress.org/issues/security/news/2004/03/18/615/think-again-bushs-war-on-terror/.

Moran, S. (2015). Kant's conception of pedagogy. *South African Journal of Philosophy*. Vol. 34/1, pp. 29–37.

Myers, D., & Pitkin, J. (2010). *Assimilation today: Evidence shows the latest immigrants to America are following in our history's footsteps*. Washington, DC: Center for American Progress.

Myre, G. (2013, April 20). Boston bombings point to growing threat of homegrown terrorism. *National Public Radio*. Retrieved from http://www.npr.org/blogs/thetwo-way/2013/04/20/177958045/boston-bombings-point-to-growing-threat-of-homegrown-terrorism.

Nakamura, D., & Harris, H. R. (2015, October 10). 20 years after the Million Man March, a fresh call for justice on the Mall. *The Washington Post*. Retrieved from https://www.washingtonpost.com/politics/20-years-after-the-million-man-march-a-fresh-call-for-justice-on-the-mall/2015/10/10/b3d8ffca-6f66-11e5-b31c-d80d62b53e28_story.html.

Napolitano, J. (2010). *Quadrennial Homeland Security Review Report (QHSR)*. Washington, DC: Government Printing Office.

Napolitano, J. (2012). *Department of Homeland Security Strategic Plan: Fiscal years 2012–2016*. Washington, DC: US Government Printing Office.

"Native Americans say US violated human rights: A Native American group is asking the international community to charge the United States with human rights violations in hopes of getting help with a land claim." (2014, April 14). *Associated Press*. Retrieved from AOL News at http://www.aol.com/article/2014/04/14/native-americans-say-us-violated-human-rights/20868905/?icid=maing-grid7 | main5 | dl19 | sec1_lnk2%26pLid%3D464622.

Nebraska Studies. The missionary spirit: The conversion struggle. *Nebraska Studies*. Retrieved from http://www.nebraskastudies.org/0400/frameset_reset.html?http://www.nebraskastudies.org/0400/stories/0401_0129.html.

Nelson, R. (2010). *A growing terrorist threat? Assessing "Homegrown" extremism in the United States*. Center for Strategic & International Studies A report of the CSIS homeland security and counterterrorism program. Washington, DC: CSIS.

Nelson, R., & Bodurian, B. (2010, March). A growing terrorist threat? Assessing "Homegrown" extremism in the United States. *Center for Strategic & International Studies A report of the CSIS homeland security and counterterrorism program*. Washington, DC. Retrieved from http://csis.org/files/publication/100304_Nelson_GrowingTerroristThreat_Web.pdf.

Nelson, S. S. (2013, September 16). German nationalists protest against Muslim immigration. *National Public Radio*. Retrieved from http://www.dailystormer.com/german-nationalists-protest-against-muslim-immigration/.

NewsOne. (2013, April 19). Muslim woman attacked after Boston Marathon bombings. *NewsOne*. Retrieved from http://newsone.com/2396424/heba-abolaban-boston-marathon-bombings-terrorist/.

Nimmo, K. (2011, July 6). Russian FSB Boss: Internet a Haven for Terrorists. *InfoWars.com*. Retrieved from http://www.infowars.com/russian-fsb-boss-internet-a-haven-for-terrorists/.

Nuzzi, O. (2015, November 16). Jeb Bush & Ted Cruz only want to save Christians. *The Daily Beast*. Retrieved from http://www.thedailybeast.com/articles/2015/11/16/jeb-cruz-only-want-to-save-christians.html.

Oakes, E. T. (2008, January 29). Atheism and violence. *First Things*. Retrieved from http://www.firstthings.com/web-exclusives/2008/01/atheism-and-violence.

Obama, B. (2011a). *Presidential Policy directive – 8: National Preparedness*. Washington, DC: Government Printing Office.

Obama, B. (2011b). *Empowering local partners to prevent violent extremism in the United States*. Washington, DC: Government Printing Office.

Obama, B. (2015, February). *National security strategy*. Washington, DC: GPO.

Obeidallah, D. (2015, May 18). America Snores When Christian Terrorist Threatens to Massacre Muslims. *The Daily Beast*. Retrieved from http://www.thedailybeast.com/articles/2015/05/18/guess-why-this-christian-terrorist-plot-against-muslims-isn-t-getting-any-press.html.

O'Connor, A. (2011, July 27). Mexican cartels move into human trafficking. *The Washington Post*. Retrieved from http://www.washingtonpost.com/world/americas/mexican-cartels-move-into-human-trafficking/2011/07/22/gIQArmPVcI_story.html.

Office of the Inspector General. (2004, April). *A review of the federal bureau of prisons' selection of Muslim religious services providers*. Washington, DC: U.S. Department of Justice.

Oliker, O. (2013, May 6). Searching for clues on the brothers Tsarnarev. *Rand*. Retrieved from http://www.rand.org/blog/2013/05/searching-for-clues-on-the-brotherstsarnarev.html.

O'Reilly, B. (2014, July 2). Talking points: America growing angrier at the federal government. *Fox News*, video available at http://www.foxnews.com/on-air/oreilly/index.html.

Owens, E. (2012, November 26). Texas school teach Boston tea party as act of terrorism. *The Daily Caller*. Retrieved from http://dailycaller.com/2012/11/26/texas-schools-teach-boston-tea-party-as-act-of-terrorism/.

Page, J., & Levin, N. (2014, June 24). Web Preaches Jihad to China's Muslim Uighurs: China Says Internet, Social Media Incite Terrorism Among Uighur Minority. *The Wall Street Journal*. Retrieved from http://www.wsj.com/articles/web-preaches-jihad-to-chinas-muslim-uighurs-1403663568.

Panza, S. (2014, July 2). Furious California citizens block buses carrying illegal immigrants, force them to turn around. *IJReview*. Retrieved from http://www.ijreview.com/2014/07/152958-even-california-citizens-are-angrily-protesting-against-obamas-plan-to-bus-illegal-aliens-all-over-america/.

Papademetriou, D. (2005, September 1). The global struggle with illegal migration: No end in sight. *Migration Information* Source, Migration Policy Institute. Retrieved from http://www.migrationpolicy.org/article/global-struggle-illegal-migration-no-end-sight.

Parikh, R. (2006). White males, racism and Christian fundamentalism in American politics. *Sulekha.com*. Retrieved from http://creative.sulekha.com/white-males-racism-and-christian-fundamentalism-in-american-politics_190267_blog.

Patten, E., & Lopez, M. H. (2013, July 22). Are unauthorized immigrants overwhelmingly democrats? *Pew Research Center*. Retrieved from http://www.pewresearch.org/fact-tank/2013/07/22/are-unauthorized-immigrants-overwhelmingly-democrats/.

Peck, M. (2013, August 20). Russia Says Cyberspace is New 'Theater of War.' *Forbes*. Retrieved from http://www.forbes.com/sites/michaelpeck/2013/08/20/russia-says-cyberspace-is-new-theater-of-war/.

Post, J. (2005, August). When hatred is bred in the bone: Psycho-cultural foundations of contemporary terrorism. *Political Psychology*, Vol. 26, No. 4, pp. 615–636.

Powell, W. (1971). *The anarchist cookbook*. Fort Lee: Barricade Books.

Preston, J. (2013, September 23). Number of illegal immigrants in U.S. may be on rise again, estimates say. *The New York Times.* Retrieved from http://www.nytimes.com/2013/09/24/us/immigrant-population-shows-signs-of-growth-estimates-show.html?_r=0.

Public Enemy. (1991). *By the time I get to Arizona.* Written by Ridenhour, C., Rinaldo, G., & Shocklee, H. Produced by Island Def Jam Group. Video available on YouTube at http://www.youtube.com/watch?v=zrFOb_f7ubw; lyrics available at http://www.publicenemy.com/album/10/34/by-the-time-i-get-to-arizona.html.

Qutb. S. (1953/2000). *Social justice in Islam.* (J. B. Hardie, & H. Algar, Trans.). Oneonta: Islamic Publications International.

Qutb, S. (1991). *The Islamic concept and its characteristics.* (Mohammed Moinuddin Siddiqui, Trans.). Plainfield: American Trust Publications.

Qutb, S. (2005) *Milestones.* (2nd Ed). Damascus: Dar al-Ilm.

"Race and Higher education: Not black and white. Asians object to affirmative action." (2014, March 22–28). *The Economist.*

Rasley, G. (2014, July 3). Murrieta shows citizens can strike back against illegal alien invasion. *Conservative HQ.* Retrieved from http://www.conservativehq.com/article/17653-murrieta-shows-citizens-can-strike-back-against-illegal-alien-invasion.

Religion Statistics. (2014). U.S. Census Bureau. Retrieved from http://www.census.gov/compendia/statab/cats/population/religion.html.

"Reports 1: Religious affiliation" and "Report 2: Religious beliefs & practices/social & political views." (2014). *Pew Forum.* Retrieved from http://religions.pewforum.org/reports.

Resnick, G. (2015, September 29). Seven times the Taliban was supposedly defeated. *The Daily Beast.* Retrieved from http://www.thedailybeast.com/articles/2015/09/29/seven-times-the-taliban-was-supposedly-defeated.html.

Rice, C. (2007). *Trafficking in persons reports.* Washington, DC: US Government Printing Office.

Rice, Z. (2016, January 20). How Fresno, California, became hotspot for anti-Sikh violence in America. *Identities.mic.* Retrieved from https://mic.com/articles/132552/how-fresno-california-became-a-hotspot-for-anti-sikh-violence-in-america#.6gvZgupNA.

Riddell, K. (2014, April 9). Sheriffs warn of violence from Mexican cartels deep into interior of U.S. *The Washington Times.* Retrieved from http://www.washingtontimes.com/news/2014/apr/9/sheriffs-warn-of-violence-from-mexican-cartels-dee/?page=all.

Robbins, L., & Hamill, S. D. (2009, April 4). Gunman kills 3 police officers in Pittsburgh. *The New York Times.* Retrieved from http://www.nytimes.com/2009/04/05/us/05pittsburgh.html.

Roberts, P. (2007). The years on: Engaging the work of Paulo Freire in the 21st Century. *Studies in Philosophy & Education.* Vol. 26, pp. 505–508.

Robertz, F. J. (2007, July 30). Deadly dreams: what motivates school shootings? [Preview]. *Scientific American.* [Excerpt from *The science of gun violence and gun control in the U.S.*] Retrieved from http://www.scientificamerican.com/article/deadly-dreams/?page=3.

Rockwell, N. (1958, 20 September). *Runaway.* Retrieved from http://www.art.com/products/p9388040471-sa-i5446828/norman-rockwell-runaway-september-20-1958.htm.

Rodgers, E. (2015, August 12). The insiders: The Black Lives Matter movement is bad for Democrats. *The Washington Post.* Retrieved from https://www.washingtonpost.com/blogs/

post-partisan/wp/2015/08/12/the-insiders-the-black-lives-matter-movement-is-bad-for-democrats/.

Roediger, D. (2005). *Working toward whiteness: How America's immigrants became white: The strange journey from Ellis Island to the suburbs.* New York: The Perseus Books Group.

Romano, J. (2015, June 20). Romano: Killer's crusade for white America defies logic. *Tampa Bay Times.* Retrieved from http://moms.tampabay.com/news/courts/criminal/romano-killers-crusade-for-white-america-defies-logic/2234485.

Rose, S. (2014, October 7). The Isis propaganda war: A hi-tech media jihad. *The Guardian.* Retrieved from http://www.theguardian.com/world/2014/oct/07/isis-media-machine-propaganda-war.

Ross, B., & Ferran, L. (2011, September 30). How Anwar al-Awlaki inspired terror from across the globe. *ABC News.* Retrieved from http://abcnews.go.com/Blotter/anwar-al-awlaki-inspired-terror/story?id=14643383.

Rubin, A. J., Blaise, L., Nossiter, A., & Breeden, A. (2016, July 15). France says truck attacker Was Tunisia native with record of petty crime. *The New York Times.* Retrieved from http://www.nytimes.com/2016/07/16/world/europe/attack-nice-bastille-day.html.

Rudolph, E. (2013, April 24). Are Christians more violent than Muslims? *Abagond.* Retrieved from http://abagond.wordpress.com/2013/04/24/are-christians-more-violent-than-muslims/.

Rustom, R. (2012, September 15). Why most terrorists are Muslims. *Islam Watch.* Retrieved from http://www.islam-watch.org/authors/142-rami/1145-why-most-terrorists-are-muslims.html.

Saad, L. (2013, October 31). U.S. crime is up, but Americans don't seem to have noticed. *Gallup.* Retrieved from http://www.theatlantic.com/magazine/archive/2009/01/the-end-of-white-america/307208/.

Said, E. W. (1978/1994). *Orientalism.* New York: Vintage Books.

Said, E. W. (1993). *Cultural imperialism.* New York: Vintage Books.

Said, E. W. (1994). *Representations of the intellectual: The Reith lectures.* New York: Vintage Books.

Said, E. W. (2004). *Humanism and democratic criticism.* New York: Columbia University Press.

Sanchez, T., & Cano, R. (2014, July 5). Dueling immigration rallies in Calif. Town: 6 arrested. *The Desert Sun.* Retrieved from http://www.desertsun.com/story/news/local/2014/07/04/murrieta-california-border-patrol-immigration-protests-undocumented-immigrants-july-fourth/12217279/.

Sakuma, A. (2015, August 6). Immigration issues dominate opening of GOP presidential debate. *MSNBC.* Retrieved from http://www.msnbc.com/msnbc/immigration-issues-dominate-opening-gop-presidential-debate.

Sankaran, K. (2003). Indian way in counterinsurgency. Efraim, I. (Ed.) *Democracies and small wars,* pp. 85–97. Portland: Frank Crass.

Savage, C. (2014, June 23). Court releases large parts of memo approving killing of American in Yemen. *The New York Times.* Retrieved from http://www.nytimes.com/2014/06/24/us/justice-department-found-it-lawful-to-target-anwar-al-awlaki.html?_r=0.

Seibert, T. (2013, February 27). Ocalan negotiations bring Turkey a step closer to peace with Kurds. *The National.* Retrieved from http://www.thenational.ae/news/world/europe/ocalan-negotiations-bring-turkey-a-step-closer-to-peace-with-kurds.

Serrano, R., Blankstein, A., & Gerber, M. (2013, June 8). Santa Monica shooting suspect, possible motive identified, officials say. *Los Angeles Times*. Retrieved from http://articles.latimes.com/2013/jun/08/local/la-me-ln-santa-monica-gunman-identified-john-zawahri-20130608.

Sewall, S. (2016, March 30). Our common struggle against violent extremism. *US Department of State*. Retrieved from http://www.state.gov/j/remarks/255314.htm.

Schanzer, D., Kurzman, C., & Moosa, E. (2010). Anti-terror lessons of Muslim-Americans. *Duke University*. Retrieved from http://www.google.com/url?sa=t&rct=j&q=&esrc=s&source=web&cd=1&ved=0CB0QFjAA&url=http%3A%2F%2Fsites.duke.edu%2Ftcths%2Ffiles%2F2013%2F06%2FSchanzer_Kurzman_Moosa_Anti-Terror_Lessons1.pdf&ei=ZqneU6uTL9PooATEiIHQBA&usg=AFQjCNETb-hEGBweLfZYZMkmPkqYfv_xpw&bvm=bv.72197243,d.cGU.

Schubert, W. H. (2008). Perspectives on the pedagogy of democracy. *Curriculum and Training Dialogue*. Vol. 10/1–2, pp. 157–164.

Schladen, M. (2014, July 2). DPS: Cartels helping immigrant children enter US illegally. *El Paso Times*. Retrieved from http://www.kfiam640.com/media/podcast-handel-on-demand-BillHandel/immigration-crisis-7a-0703-24985857/.

Schoch, J. (2012, November 9). 20 athletes we wish were better role models. *Bleacher Report*. Retrieved from http://bleacherreport.com/articles/1394702-20-athletes-we-wish-were-better-role-models.

Schroeter, S. (2013). "The way it works" doesn't: Theatre of the oppressed as critical pedagogy and counternarrative. *Canadian Journal of Education*. Vol. 36/4, pp. 394–415.

Schmidt, M. S., & Perez-Pena, R. (2015, December 4). F.B.I. treating San Bernardino attack as terrorism case. *The New York Times*. Retrieved from http://www.nytimes.com/2015/12/05/us/tashfeen-malik-islamic-state.html.

Sergie, M. A., & Johnson, T. (2015, March 5). Boko Haram. *Council on Foreign Relations*. Retrieved from http://www.cfr.org/nigeria/boko-haram/p25739.

Shapira, I. (2010, March 7). Pentagon shooter's spiral from early promise to madness. *The Washington Post*. Retrieved from http://www.washingtonpost.com/wp-dyn/content/article/2010/03/06/AR2010030602537.html.

Shrestha, N. (2010, September 29). Explore other cultures to understand your own. *Collegiate Times*. Retrieved from http://www.collegiatetimes.com/opinion/columnists/article_8c7d4da2-8ff9-548f-857e-03b9384e2193.html.

Silsby, G. (2013, August 7). Why people take the risk of illegal immigration. *Futurity*: University of Southern California Study. Retrieved from http://www.futurity.org/why-people-take-the-risk-of-illegal-immigration/.

Singh, J. (2014, June 16). Robert Bergdhal's beard is not the threat. *Huffington Post*. Retrieved from http://www.huffingtonpost.com/jasjit-singh/robert-bergdahls-beard-is_b_5500749.html.

Sizgorich, T. (2008). *Violence and belief in late antiquity: Militant devotion in Christianity and Islam (Divinations: Rereading late ancient religion)*. Philadelphia: University of Pennsylvania Press.

Sloan, A. A. A., & Al-Ashanti, A. (2011). *A critique of the methodology of Anwar Al-Awlaki and his errors in the Fiqh of Jihad*. Leyton: Jamiah Media.

Snowden, P. (2014). The revolution *will* be uploaded: Vernacular video and the Arab Spring. *Culture Unbound*. Vol. 6, pp. 401–429.

Snyder, M. (2013, August 10). 19 very disturbing facts on illegal immigration every American should know. *Right Side News*. Retrieved from http://www.rightsidenews.com/2013081033026/us/homeland-security/19-very-disturbing-facts-on-illegal-immigration-every-ameri can-should-know.html.

Soergel, A. (2015, February 3). Better test scores could mean trillions of dollars for the U.S. economy. *US News & World Report*. Retrieved from http://www.usnews.com/news/arti cles/2015/02/03/better-test-scores-could-mean-trillions-of-dollars-for-the-us-economy.

Southern Poverty Law Center (SPLC). (2009, February 26). Hate group numbers up by 54% since 2000. *Southern Poverty Law Center*. Retrieved from http://www.splcenter.org/get-in formed/news/hate-group-numbers-up.

Sonner, S. (2014, July 10). Report shows how Cliven Bundy has emboldened right-wing extremists. *Huffington Post*. Retrieved from http://www.huffingtonpost.com/2014/07/10/cliven-bundy-report_n_5574512.html.

Squires, N. (2008, October 5). Protests in Italy against escalating racism. *The Telegraph*. Retrieved from http://www.telegraph.co.uk/news/worldnews/europe/italy/3141066/Protests-in-Italy against-escalating-racism.html.

Stern, J. (2000). *The ultimate terrorists*. Boston: Harvard University Press.

Stavridis, J., & Girrier, R. (2007). *Watch officer's guide* (15th Ed.). Newport: Naval Institute Press.

Straziuso, J., Forliti, A., & Watson, J. (2012, January 14). Al Shabaab's American recruits in Somalia. *Huffington Post*. Retrieved from http://www.huffingtonpost.com/2012/01/14/americans-al-shabaab_n_1206279.html.

Takeda, A. (2015, July 16). Colorado Theater Shooter James Holmes Found Guilty of First-De gree Murder. *US Weekly*. Retrieved from http://www.usmagazine.com/celebrity-news/news/colorado-theater-shooting-verdict-james-holmes-found-guilty-of-murder-2015167.

Taraby, J. (2013, August 14). A rare meeting with reclusive Turkish spiritual leader Fethullah Gulen. *The Atlantic*. Retrieved from http://www.theatlantic.com/international/archive/2013/08/a-rare-meeting-with-reclusive-turkish-spiritual-leader-fethullah-gulen/278662/.

Tashman, B. (2011, March 29). Tea party group warns of white "extinction" in America. *Right Wing Watch*. Retrieved from http://www.rightwingwatch.org/content/tea-party-group-warns-white-extinction-america.

Thaler, D., Brown, R. Gonzalez, G., Mobley, B., & Roshan, P. (2013). *Improving the U.S. military's understanding of unstable environments vulnerable to violent extremist groups: Insights from social science*. Santa Monica: RAND.

"The church and racism: Toward a more fraternal society." (1997.). *Political Commission Jus tice and Peace*, Eternal World Television Network (EWTN), Global Catholic Network. Retrieved from http://www.ewtn.com/library/curia/pcjpraci.htm.

"The path of least resistance: The republicans may be groping their way to compromise." (2014, February 8). *The Economist*.

"The Dish: Biased and Balanced." (2014). Retrieved from http://dish.andrewsullivan.com/2014/04/28/the-pernicious-poison-of-palin-ctd.

The White House. (2015, February 18). Fact sheet: The White House Summit on counter ing violent extremism. *Office of the White House Press Secretary*. Retrieved from https://

www.whitehouse.gov/the-press-office/2015/02/18/fact-sheet-white-house-summit-coun
tering-violent-extremism.

Thompson, P. (2010, May 16). Autistic child charged with terrorism over school drawing. *The Telegraph*. Retrieved from http://www.telegraph.co.uk/news/worldnews/northamerica/ usa/7731513/Autistic-boy-charged-with-terrorist-offence.html.

Tiger, C. (1999). *The classic treasury of Aesop's fables*. (Caroline E. Tiger, Ed.). Philadelphia: Running Press.

Toews, V. (2013). *2013 public report on the terrorist threat to Canada*. Canada; Ministry of Public Safety.

Tone, H., & Uwimana, S. (2013, February 1). 10 myths conservative media will use against immigration reform. *Media Matters for America*. Retrieved from http://mediamatters.org/ research/2013/02/01/10-myths-conservative-media-will-use-against-im/192494.

Tse-tung, M. (2012). On guerrilla warfare. San Bernardino: Import Books.

Tures, J. (2009). Do terrorists win elections? *Homeland Security Affairs*, September. Vol. V, No. 3. Retrieved from http://www.hsaj.org/?fullarticle=5.3.5.

Tzu, S. (1994). *The art of war*. (R. D. Sawyer, Trans.). New York: Fall River Press.

U.S. Census Bureau. (2012). Statistical abstract of the United States: 2012. U.S. Census Bureau. Retrieved from http://www.google.com/url?sa=t&rct=j&q=&esrc=s&source=web&cd= 1&ved=0CB0QFjAA&url=http%3A%2F%2Fwww.census.gov%2Fprod%2F 2011pubs%2F12statab%2Fpop.pdf&ei=UHDeU8n9F8XaoATLr4D4DQ&usg=AFQ jCNHabHgDXuO-kS1UMDIUFyYAbw8CSQ&bvm=bv.72197243,d.cGU.

U.S. Department of Health and Human Services (USDHHS). (2016, June 23). Community immunity. Retrieved from http://www.vaccines.gov/basics/protection/.

Utley, R. M., & Washburn, W. E. (2002). *Indian wars*. New York: American Heritage Press.

Vadum, M. (2015, October 9). The Million Man March comes to Washington: Violence on the Horizon? *Front Page magazine*. Retrieved from http://www.frontpagemag.com/fpm/260399/ million-man-fraud-comes-washington-matthew-vadum.

Venugopal, A. (2011, May 24). Immigrants assimilate more successfully in the U.S. than in Europe: Report. *WNYC*. Retrieved from http://www.wnyc.org/story/136690-immigrants-as similate-more-successfully-us-europe-according-report/.

Vetter, R. (2013, August 5). Border security costs taxpayers $12 Billion. *IVN*. Retrieved from http://ivn.us/2013/08/05/border-security-costs-taxpayers-12-billion-2/.

Vigdor, J. (2008). *Measuring immigrant assimilation in the United States*. Manhattan: Center for Civic Innovation.

Vinzant, J. H. (2006). *Supreme Court interpretation and policy making in American Indian Policy*. Dissertation, Southern Illinois University, UMI Number: 3229889

Von Clausewitz, C. (1976/2008). On war. (M. Howard, & P. Paret, Trans. & Eds.). Princeton: Princeton University Press.

Voorhees, J. (2013, April 23). Slatest PM: How the Tsarnaev Brothers learned to make their bombs. *The Slate*. Retrieved from http://www.slate.com/blogs/the_slatest/2013/04/23/ inspire_magazine_tsarnaev_brothers_used_al_qaida_magazine_for_directions.html.

Walser, R., McNeill, J. B., & Zuckerman, J.. (2011). The human tragedy of illegal immigra-tion: Greater efforts needed to combat smuggling and violence. *The Heritage Foundation*.

Retrieved from http://www.heritage.org/research/reports/2011/06/the-human-tragedy-of-il legal-immigration-greater-efforts-needed-to-combat-smuggling-and-violence.

Warrick, J. (2015). *Black flags: The rise of ISIS*. New York: Doubleday.

Watanabe, T. (2015, November 20). Occidental College protesters to end sit-in, vow to keep fighting bias. *The Los Angeles Times*. Retrieved from http://www.latimes.com/local/lanow/la-me-ln-oxy-protest-ends-20151120-story.html.

Watson, J. (2014, July 2). Buses with migrant families rerouted amid protest. *Associated Press*. Retrieved from http://talkingpointsmemo.com/news/buses-with-migrant-families-rerout ed-protests.

Weathers, C. (2014, June 4). Jon Stewart chides Fox news: You'd like Bob Bergdahl's beard if Hewas on 'Duck Dynasty.' *Alternet*. Retrieved from http://www.alternet.org/news-amp-pol itics/jon-stewart-chides-fox-news-youd-bob-bergdahls-beard-if-he-was-duck-dynasty.

Wellman, J. (2013, July 7). Should Christians have non Christian friends? *What Christians Want to Know*. Retrieved from http://www.whatchristianswanttoknow.com/should-chris tians-have-non-christian-friends/.

Werner, E., & Caldwell, A. A. (2014, July 14). Possible compromise emerges on border secu rity. *Associated Press*. Retrieved from http://www.aol.com/article/2014/07/10/possible-com promise-emerges-on-border-request/20928845/?icid=maing-grid7 | main5 | dl17 | sec1_ lnk2%26pLid%3D500053.

Wilber, D. Q. (2010, January 7). Von Brunn, white supremacist Holocaust museum shooter, dies. *The Washington Post*. Retrieved from http://www.washingtonpost.com/wp-dyn/con tent/article/2010/01/06/AR2010010604095.html.

Williams, P. (2007). *The day of Islam; The annihilation of America and the western world*. New York: Prometheus Books.

Williams, P. (2014, May 30). Florida Man Identified as Syria Suicide Bomber. *NBC News*. Retrieved from http://www.nbcnews.com/news/investigations/florida-man-identified-syr ia-suicide-bomber-n118926.

Wolf, N. (2015, February 20). Chilling report details how Elliot Rodger executed murderous rampage. *The Guardian*. Retrieved from https://www.theguardian.com/us-news/2015/feb/20/mass-shooter-elliot-rodger-isla-vista-killings-report.

Woodyard, C., & Heath, B. (2015, December 3). San Bernardino shooters lived a double life. *USA Today*. Retrieved from http://www.usatoday.com/story/news/2015/12/03/san-ber nardino-shooter/76710658/.

Woodsome, K. (2013, April 26). Immigration shapes US political parties as much as demograph ics. *Voice of America*. Retrieved from http://www.voanews.com/content/immigration-shapes-us-parties-as-much-as-demographics/1649600.html.

Wright, B. (1916). *The real Mother Goose* (Blanche F. Wright, Illus.). New York: Scholastic, Inc.

Zakaria, F. (2013, January/February). Can America be fixed? The new crisis of democracy. *For eign Affairs*.

Zalikind, S. (2015, June 22). How ISIS's 'Attack America' Plan Is Working. *The Daily Beast*. Retrieved from http://www.thedailybeast.com/articles/2015/06/22/how-isis-s-attack-amer ica-plan-is-working.html.

Zein, Q. (2007, May 14). The list: The world's fastest growing religions. *Foreign Policy*. Retrieved from http://www.foreignpolicy.com/articles/2007/05/13/the_list_the_worlds_fastest_growing_religions.

Ziv, S. (2014, November 25). Report details Adam Lanza's life before Sandy Hook. *US Newsweek*. Retrieved from http://www.newsweek.com/report-details-adam-lanzas-life-sandy-hook-shootings-286867.

Zorn, J. (2001). Henry Giroux's pedagogy of the oppressed. *Academic Questions*. Fall.

· 2 ·

THE FACE OF AMERICA'S THIRD CIVILIZATION

Mismanaging America's Demographic Shift and the Rise of Violent Extremism

Overview

America's civilizational profile is changing as the demographic shift in America is creating a new collective face that represents America. Along with the loss of a European-based identity, America's cultural and religious preferences of the last century are giving way to a national identity that is multihued (Krukenberg, 2008). Mismanaging this civilizational change will create conditions facilitating the growth of violent extremism in America. This section explores the factors that create threats of violent extremism coming from more than the jihadi-based terrorist groups that the media prefers to cover in an unbalanced coverage of religious-based violent extremism (Jurgensmeyer, 2000; 2003). There is also a growing threat of violent extremism from a White supremacist movement that does not want to relinquish the control of its European-based, Christian-driven, ideological regime. Their goal is regime continuity through entrenchment of the institution of hegemonic banking. It will take a deep understanding of the demographic shift's unavoidable changes to social practices, customs, and identity to produce conditions indicative to more or less violent extremism in America's future.

According to the U.S. Census Bureau (2012), the demographic shift in America has risen from about one in eight people being non-White in 1900 to about one in four people being non-White in 2000. Figure 2.1 illustrates the change in the ratio of non-White Americans in the 100 years from 1900 to 2000. The ratio of White compared to non-White Americans doubled during the period reviewed. Within this ratio change, the Hispanic population exceeded growing twice in size from 1980 to 2000. A consideration that requires attention is the growing trend in non-White Americans is the report from the U.S. Census Bureau (2012) that the White population grew slower than all other races from about 1950 to 2000. Additionally, reported was the minority population growing at a rate eleven times faster than the White population from 1980 to 2000.

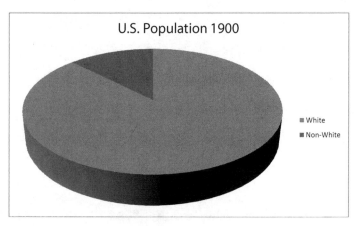

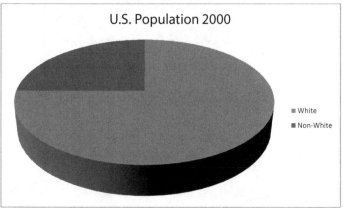

Figure 2.1: Demographic Shift in the United States, 1900–2000.
Source: Author, Copyright 2015

Discussed later in this section are the racial enclaves that exist within America. The U.S. Census Bureau (2012) confirmed these segregative tendencies saying that Blacks and Asians are the most regionally concentrated races with Blacks living in the south and Asians in the west. Understand that the U.S. Census Bureau's current methodologies do not capture many of the ethnic data addressed in this book.

Driving contemporary debate on immigration are those that seek to enter America as refugees seeking asylum. According to the Department of Homeland Security, refugees coming to America grew from 28,286 in 2003 to 69,909 in 2013. Figure 2.2 shows a disaggregated illustration of the 69,909 refugees entering America in 2013. The largest growth seen is in refugees during this period is in refugees from Asia. The most significant increase experienced in refugees from 2012 to 2013 was from Africa, Asia, and North America. In 2013, countries that had more than 500 refugees enter America were Afghanistan with 661 refugees, Bhutan with 9,134 refugees, Burma with 16,299 refugees, Congo with 2,563 refugees, Cuba with 4,205 refugees, Eretria with 1,824 refugees, Ethiopia with 765 refugees, Iran with 2,579 refugees, Iraq with 19,478 refugees, and Somalia with 7,608 refugees.

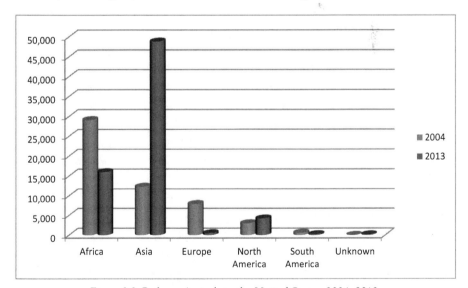

Figure 2.2: Refugee Arrivals in the United States, 2004–2013.
Source: Author, Copyright 2015

America affirmatively granted 15,266 people with asylum in 2013. Those countries that had more than 1,000 people granted asylum were from Africa with 4,844 people, Asia with 7,579 people, and North America with 1,152 people. From these people granted asylum, the largest populations were from China with 4,072 people and Egypt with 3,102 people. Except for Iran, which had 612 people granted asylum, the rest of the countries had less than 500 people granted asylum. The data on immigration clearly shows that people are entering America from all over the world. Not counted in this data are those that enter America illegally or stay beyond their legal dates of entry. The remainder of this segment and the next will weave together a tapestry of how immigration affects the development and use of violent extremism. The analysis will contain the voice of many actors in the immigration and security arenas that exist in America; many linked to violent extremism—a notion not previously explored widely in the literature on security studies.

Violent Extremism in Response to a Demographic Shift

The face of America is changing for the third time since humans first populated North America. Long gone from America is the Norman Rockwell version of a predominantly Anglo-American landscape. America's collective face is giving way to a distinct character that is multihued (Kruckenberg, 2008) as immigration and inter-race marriages are on the rise. Particularly salient is the recent mass migration of people from the areas decimated by wars in the Middle East. Creating a social divide are the various non-European and non-Christian cultures trying to meld with American culture. Events like a teacher in Irving, Texas accusing her teenaged Muslim student of making a bomb instead of recognizing it as only a homemade clock point to an inability of some mainstream Americans to blend foreign cultures into their idea of Americanism. Notwithstanding the smiles and speeches of many Americans in public venues, insincere acts show that assimilation of non-European immigrants is proving to be as challenging as stuffing a square peg into a round hole.

A contemporary Rockwellian portrait of the *Runaway* (Rockwell, 1958) would have Officer Chan talking to a boy whose name is Pedro, as the shop owner Mohamed, serves them from behind his counter. This modernized portrait begs the question of researchers in many disciplines: How will America's new civilization change the society and culture that has ruled in America for over two centuries. Therefore, understanding how the variables contributing to the transformation of America's third identity can influence the probability of America experiencing an increase in violent extremism is pertinent to current leaders and academia. The intent is not to be alarmist in this book, but to explore factors that enable violent extremism to flourish in contemporary society.

Violent extremism is a form of hate terrorism that is on the rise in America as seen in the murders committed by Dylann Roof at the Emanuel African Methodist Episcopal Church in Charleston, South Carolina in June of 2015 (Corasanti, Perez-Pena & Alvarez, 2015). With almost as many definitions for terrorism as there are books printed on the subject, terrorism will not be a focal word in this book as the emphasis is on violent extremism. The working definition for violent extremism is any phenomenon that creates fear within a society using extreme violence, imagined or real, as part of its operational methodology. This broad definition alleviates the difficulty of knowing how the future will characterize terrorism. Since terrorism has become the term-du-jour to describe anything from bullying at an elementary school to disagreeing with ruling governments, it would not be prudent to limit violent extremism with a precise prescription of terrorism. Combating violent extremism needs to concentrate on the criminal and noncriminal acts of using violence. Understanding the root causes of violent extremism aids in developing strategies and tactics to prevent or respond to this form of terrorism. Therefore, in exploring the face of America's third civilization, this book concentrates on the diaspora, tribalism, multihued culturalism and the internet as primary factors responsible for America's new identity in conjunction with being some of the factors responsible for violent extremism.

America has long been home to immigrant populations and cultures. These immigrants came primarily from Europe in the last two centuries. The consequence of this migration caused America to become a nation known for its blond-haired, blue-eyed, Christian-believing people that stood as a banner of hope for many people throughout the world. This image has changed over the last couple of decades that have seen the American demographic transform as the Hispanic population is quickly becoming the new majority in population as well as in political power. Additionally, the Asian population is on the rise and starting to flex their collective political muscle in educational and political arenas (Lowe, 1996; "Race and higher education," 2014). The demographic change in America is currently undergoing a process experienced in Europe with its Asian population ("A post-colonial France," 2014). Key among the European experience has been the well-documented ethnic ghettos and rise in homegrown terrorists from within the diaspora (Nelson & Bodurain, 2010). What can American leaders learn from the European experience and how will the changing American demographic impact its formally homogenous society? Answering this question can prepare America for the expected rise in extreme violence within its borders.

In looking at Europe as a textbook, Americans have to understand what Europeans consider Asians. The concept of Asian is inclusive of people from the classical concept of Occidentals as opposed to Orientals. The significance in this disaggregation of cultures is an, *Us* versus *Them* attitude, in which the lesser cultures of the Orient are people from the Middle East, Asia and the Subcontinent—all geographic areas that have suffered under European colonialism. A notable difference between Occidentals and Orientals within this ideology is that the Orientals are less than the European-based cultures (Said, 1978/1994), a point seen in a contemporary study by the *Faith & Heritage Newsletter* that supports the preservation of Occidental Christianity as the dominant model of society (Adi, 2012). Those losing or perceived to be losing hegemonic authority will fight for the maintenance of their regime. Likewise, those who see no other recourse except to fight to achieve equality within their societies, see the use of violence as acceptable.

The Faces of American Civilizations

America has experienced two distinct civilizations within our known history, each with their own identity and generic distinctive face. Currently, America is in the process of transforming into its third civilization; and as in the previous metamorphous, the face of the average *American* is changing. The face of America's first civilization is that of the early indigenous people that inhabited the North American continent prior to the Europeanization phase of America's second civilization ("Measuring America," 2015). The Native American population suffered decimation as America became Europeanized through a series of events resulting in the indigenous population being victims of genocide at worst or shuttered in reservations, an outcome that ensured the European social, cultural, and religious belief systems were dominant for the remainder of the next couple of centuries (Utley & Washburn, 2002).

Conspicuous in a review of the history detailing the transition from one cultural collective face to another is the violence associated with the change in civilizations. At present, America is in the throes of evolving into its third civilization. It is clear that the third face of America's civilization will not be that of a Christian, European-based identity. Demographic and immigration data point to an emerging American face influenced by non-Europeanism and multihueism, which includes people of non-European and or mixed racial extractions. The question that requires further exploration is what kind of violence will accompany this evolutionary stage of America's cyclical identity?

Since the contemporary fabric of American identity now includes threads of people that are distinctly neither Anglo-Saxon in extraction or Judeo-Christian in faith, there needs to be a societal acknowledgment that America is changing (Kotkin, 2010). This is something that the current European-based majority is having difficult grasping, as extreme Christian fundamentalists and White supremacists form dyadic social barriers letting the multihues know they are not part of the majority or their version of America (Parikh, 2006; Corasanti, Perez-Pena & Alvarez, 2015).

These actions are consistent with oppression as one class of citizens sees itself as superior to another within a same or linked society. Acts of banking hegemony maintain oppression by the elite class, in this case softening the term *oppressed* with the use of *minority*. The conscious effort to ignore the rise of minority people disregards, through a deeply imbedded prejudice, the use of masking to politically excuse oppression through terms like *unconscious bias* (Lublin, 2104) that excuses racism, prejudices, and oppression. Disingenuous use of linguistics promotes a *neo-plantationist* (Goldberg & Griffey, 2010) attitude that excuses a true acceptance of the growing minority in the leadership of Americanism, an exercise meant to ensure regime continuity for the ruling hegemonic class. Consider how pundits supporting hegemonic continuity use the media to reveal to the oppressed minority that they cannot be suffering prejudice because they—*the hegemonic elite*—said so. Reflect also on how some in the conservative American media posited that the perceived racism (Vadum, 2015) discussed at the twentieth anniversary of the Million Man March in Washington, DC was nonexistent (Nakamura & Harris, 2015). This is hard to believe considering the thousands that attended the rally and *owned* their feelings of racial unfairness as a product of oppression. The presumptiveness of leading conservative media reporters to deny this claim is paramount with paternalism in which, a superior dictate to the dependent how they feel.

In a similar vein, a U.S. Supreme Court Justice recently revealed this perception when the media-raised questions about his personal experiences and opinion on prejudicial practices in America (Lengall, 2014). The negative responses to Justice Thomas' comments in the media (Mears, 2014) brought visibility to the invisible hegemonic-hand that rules America practically unchallenged. An example of this invisible hegemonic hand was noted by critics that quickly noticed a selfie by Paul Ryan with Capitol Hill interns in 2016 had a distinctive lack of diversity among those being earmarked for careers in government (Lampen, 2016). Explaining away such a notable lack of inclusion for interns will be hard to justify.

On a positive note, unlike the migration of Asians to Europe, America has had an advantage in the last century in that immigrants have partially assimilated into the amalgamated cultures that defined America by the second generation in the last wave of immigrants (Greenman & Xie, 2008). The question that America now faces is if the current Americanization of immigrants will be as accepting of those with different physical features, faiths, and customs. Unfortunately, the exponential fear factor created by ideas of terrorism is letting a few incidents define, almost to a categorical imperative, entire ethnic and religious populations as being terrorists, a practice that hinders the acceptance of non-Europeans into American culture (Jenkins, 2010a). The inability of the mainstream American society to divorce ideas of terrorism from the purpose of a sole religion will prove to be a lasting scare on America's new face as the xenophobia will cause people to act out with extreme violence to find their ideas of freedom and humanness.

Faith, Conversion, and Fundamentalism

The power of the Bible as a symbolic representation of America's Christian-based government is giving way to the partial acceptance of other religions as long as there is no conflict with the dominate Christian faith-based authority in the nation. For those Christian fundamentalists that see other religions as a threat to America, their extreme actions can prove to be fatal to many innocent Americans ("Almost 100 hate crimes," 2014). The shift in the American identity through differing faiths is tolerated on a pedestrian level; however, it is not yet fully accepted as part of the accepted governmental structure as evidenced by the swearing in of Keith Ellison who used the Quran to take his oath of office (Fischer, 2007).

Apparent in the media criticism of Ellison's decision not to use the Bible was the absence of acceptance from pro-Christians on what represents a person's honor, morality, ethics, ideology, and commitment to a government. Instead, Christian fundamentalists concentrated on the lack of a representation of the presumptive collective national belief system in attaining a government office. In this case, the symbolism of duty did not rely on capability or character, but rather on the idea of the illustrative faith behind demonstrative acts associated with an office (Goldfarb, 2006). Ellison's actions of using a Quran were antihegemonic and threatened the future governmental control in America.

Christianity is losing its place in America as the sole symbol of ethical and moral behavior. Differing religious beliefs are far from the signs of being a disqualifier for being a good citizen since the loyalties assumed by the person are to a nation—at least in a professed secular society. Loyalty to a faith can coexist with loyalty to a nation. In Ellison's case, a pro-Christian ideology mitigated the offense to their idea of government by noting the Quran used in the ceremony had belonged to Thomas Jefferson, a tactic that seem to place Christianity once again in the dominant position of governing America (Kirby, 2015). Appending reference to Ellison's swearing in with Thomas Jefferson's Quran (Artsinger & Roberts, 2007) is analogous with hyphenating an American's identify with that of a person's racial extraction in which subservience is domineered by Western authority.

The conversion of former Christians to other religions, especially Islam, is synonymous with treason by many Christian fundamentalists (Christian Broadcasting Network, 1990). The same is true of Islamic fundamentalists who view Muslims converting to Christianity (Admin, 2014). In the tradition of observing America through the Anglo-Christian lens of intolerance, reasons for conversions fragment what can only be one right way for America to exist. Such thinking ignores the reason why people convert to any religion: which is that of searching for something that is not in their current lives (Anonymous, 2012). Interestingly, the question of conversion in the opposite direction from another religion to Christianity becomes salvation though not necessarily complete acceptance ("The church and racism," 1997).

Another skewed national perspective is the relationship between faith and patriotism in relation to how the nation defines and responds to terrorism. Faith alone should not be a qualifier in determining guilt in acts of terrorism, yet it has proven itself true in more cases than the mainstream media will admit. How many people complained about Christians being the source of evil when Timothy McVeigh bombed the Murrah Federal building in Oklahoma City? So far, the Christian faith has not been as much a qualifier for evil as is the use of Islam in the American media. The divide between differing faith systems requires decoupling from the assumed motivation of criminal acts, terrorism included. Using faith to underscore criminal activity only adds to the identity inequality among the people of America.

The ebb of receding Christianity is a concern for many leaders of Christianism ("The dish," 2014). Taking a stance on the politicization of the Christian faith, some Christians want to place a distance between their beliefs and the corruption of society under the banner of Christianity. The Christian monopoly though, is still giving way to people leaving religion altogether or conversion to other religions that are of non-Christian belief systems ("Reports 1 & 2," 2014). The market for religion is competitive and a sure way for building and maintaining religion is through the building of larger families, a practice observed by the Pew Forum when reporting on the growth of Mormons and Muslims ("Reports 1 & 2," 2014). If spreading a host religion were part of the faith's core precepts, this fact would support a solid growth strategy relying on cradle to grave adherence to a specific belief system. Faith systems are important to any country because they provide morals, collective belief, and political and financial power to the leaders. Therefore, if a person is not born into a faith system, conversion is the other way of attracting new members. The remedy provided by religion to converts, or to sustain current congregations, is to provide the hopes promised by the faith system. Being a Christian, but never really accepted in all aspects of the faith could cause many disenfranchised believers to look for a faith system where acceptance, identity, and belonging are more real than that currently experienced in many Christian churches.

The U.S. Census Bureau's report (2014) on religion reported the fastest growing religion throughout the world (Zein, 2007) and in America is Islam. Islam's growth is creating fear in many Americans that perceive Muslims as incapable of being truly American (Esposito, 2010). This fear fuels the anticipated and unwelcoming position many Americans hold toward immigrants. To these people, an American world without Christianity as the lighthouse of identity and authority is unthinkable (Williams, 2007). These fears point to the declining of America's second civilization as many people have learned that spiritual salvation also exists in non-Christian faith systems. This practice is not wrong, nor does it deserve the label of un-Americanism by the religions that are losing their congregations of believers to conversion. Making enemies of different religions or people that choose either to convert or not to believe in a spiritual faith provides the foundation for hate on many levels. Fundamentalism as an extreme practice for any religion is the root of future violence.

Diaspora and Tribalism

As the American population continues to grow dramatically over the coming decades there is concern that the demographic change will experience a disproportionate growth from immigration. The concern being, that the migration to America will largely be from developing countries (Kotkin, 2010) where the cultural practices are not always supportive of traditional American values. The apprehension in this scenario is that Europe has experienced much trouble with the diaspora assimilating into the established traditional European culture (Hoffman, Rosenau, Curiel & Zimmermann, 2007). More troubling is the growing threat from European diaspora adding to the ranks of domestic terrorist organizations and in jihadi-based conflicts around the world (Huffman, 2011). While there has been a limited number of America's diaspora joining terrorist ranks overseas (Jenkins, 2010b) there is unease about these veteran jihadists returning home to spread their violence like many of their European counterparts have done in France, Belgian, and England (Jenkins, Liepman & Willis, 2014). This trend is real and is likely to grow as a wedge divides the civilizational gap between the European and Asian cultures; both sides fighting for their core beliefs as each see the opposite side imposing unwanted sociopolitical and faith-based belief systems on the other. Exacerbating this situation is the recent influx of refugees into Europe from Syria. As the refugees flee one war torn country are they just migrating their violence to a new locale, as the honeymoon period of welcome soon wears off in their new homes. History is replete with examples of how refugee camps breed extremist thoughts in the minds of the young and restless people denied the basics of human existence.

The experiences of diaspora in the insurgencies in Turkey and India (Sankaran, 2003; Aydinli & Ersel, 2003), point to the potential support systems exploitable, if the diaspora in America decide they want to change their contemporary culture to one that aligns to their home cultures. The support could be from the pressure the international community places on America or, at the far right of the spectrum, actually arming and supporting a terrorist movement within America. If this were to occur, it would be hard to totally eliminate a terrorist movement as the terrorists could move through and hide among the diaspora that may not believe in their cause but remain silent in an effort to protect their people from the patronizing and unwelcoming imposition of oppressive American hegemony.

A unique result of the Americanization of immigrants is the dynamic identity drawn from the diverse cultures, faiths and belief systems that add to the ideas and practices of being American, or at least a traditional twentieth century American (Roediger, 2005). The success of European Americanization may not be as available to non-Europeans wishing for the same acculturation as the preceding wave of immigration in the previous century.

This can partially explain why many non-Europeans wish to create self-supporting tribal colonies within larger Americana as older generations hold on to the unique language and customs from their homeland. Witness the various cultural enclaves hosted by larger cities throughout the United States like Little Tokyo, China Town, Korea Town, Little Saigon, Little Armenia, Little Manila, Thai Town, Little Arabia, and Little Somalia to name a few. Each culturally based town supports tribalism through the rich and vibrant cultures preserved within American society. A further negative side of tribalism is that practices created by the second American civilization institutionalized poor educational and workforce options for the emerging cultural enclaves, a practice synonymous with the reservation system that continues to disparage the Native American populations (Vinzant, 2006). Will the *Little-Towns* become the neo-reservationist practices of the twenty-first century as the declining mainstream of America sees false value in keeping *them* in their own towns, when it is much better to have *them* away from mainstream traditional America?

The danger in tribal enclaves is that the support system that aids in providing a comfort zone also delays the assimilation process of successive generations into Americanism—especially in developing new versions of an amalgamated Americanism (Lazear, 2005). This cultural bunkering by diaspora can lead to the social hobbling of the second generation of immigrants ("Mobility measured," 2014) as they discover a conflict between their two separate cultures where they are members of both cultures yet, at the same time, a member of neither. Adding to the identity crises within the diaspora is the increasing gap in the educational preparation of the immigrant populations.

Adding to this is the reality that American schools do not keep pace with the distinction of being the leading global power (Mehta, 2013). The dominant systemic pedagogy enshrined in curricular themes subliminally enforces a caste system that ensures a masked oppression under the umbrella of aid and assistance (Illich, 2000). All these variables feed into a growing population of people who are not finding the American dream. Instead, they are harvesting the sour emotions of being second-class citizens with little option to gain a respectable identity that fits into the model of traditional American success. The outcomes experienced by these people seem to remind them of their inferiority within American culture. The act of transformation then cannot come from the immigrants alone but also from the America that is changing as it creates the third civilization's new face. A representative America of the future cannot expect the character of Americanism that has prevailed for the last 300 years to continue. Contemporary campaigns to stress tolerance are not the answer. Inclusion is the best approach to ensuring safety and security in a multihued (Krukenberg, 2008) America.

The question facing America is how many generations need to pass before the non-European wave of immigration completely assimilates into Americana. It took two to three generations for new Europeans to become part of the America their ancestors viewed as the land of opportunity (Roediger, 2005). The most visible feature in comparing the systemic goals of acculturation is the aspiration of gaining currency by becoming as close as possible to the traditional version of an American as possible (Leong, 2013). This cannot be a current goal as the currency of ethnicity in many immigrants is not available to non-Europeans, or even to those of mixed race. Consider President Obama and his characterization in the media. Identity for mixed race people is often with the non-European character of the birth and ignores the harmonizing of the parents that make up many American citizens. Such reference denies mixed race people, President Obama included, full access to being an American through the lens of a traditional European-based identity. Is being a multihued person becoming a mark of second-class citizenry? Will the term biracial become synonymous with the pejorative practices of calling someone a mulatto in the previous century?

Another form of tribalism is the growing income gap in America. This became evident in how the government responded to natural disasters such as Hurricane Katrina. A majority of the victims were those that did not have a means to escape to safety or were unprepared due to lower levels of income and or education (Cooper & Block, 2006). Added to this is the treatment of other ethnicities in equality and access (Lazear, 2005). Though not new to the shores of America, older ethnic groups struggle with American identity and acceptance much like those newly reporting immigrants (Lazear, 2005; Leong, 2013). When a disaster exemplifies this separation, it does not reveal the best of Americanism.

The emotive understanding many non-Whites have come to realize is that the hyphen separating *American* from the source of a person's ethic extraction is in reality an inaccessible bridge to being American. The designation, forced on immigrants regardless of their generation, serves as a diminutive punctuation to something other than full membership in a Europeanized America. In place of full acceptance is the distinction of being an American-lite. Think of the following, does a person with the surname of Adler routinely identify themselves as a German-American on the myriad of forms required of citizens in an American lifestyle.

Rise of Homegrown Violent Extremism in America

Much of the literature on homegrown terrorism focuses on the narrow view of Muslims as the source—to some, the sole source—of future threats to the homeland. This is not a realistic position to pursue nor does it add to the pedagogy of academic rigor in exploring the seeds of violent extremism. Believing in these stereotypical perceptions of Muslims strengthens hegemonic banking though oppressive prejudicial actions by mainstream America. There are plenty examples of Christian, Hindu, and Buddhist zealots becoming terrorists within the borders of their host nations, America included. Concepts of power and freedom are root causes of such violence.

In America, it appears that acts of extreme violence by a White citizen escape the label of terrorism. In its place, the label of a criminal act detracts from the label of terrorism, even when religion and politics is at the core of the crime (Corasanti, Perez-Pena & Alvarez, 2015; "Authorities say hate," 2014). These patterns in a biased portrayal of criminal activity do not escape the attention of those with a more discerning outlook on the phenomenon of terrorism (Friedersdorf, 2012). Consider if street gangs are included in the greater definition of terrorism, including violent extremism. Will the concern for knowing the faith systems of the gang members be newsworthy? It has not so far, other than mentioning those gang members that convert to Islam while in prison. Look at how the conversion of prisoners to Islam draws serious concern from America's prison system in the Office of the Inspector General (2004). Drawn out in a Department of Justice report (2004) is the concern the government had about the trustworthiness of the prison chaplains serving the Muslim population. While rehabilitation of prisoners is a primary concern of the penal system, is it right to deny a prisoner a faith because it does not meet every principle identified through a Christian lens. Such practices further feed the religious tyranny of one faith over all other faiths. For the prisoners converting to Islam, what are they learning about their American custodians and equality? It can be that irrespective of rehabilitation, as a non-White, non-Christian person they will never be a completely American, regardless of where they were born. What recourse is there for people marginalized in this manner?

Even though research is inconclusive on the potential threat from homegrown terrorism, the pattern of terrorist attacks in the homeland, dictate that the eventuality of homegrown terrorism, particularly violent extremism, will increase in the number of occurrences and/or the level of destruction (Brooks,

2011). The fact that the subject is even being discussed serves to create an environment of institutionalized fear. Criminal and terrorist acts are not new to America. Fear and terror has been, especially since 9/11, focused on a narrow part of the entire phenomenon of violence as terror. The operative expression of linguistics associates fears with the narrow focus of Islamist or jihadi-based terrorism. Linking the collective fear America has to Islamic-based terrorism has been the one event that has drastically changed how the American government views privacy and security. Is the US PATRIOT Act, or its reinvented USA Freedom Act, actually preventing terrorism within our borders or sowing the seeds of potential violent extremism of the future? Homegrown terrorism has been part of Americana since before the Boston Tea Party and it will continue to be part of the culture. The depth and reach of future terrorism will largely be contingent on how the American government reacts to the transformation to America's third civilization.

The Al Qaeda model of terrorism changed the basic infrastructure of future terrorist organizations. The extreme violence of the Islamic State replaced the Al Qaeda model of terrorism as the next threat to America (Dassanayake, 2015). Their maximization of the internet (Coughlin, 2014) has created for terrorism, the power of an anti-Westernization campaign based on wide and divergent social support (Cronin, 2006). These elements could keep terrorism alive as the ideas of the Islamic State and other groups continue exist beyond the death of their targeted leaders. Reflect on how the death of bin Laden did not stop terrorism or destroy Al Qaeda. The contemporary ideology-based threats against America are able to survive without borders or a shelf life. Ideology is difficult to exterminate. If terrorist ideologies couple with faith and cultural identity, the task is even more challenging. The battles of homegrown terrorism can take place from anywhere in the world. No longer is one leader required to be at the helm of a terrorist group for it to function. Actually, the most recent events of homegrown terrorism in America point to individuals acting without a terrorist group for support or leadership (Jenkins, 2011). This tendency supports the future of terrorism, or one category of it. The rise of one person or teams acting autonomously to perpetrate violent extremism is changing how security professionals respond to terrorism. This type of threat remains largely unnoticed until after the terrorist event occurs.

Although there is still debate on the threat from homegrown terrorism, recent incidents have proven the threat from violent extremism is real as evidenced in the numerous mass shootings experienced in America

(Brooks, 2011; Johnson, 2011; Inserra, 2015). By the middle of 2015, American authorities responded to over sixty terrorist plots within the nation's borders (Inserra, 2015). These arrests have proven that Americans have the lethal potential to make violent extremism a reality in any hometown (Jenkins, 2011; Carafano, Bucci & Zukerman, 2012; Inserra, 2015). The primary obstacle in combating terrorism is that the majority of the sensational attacks go unnoticed as planning and execution is in isolation—the individual actor phenomenon—an element that makes it difficult for authorities to counter before an event occurs (Jenkins, 2011; Carafano, Bucci & Zukerman, 2012; Inserra, 2015). The call for increasing the understanding of how terrorism nurtures in a society cannot be limited to the military as many lessons learned from events call for sharing of information across civil and military disciplines responsible for planning, protecting, responding to and recovering from terrorist attacks (Thaler, Brown, Gonzales, Mobley & Roshan, 2013).

One consideration is in developing the capability for detecting these individual actors. A vulnerability that exists in America is in the capability of identifying the individual actor. If authorities can identify an individual prone to using extreme violence, particularly through the internet, so too can terrorists. The internet is a mechanism to support and bring together the individual actors to aid them and possibly control them in making their attacks more dramatic. Much of the future antiterrorism efforts will take place over the internet, a place where actions and identities remain hidden from sight until the actual terrorist attack.

Homegrown violent extremism in the future will have various casual factors, as violence becomes the action of choice to have a voice heard. These factors could be the result of social, religious, or political disagreement that bring together the three sides of the hegemonically provoked violent extremism triangle. At the root of these concerns is the idea of equality and identity within the hegemonic society. America cannot excuse the reality of government-sponsored terrorism in the future, as this form of terrorism has been in existence for millennia and is, in a sense considered homegrown. This occurs when the existing sovereign powers are threatened and they take drastic actions to save their regime. In America's case, the threat could be the possible internal transformation from the Euro-Christian-based identity of America's second civilization to a new multiethnic, multireligious multihued identity of the nation's third civilization.

Enriching America's Third Civilization

Instead of fearing what America may become as it changes identity, the people of America should appreciate the benefits of the growing diversity. Much like the wave of Europeanization that swept the shores of the budding second civilization of America, the changes expected of the future can draw strength from the changing environment. The diversity (Churchill, 2006) creating the transformation is like a double-edged axe that if, wielded incorrectly can injure the bearer of the weapon. Similarly, rejecting the value of the growing diversity in America creates differences in the current and emerging Americanism that can be the root of future sociopolitical problems.

Democracy in America is also changing, as the majority is taking notice of the growing power of the minority. The transformation in America (Zakaria, 2013) mirrors activities around the world as the last vestiges of colonialism are declining. The politically astute have realized that wooing minority constituencies can improve political outcomes (Ansolabehers, Persily & Stewart, 2010; Blake, 2015). There also exists the eventuality that the minority voters may elect to take America in a different direction as divergent views become more conventional. The future notions of American democracy will not be those of the last century. The democracy of the next American civilization has the potential to grow into a valuable currency consumed throughout the world or, it can become more sterile and constricted, becoming synonymous more with tyranny than a government by and for the people. Consider what is occurring in the 2016 presidential elections.

Unfortunately, America's historical actions focus on regime continuity and not reliability. It is hard to think of a non-European community that received aid from America without a string attached ensuring servitude to Americanism. After centuries of struggle, Native Americans continue to be victims to European-based expansionism as the government ignores treaties it made concerning land rights as well as the courts refusing to hear petitions to receive justice (Vinzant, 2006; "Native Americans say," 2014). America's poor practice of equality toward Native Americans has yet to heal old wounds and this is not lost on other minority groups that have become Americans (College Board, 2014). Equality may be realized when more minority people become leaders in government and judicial positions. This development would present the opportunity to view and practice Americanism from a wider perspective than that practiced by the current majority population. This trend of disenfranchising non-Europeans continues against Muslims in America that feel they wear a label that reads *terrorist*, because of their faith and customs (Kaleem, 2014).

While traditional America realizes that the minority will soon sway the country's direction ("The path of least resistance," 2014) they need to direct their concern to how the nation is changing, rather than making compromises to fit their narrow view of the sociopolitical environment America used to be. It is not too much of a leap in declaring that in the next election many in the current majority will be making alliances with the varied ethic constituencies just to have a seat at the table. The relinquishing of power, even within an unstoppable evolutionary process is never easy. It took the Europeanization of America over 100 years to gain control of the land and people (Utley & Washburn, 2002).

An option would be to find value in immigration, like that of the Europeanization of America. Without question, immigration reform would strengthen America by creating value out of a large migrant and professional workforce that this nation requires for its thriving economy (Aguila & Godges, 2013). Employment also gives purpose that often raises a person's ambitions above the lure of becoming a terrorist (Berrebi & Ostwald, 2013). However, the creation of pathways is important for the best and the brightest to study at the nation's best colleges. Minorities becoming part of the intelligentsia can keep America vibrant through the value of diverse ethnicities. The balance between opportunity and ability can close the income inequality gap. Disregarding the education of minorities is a phenomenon that culturally supports the precepts of neo-plantationism/reservationism.

Discounting the benefits of a multicultural nation will hamper America's third civilization from sustaining the position of leadership it now enjoys in the world. Terrorism is the current threat to all nations (Combs, 2013). Wars between nations are giving way to wars of regime survival. If America wants to avoid the damage of insurrection, rebellion, and social movements against the incumbent government, it will need to incorporate the varied people, their cultures and belief systems into an inclusive and working machination that exists on a level of acceptability not practiced today. It would be just as prudent to explore ways to develop the values of the emerging third civilization as it is in developing methods to combat terrorism.

The Internet and Violent Extremism

The internet is a new theater to wage war (Peck, 2013). Not only is the anonymity of this virtual space a place to attack the infrastructure of governments, it is a place to spread ideology and attract recruits to terrorist causes. The Islamic State mastered the internet and social media long before the American government took this threat as a serious matter. Not only has Islamic State recruited Americans to fight in its wars (Bothelho & Sciutto, 2014); it has also recruited Americans to commit acts of violent extremism in America (Zalikind, 2015). The Islamic State is not the first terrorist group to recruit Americans to fight for a jihadi cause. Al Nusra recruited an American that became a suicide bomber in the war against Syrian forces (Williams, 2014).

The internet is facilitating violent extremism by allowing the spread of ideology across the internet. Even in the face of a death sentence, Nidal Hasan, seeks to be part of the Islamic State (Chumley, 2014) even though his violent extremism was in response to his communications with Al Qaeda leader Anwar al-Awlaki; an American eventually killed by an American drone strike (Johnston & Shane, 2009). The internet also aided the Tsarnaev brothers in learning how to make the two bombs they exploded during the 2013 Boston Marathon (Voorhees, 2013).

Again, America needs to take caution not to concentrate solely on jihadi-based violent extremism when considering the internet. The internet serves as a conduit to spread violent extremism by Christian fundamentalists too. Unfortunately, authorities often downplay terrorist acts planned by non-Islamist people. Why were the American media and courts not as lenient on Noelle Velentzas and Asia Siddiqui, who planned to bomb New York (Dienst, Valiquette, Nious & Milliman, 2015) as they were with a Robert Doggart (Obeidallah, 2015), in planning terrorist attacks in the same city? The differences between the two cases are that the women were Muslim and the man a Christian.

Just as the Islamic State is using the internet to call for the killing of Americans (Rose, 2014), there has long been an internet-based call to reinstate White supremacy in America as evidenced by the aftermath of Dylann Roof's racially motivated killings in Charleston in June 2015 (Romano, 2015). The internet is largely lawless as the breadth and depth of the virtual world is manipulatable by almost anyone with the will to post a message. Governmental control in places like India (Marszal, 2014; Glanz, Rotella & Sanger, 2014), China (Page & Levin, 2014), and Russia (Nimmo, 2011) has not prevented the internet from use as a venue to plan terrorist attacks. America has to do more than just create phony websites to trick terrorists of its intentions (Kaplan, 2009). The danger in policing the internet is that the web is considered sacred territory by many right-to-privacy advocates, as demonstrated by the actions of Edward Snowden (Matthews, 2015). Those wishing to carry out acts of violent extremism will exploit the internet to its maximum capability as they push the envelope of capabilities.

Conclusions: The Calculus of Convergent Variables in Creating Homegrown Terrorism

Even though many of the examples in this section are stand-alone events, they do provide illustration of what can occur on a larger scale if the policies of the current American practices toward minorities and non-Christian communities continue to worsen. As a worst-case scenario, the convergence of two or more of the contributing variables may cause a concerted rise in homegrown terrorism within America as people see resignation as a road to using extreme violence. This section briefly highlighted several, though not all inclusive, variables that can lead to homegrown terrorism and violent extremism. The fact is that it only takes one of these variables, or one not identified in this book, to motivate a person or group to commit an act of violent extremism. In that one act, fear will be created that will be greater than the actual damage from the attack. As America reaches another crossroads in its history, it is time for America to real-ize what its national identity is in the eyes of its entire population. Gone from our shores, or should be gone, is the rationale of the "three-fifths" mindset (Jill-son, 2009). A continuance of the founding convictions on peoples and cultures being unequal should not be part of America's third civilization, whether insti-tutionalized, or concealed behind disingenuous laws and accepted practices.

A true danger would come from a person that manipulates the anxieties of the American people by maximizing their fears of an emerging and uncertain change in American culture. By exploiting the fears created by cultural survival, a person could draw power from the people and create a state much like that of Adolph Hitler. Likewise, there is the prospect of a person maximizing the power of inequality and converges the fears of noninclusion to rise against the American government much like Abdullah Ocalan did in Turkey (Seibert, 2013). Avoiding both scenarios is beneficial to America as it transforms into the next civilization.

The power of Americanization, drawn from its diverse demography is the best protection from tribalism turning into homegrown terrorism. Guarding against the isolation of tribalism the nation needs to concentrate on accul-turation of the various diaspora through education, employment and a respect for the values other cultures bring to Americanism. Additionally, the dispar-ity in responding to disasters needs the attention of equity in response. The governmental responses to Katrina were dismal. Response and aid revealed an institutional approach to disaster delineated by race (Cooper & Block, 2006). The culture and policies of Americanism drew the lines of distinction long before Hurricane Katrina landed on shore.

Faith will always be contentious in society as the purpose is rooted not only in presumed souls saved but also in the associated powers received through controlling political structures, culture, and funding. It is not wrong for a religion to have as its goal the conversion of nonbelievers. This model finds acceptance in most cultures throughout history. Likewise, the supplanting of one faith by another usually has both sides carrying a banner calling the other evil. Without an acceptance of religion across faiths, religion will continue to skew how terrorism is perceived on American shores and abroad.

Even though contemporary research is inconclusive on the potency of homegrown terrorism (Inserra, 2015), if any of the recent thwarted terrorist plots succeeded, it would have launched the American society into a frenzy supporting institutionalized fear. As the boundaries between aged definitions of terrorism become more blurred with the world growing smaller, researchers, especially those focusing on American homegrown terrorism, must shed the narrow view of homegrown terrorism being an Islamic phenomenon. Violence is violence regardless of race, religion or ethnicity. Violent extremism around the world makes this point clear enough (Husain, 2013).

Preventing violent extremism in America requires an all-terror approach that considers all criminal and potential criminal activities whether committed by a person or state. The combined factors of social dissatisfaction, religious motivation, criminal gain, and personal vengeance need to be considered as empowering people to become terrorists; not just belonging primarily to one misunderstood religion.

American leaders can learn from their experiences in Iraq and Afghanistan. Conduct in political, social, and faith polices actually drove many disenfranchised people to become or support terrorism as American oppression had little option for other actions. The continued actions of the cultural practices of America's second civilization could prove to be one of the primary motivators in the creation of and continuance of homegrown terrorism in the homeland.

References

"A post-colonial France: A chronicle of years of fire, France's relationship with its Arab population is defined by hatred and hurt." (2014, March 1). *The Economist*.

Adi. (2012, September 19). Characteristics inherent to the Occidental and Oriental races: A comparative study. *Faith & Heritage*. Retrieved from http://faithandheritage.com/2012/09/characteristics-inherent-to-the-occidental-and-oriental-races-a-comparative-study/.

Admin. (2014, November 4). '350 million Muslims secretly live as Christian converts.' *Muslim World Press, Statistics*. Retrieved from https://muslimstatistics.wordpress. com/2014/11/04/350-million-muslims-are-secretly-living-lives-as-christian-converts/ comment-page-1/.

Aguila, E., & Godges, J. (2013). *Heavy lift: Truly comprehensive immigration reform would span the migrant labor lifecycle*. Rand Review, pp. 18–26.

"Almost 100 hate crime killings linked to one website: Report." (2014, April 18). *The Guardian*. Retrieved from the Huffington post at http://www.huffingtonpost.com/2014/04/08/ hate-crimes-linked-to-website_n_5173944.html?icid=maing-grid7 | main5 | dl7 | sec1_ inl2%26pLid%3D466548.

Anonymous. (2012, September 14). Converting to Islam: "I'm a 17-year-old Latin-American girl who switched from Christianity to Islam." *Huffington Post*. Retrieved from http://www. huffingtonpost.com/2012/09/12/converting-to-islam_n_1877655.html.

Ansolabehers, S., Persily, N., & Stewart, C. III. (2010, April). Race, region, and vote choice in the 2008 election: Implications for the future of Voting Rights Act. *Harvard Law Review*, Vol. 123, No. 6, pp. 1386–1436.

Artsinger, A., & Roberts, R. (2007, January 2007). But it's Thomas Jefferson's Koran! *The Washington Post*. Retrieved from http://www.washingtonpost.com/wp-dyn/content/arti cle/2007/01/03/AR2007010300075.html.

"Authorities say hate motivated Kansa shooting." (2014, April 14). *Associated Press*. Retrieved from http://www.aol.com/article/2014/04/14/suspect-in-killings-at-kansas-jewish-centers-has-hate-filled-his/20868805/?icid=maing-grid7 | main5 | dl6 | sec1_lnk2%26plid%3D464554.

Aydinli, O., & Ersel, U. (2003). Winning a low intensity conflict: Drawing lessons from the Turkish case, pp. 101–118. In Efraim, I. (Ed.), *Democracies and small wars*. Portland: Frank Crass.

Berrebi, C., & Ostwald, J. (2013, February). *Terrorism and the Labor Force: Evidence of an effect on female labor force participation and the labor gender gap*. RAND Working Paper, Santa Monica: RAND.

Blake, A. (2015, January 6). The GOP's major 2016 problem—in 3 maps. *The Washington Post*. Retrieved from http://www.washingtonpost.com/news/the-fix/wp/2015/01/06/the-gops-2016-problem-in-3-maps/.

Bothelho, G., & Sciutto, J. (2014, August 27). Slain ISIS jihadi among more than 100 Americans fighting with militants in Syria. *CNN*. Retrieved from http://www.cnn. com/2014/08/26/world/meast/syria-american-killed/.

Brooks, R. A. (2011). Muslim 'homegrown' terrorism in the United States: How serious is the threat? *International Security*. Vol. 36, No. 2 (Fall), pp. 7–47.

Carafano, J., Bucci, S., & Zukerman, J. (2012, April 25). *Fifty terror plots foiled since 9/11: The homegrown threat and the long war on terrorism*. The Heritage Foundation. Retrieved from http://www.heritage.org/research/reports/2012/04/fifty-terror-plots-foiled-since-9-11-the-homegrown-threat-and-the-long-war-on-terrorism.

Christian Broadcasting Network. (1990). Q & A: Why are so many westerners converting to Islam? Retrieved from http://www.cbn.com/spirituallife/onlinediscipleship/understandin-gislam/why_are_westerners_converting.aspx.

Chumley, C. K. (2014, August 29). Fort Hood shooter Nidal Hasan petitions to be 'citizen' of Islamic State. *The Washington Times*. Retrieved from http://www.washingtontimes.com/news/2014/aug/29/fort-hood-shooter-nidal-hasan-petitions-be-citizen/.

Churchill, R. P. (2006). *Human rights and global diversity*. Upper Saddle River: Pearson Education.

College Board. (2014). *Major profile, American Indian Studies* webpage at https://bigfuture.collegeboard.org/majors/area-ethnic-cultural-gender-studies-ethnic-cultural-minority-gender-group-studies-american-indian-studies.

Combs, C. C. (2013). *Terrorism in the twenty-first century* (7th Ed.). Boston: Pearson.

Cooper, C., & Block, R. (2006). *Disaster: Hurricane Katrina and the failure of Homeland Security*. New York: Henry Holt and Company, LLC.

Coughlin, C. (2014, November 5). How social media is helping Islamic State to spread its poison. *The Telegraph*. Retrieved from http://www.telegraph.co.uk/news/uknews/defence/11208796/How-social-media-is-helping-Islamic-State-to-spread-its-poison.html.

Corasanti, N., Perez-Pena, R., & Alvarez, L. (2015, June 18). Church massacre suspect held as Charleston grieves. *The New York Times*. Retrieved from http://www.nytimes.com/2015/06/19/us/charleston-church-shooting.html?_r=0.

Cronin, A. K. (2006, Summer). How al-Qaeda end: the decline and demise of terrorist groups. *International Security*, Vol. 31, No. 1, pp. 7–48.

Dassanayake, D. (2015, February 13). Islamic State: What is IS and why are they so violent? *Express*. Retrieved from http://www.express.co.uk/news/world/558078/Islamic-State-IS-what-is-ISIS-why-are-ISIL-so-violent.

Dienst, J., Valiquette, J., Nious, K., & Millman, J. (2015, April 3). 2 Queens women accused of plotting to plant bombs in U.S. talked suicide attacks, had propane tanks: Complaint. *NBC New York*. Retrieved from http://www.nbcnewyork.com/news/local/Terror-Arrest-New-York-FBI-NYPD-Police-297422441.html.

Esposito, J. L. (2010). *The future of Islam*. New York: Oxford Press.

Fischer, A. (2007, January 3). News from the Library of Congress. *Library of Congress*. Retrieved from http://www.loc.gov/today/pr/2007/07-001.html.

Friedersdorf, C. (2012, August 8). Why the reaction is different when the terrorist is white. *The Atlantic*. Retrieved from http://www.theatlantic.com/politics/archive/2012/08/why-the-reaction-is-different-when-the-terrorist-is-white/260849/.

Glanz, J. Rotella, S., & Sanger, D. E. (2014, December 21). In 2008 Mumbai Attacks, Piles of Spy Data, but an Uncompleted Puzzle. *The New York Times*. Retrieved from http://www.nytimes.com/2014/12/22/world/asia/in-2008-mumbai-attacks-piles-of-spy-data-but-an-uncompleted-puzzle.html?_r=0.

Goldberg, D., & Griffey, T. (Eds.) (2010). *Black power at work: Community control, affirmative action, and the construction industry*. Ithaca: Cornell University Press.

Goldfarb, Z. (2006, December 21). Va. Lawmaker's remarks on Muslims criticized. *The Washington Post*. Retrieved from http://www.washingtonpost.com/wp-dyn/content/article/2006/12/20/AR2006122001318.html.

Greenman, E., & Xie, Y. (2008, March). Is assimilation theory dead? The effect of assimilation on adolescent well-being. *Social Science Research*, Vol. 31, No. 1, pp. 100–13. Retrieved from http://www.ncbi.nlm.nih.gov/pmc/articles/PMC2390825/.

Hoffman, B., Rosenau, W., Curiel, A., & Zimmermann, D. (2007). *The radicalization of Diasporas and terrorism: A joint conference by RAND corporation and the Center for Security Studies, ETH Zurich.* Santa Monica: RAND.

Huffman, A. O. (2011). *Homegrown terrorism in the United States: Comparing radicalization trajectories in Britain and America* (Master's thesis). Retrieved from http://respository.library.georgetown.edu/bitstream/handle/10822/553516/huffmanAlexia.pdf?sequence=1.

Husain, E. (2013, September. A global venture to counter violent extremism. *Council on Foreign Relations.* Retrieved from http://www.cfr.org/radicalization-and-extremism/global-venture-counter-violent-extremism/p30494.

Illiach, I. (2000). *Deschooling society.* London: Marion Boyers Publishers.

Inserra, D. (2015, June 8). 69th Islamist terrorist plot: Ongoing spike in terrorism should force Congress to finally confront the terrorist threat. *The Heritage Foundation.* Retrieved from http://www.heritage.org/research/reports/2015/06/69th-islamist-terrorist-plot-ongoing-spike-in-terrorism-should-force-congress-to-finally-confront-the-terrorist-threat.

Jenkins, B. M. (2010). *Would-be warriors: Incidents of jihadist terrorist radicalization in the United States since September 11, 2001.* Santa Monica: RAND.

Jenkins, B. M. (2011). *Stray dogs and virtual armies: Radicalization and recruitment to jihadist terrorism in the United States since 9/11.* Santa Monica: RAND.

Jenkins, B. M., Liepman, A., & Willis, H. (2014). *Identifying enemies among us: Evolving terrorist threats and the continuing challenges of domestic intelligence collection and information sharing.* Santa Monica: RAND.

Jillson, C. (2009). *American Government: Political development and institutional change* (5th ed.). New York: Taylor & Francis.

Johnson, T. (2011, September 30). *Threat of homegrown Islamist terrorism.* Council on Foreign Relations. Retrieved from http://www.cfr.org/terrorism/threat-homegrown-islamist-terrorism/p11509.

Johnston, D., & Shane, S. (2009, November 9). U.S. Knew of Suspect's Tie to Radical Cleric. *The New York Times.* Retrieved from http://www.nytimes.com/2009/11/10/us/10inquire.html.

Jurgensmeyer, M. (2000). *The global rise of religious violence.* Berkeley: University of California Press.

Juergensmeyer, M. (2003). *Terror in the mind of god.* (3rd ed.). New York: University of California Press.

Kaleem, J. (2014, October 6). Here's why these Muslims are refusing to criticize ISIS. *Huffington Post.* Retrieved from http://www.huffingtonpost.com/2014/10/06/muslims-condemn-isis-debate_n_5927772.html.

Kaplan, E. (2009, January 8). Terrorists and the internet. *Council on Foreign Relations.* Retrieved from http://www.cfr.org/terrorism-and-technology/terrorists-internet/p10005.

Kirby, S. M. (2015, April 19). Congressman Ellison and Jefferson's Koran: What does Ellison know about the Koran he used for his ceremonial swearing-in? *Front Page Magazine.*

Retrieved from http://www.frontpagemag.com/fpm/255250/congressman-ellison-and-jef fersons-koran-dr-stephen-m-kirby.

Kotkin, J. (2010, August). The changing demographics of America: The United States popu-lation will expand by 100 million over the next 40 years. Is this a reason to worry? *Smith-sonian Magazine*. Retrieved from http://www.smithsonianmag.com/40th-anniversary/ the-changing-demographics-of-america-538284/.

Krukenberg, K. A. (2008, April). *Multi-hued America: The case for the civil rights movement's embrace of multiethnic identity*. From the selected works of Kamaria A. Kruckenberg. Retrieved from http://works.bepress.com/cgi/viewcontent.cgi?article=1000&context=kamaria_krucken berg.

Lampen, C. (2016, July 18). Can you spot the reason people are upset about Paul Ryan's latest Instagram post? *AOL News*. Retrieved from http://www.aol.com/article/2016/07/18/can-you-spot-the-reason-people-are-upset-about-paul-ryans-lates/21433945/.

Lazear, E. P. (2005, March). *Mexican assimilation in the United States*. Research report for the Hoover Institute and Graduate School of Business, Stanford University.

Lengall, S. (2014, February 12). Supreme Court Justice Clarence Thomas: racism worse now than era segregated South. *Washington Examiner*. Retrieved from http://washingtonexaminer.com/ supreme-court-justice-clarence-thomas-racism-worse-now-than-era-of-segregated-south/ article/2543918#null.

Leong, N. (2013, June). Racial capitalism. *Harvard Law Review*, Vol. 126, No. 8, pp. 2152–2226.

Lowe, L. (1996). *Immigrant Acts: On Asian American cultural politics*. Durham: Duke University Press.

Lublin, J. S. (2014, January 9). Bringing hidden biases into light: Big businesses teach staffers how 'unconscious bias' impacts decisions. *The Wall Street Journal*. Retrieved from http:// online.wsj.com/news/articles/SB10001424052702303754404579308562690896896.

Marszal, A. (2014, June 6). Sword fight at India's Golden temple on raid anniversary. *The Tele-graph*. Retrieved from http://www.telegraph.co.uk/news/worldnews/asia/india/10880015/ Sword-fight-at-Indias-Golden-Temple-on-raid-anniversary.html.

Matthews, C. (2015, June 5). Edward Snowden: Privacy remains 'under threat.' *Fortune*. Retrieved from http://fortune.com/2015/06/05/edward-snowden-privacy-oped/.

Mears, B. (2014, February 12). Analysis: Justice Thomas comments spark fresh debate on race. *CNN Politics*. Retrieved from http://www.cnn.com/2014/02/12/politics/clarence-thomas-racism/.

"Measuring America: The decennial census from 1790 to 2000." (2015). *U.S. Census Bureau*. Decennial Census data. Retrieved from https://www.census.gov/history/www/programs/ demographic/decennial_census.html.

Mehta, J. (2013, May/June). Why American education fails: And how lessons from abroad could improve it. *Foreign Affairs*. Vol. 92, No. 3.

"Mobility measured: America is no less socially mobile than it was a generation ago." (2014, February 1). *The Economist*.

Nakamura, D., & Harris, H. R. (2015, October 10). 20 years after the Million Man March, a fresh call for justice on the Mall. *The Washington Post*. Retrieved from https://www.washing tonpost.com/politics/20-years-after-the-million-man-march-a-fresh-call-for-justice-on-the-mall/2015/10/10/b3d8ffca-6f66-11e5-b31c-d80d62b53e28_story.html.

"Native Americans say US violated human rights: A Native American group is asking the international community to charge the United States with human rights violations in hopes of getting help with a land claim." (2014, April 14). *Associated Press*. Retrieved from AOL News at http://www.aol.com/article/2014/04/14/native-americans-say-us-violated-human-rights/20868905/?icid=maing-grid7 | main5 | dl19 | sec1_lnk2%26pLid%3D464622.

Nelson, R., & Bodurian, B. (2010, March). A growing terrorist threat? Assessing "Homegrown" extremism in the United States. *Center for Strategic & International Studies A report of the CSIS homeland security and counterterrorism program*. Washington, DC. Retrieved from http://csis.org/files/publication/100304_Nelson_GrowingTerroristThreat_Web.pdf.

Nimmo, K. (2011, July 6). Russian FSB Boss: Internet a Haven for Terrorists. *InfoWars.com*. Retrieved from http://www.infowars.com/russian-fsb-boss-internet-a-haven-for-terrorists/.

Obeidallah, D. (2015, May 18). America Snores When Christian Terrorist Threatens to Massacre Muslims. *The Daily Beast*. Retrieved from http://www.thedailybeast.com/articles/2015/05/18/guess-why-this-christian-terrorist-plot-against-muslims-isn-t-getting-any-press.html.

Office of the Inspector General. (2004, April). *A review of the federal bureau of prisons' selection of Muslim religious services providers*. Washington, DC: U.S. Department of Justice.

Page, J., & Levin, N. (2014, June 24). Web Preaches Jihad to China's Muslim Uighurs: China Says Internet, Social Media Incite Terrorism Among Uighur Minority. *The Wall Street Journal*. Retrieved from http://www.wsj.com/articles/web-preaches-jihad-to-chinas-muslim-uighurs-1403663568.

Parikh, R. (2006). White males, racism and Christian fundamentalism in American politics. *Sulekha.com*. Retrieved from http://creative.sulekha.com/white-males-racism-and-christian-fundamentalism-in-american-politics_190267_blog.

Peck, M. (2013, August 20). Russia Says Cyberspace is New 'Theater of War.' *Forbes*. Retrieved from http://www.forbes.com/sites/michaelpeck/2013/08/20/russia-says-cyberspace-is-new-theater-of-war/.

"Race and Higher education: Not black and white. Asians object to affirmative action." (2014, March 22–28). *The Economist*.

Religion Statistics. (2014). U.S. Census Bureau. Retrieved from http://www.census.gov/compendia/statab/cats/population/religion.html.

"Reports 1: Religious affiliation" and "Report 2: Religious beliefs & practices/social & political views." (2014). *Pew Forum*. Retrieved from http://religions.pewforum.org/reports.

Rockwell, N. (1958, 20 September). *Runaway*. Retrieved from http://www.art.com/products/p9388040471-sa-i5446828/norman-rockwell-runaway-september-20-1958.htm.

Roediger, D. (2005). *Working toward whiteness: How America's immigrants became white: The strange journey from Ellis Island to the suburbs*. New York: The Perseus Books Group.

Romano, J. (2015, June 20). Romano: Killer's crusade for white America defies logic. *Tampa Bay Times*. Retrieved from http://moms.tampabay.com/news/courts/criminal/romano-killers-crusade-for-white-america-defies-logic/2234485.

Rose, S. (2014, October 7). The Isis propaganda war: A hi-tech media jihad. *The Guardian*. Retrieved from http://www.theguardian.com/world/2014/oct/07/isis-media-machine-propaganda-war.

Said, E. W. (1978/1994). *Orientalism*. New York: Vintage Books.

Sankaran, K. (2003). Indian way in counterinsurgency. Efraim, I. (Ed.) *Democracies and small wars*, pp. 85–97. Portland: Frank Crass.

Seibert, T. (2013, February 27). Ocalan negotiations bring Turkey a step closer to peace with Kurds. *The National*. Retrieved from http://www.thenational.ae/news/world/europe/oca lan-negotiations-bring-turkey-a-step-closer-to-peace-with-kurds.

Thaler, D., Brown, R. Gonzalez, G., Mobley, B, & Roshan, P. (2013). *Improving the U.S. military's understanding of unstable environments vulnerable to violent extremist groups: Insights from social science*. Santa Monica: RAND.

"The church and racism: Toward a more fraternal society." (1997). *Political Commission Justice and Peace*, Eternal World Television Network (EWTN), Global Catholic Network. Retrieved from http://www.ewtn.com/library/curia/pcjpraci.htm.

"The path of least resistance: The republicans may be groping their way to compromise." (2014, February 8). *The Economist*.

"The Dish: Biased and Balanced." (2014). Retrieved from http://dish.andrewsullivan. com/2014/04/28/the-pernicious-poison-of-palin-ctd.

U.S. Census Bureau. (2012). Statistical abstract of the United States: 2012. U.S. Census Bureau. Retrieved from http://www.google.com/url?sa=t&rct=j&q=&esrc=s&source= web&cd=1&ved=0CB0QFjAA&url=http%3A%2F%2Fwww.census.gov%2Fprod%2F 2011pubs%2F12statab%2Fpop.pdf&ei=UHDeU8n9F8XaoATLr4D4DQ&usg=AFQjCN HabHgDXuO-kS1UMDIUFyYAbw8CSQ&bvm=bv.72197243,d.cGU.

Utley, R. M., & Washburn, W. E. (2002). *Indian wars*. New York: American Heritage Press.

Vadum, M. (2015, October 9). The Million Man March comes to Washington: Violence on the Horizon? *Front Page magazine*. Retrieved from http://www.frontpagemag.com/fpm/260399/ million-man-fraud-comes-washington-matthew-vadum.

Vinzant, J. H. (2006). *Supreme Court interpretation and policy making in American Indian Policy*. Dissertation, Southern Illinois University, UMI Number: 3229889

Voorhees, J. (2013, April 23). Slatest PM: How the Tsarnaev Brothers learned to make their bombs. *The Slate*. Retrieved from http://www.slate.com/blogs/the_slatest/2013/04/23/ inspire_magazine_tsarnaev_brothers_used_al_qaida_magazine_for_directions.html.

Williams, P. (2007). *The day of Islam; The annihilation of America and the western world*. New York: Prometheus Books.

Williams, P. (2014, May 30). Florida Man Identified as Syria Suicide Bomber. NBC News. Retrieved from http://www.nbcnews.com/news/investigations/florida-man-identified-syr ia-suicide-bomber-n118926.

Zakaria, F. (2013, January/February). Can America be fixed? The new crisis of democracy. *Foreign Affairs*.

Zalikind, S. (2015, June 22). How ISIS's 'Attack America' Plan Is Working. *The Daily Beast*. Retrieved from http://www.thedailybeast.com/articles/2015/06/22/how-isis-s-attack-amer ica-plan-is-working.html.

Zein, Q. (2007, May 14). The list: The world's fastest growing religions. *Foreign Policy*. Retrieved from http://www.foreignpolicy.com/articles/2007/05/13/the_list_the_worlds_fastest_growing_ religions.

· 3 ·

HOMEGROWN VIOLENT EXTREMISM
AS AN IED

Part I—U.S. Immigration Policy

Background

Among the many issues facing homeland security is the threat from home-grown terrorism (Napolitano, 2010), notably violent extremism (Obama, 2011b). Internal threats to America span several of the core mission areas for homeland security as detailed in the 2014 Quadrennial Homeland Security Review Report (Johnson, 2014). These mission areas support the overall maturation and strengthening the Homeland Security Enterprise:

- Preventing terrorism and enhancing security
- Securing and managing borders
- Enforcing and administering immigration laws
- Safeguarding and securing cyberspace
- Strengthening national preparedness and resilience

Immigration then, is a significant contributing factor to the potential for homegrown terrorism. However, this is not new to scholars and practitioners in the homeland security sector. What is alarming is how the current and past administrations have purposefully made decisions that add stress to the political system that drives the nation, and subsequently the people, as their fears of mismanaging immigration percolates to the point unintended and possibly violent actions occur.

The systems challenged by contemporary governance range far beyond the desks of elected officials in Washington, DC. The fear and violence created by terrorism affects the daily lives of all in America. Within each social system, there exist mechanizations supported by a myriad of components that need caring for the oiled parts to work as efficiently as possible (Kettl, 2014). This though, does not appear to be a concern for many lawmakers beyond rhetorical comments in the media. Within immigration as a system, this goes beyond the laws and executive direction of the president that dictate the rules and practices in managing immigration (Executive Office of the President, 2010). It also includes the people impacted by the immigration policies. They are in essence the wheels and cogs of the system and they can either sustain or hamper the system's performance. Thus, in developing a picture of immigration policy's impact on the homeland security enterprise the phenomenon contains multiple perspectives to provide a parsimonious but informative piece of literature. In keeping with the theme of violent extremism, this section of the book will use the example of an improvised explosive device (IED) to illustrate the components contributing to the potential volatility resulting from the overarching dilemma on immigration illustrated in Figure 3.1.

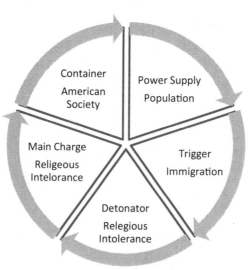

Figure 3.1: Immigration as IED Components.
Source: Author, Copyright 2015

An IED is unique because they contain five basic components in a handmade explosive (Freudenrich, 2015). The socio-religio-political component categories of the analogous IED portrayed below reveal how the American society, culture, and belief systems converge to create situations that can become volatile.

- Power Supply—The American population serves as the element providing power to the social IED.
- Trigger—The current immigration policy serves as the triggering system of the social IED.
- Detonator—Religious intolerance will be the spark that detonates the social IED.
- Main Charge—Anti-immigration attitudes serves as the social IED's main charge.
- Container—The vessel that holds these components together is the American society.

For all reasonable purposes, the debate on illegal immigration is fait accompli and awaits a mechanism to legalize a majority of the estimated 12 million people currently living without proper documentation within America's borders (Preston, 2013). Many of these illegal immigrants support a second generation of children with no legal status, yet in 2013, they received presidential notice and protection as the nation moved closer to developing a solution to the immigration debate (Dinan, 2013b). However, therein lays the foundation for analogy of homegrown violent extremism as an IED. Instead of concentrating on the flame that burns brightest, such as the Tsarnarev brothers (Oliker, 2013), academia and practitioners similarly need to focus on how the components of American immigration—the societal IED—come together to construct terrorism (Nelson, 2010).

In order to explore the phenomenon of immigration's impact on homegrown violent extremism, this part of the book presents a concept of the potential problem via a trilogy of compositions titled: *Homegrown Violent Extremism as an IED*. This trilogy explores the effect of immigration on the national homeland security enterprise. The overarching question driving the trilogy is about immigration practices in the homeland security enterprise. Thus, the question asked in this interrogative is if American policies are actually fueling future violent extremism by its immigration practices. Immigration, throughout the history of man, has had unintended consequences as people strive to share limited space, resources, and political powers.

Part I explores, the foundations of American immigration policy and acculturation, particularly how failure to acculturate can lead to violence. Part II concentrates on anti-immigration attitudes in America ("Anti-immigration groups," 2001). Specifically, how discontentment with the current enforcement of immigration law fuels violence against immigrants as well as the government. As example, consider a Tea Party website (Ferrechio, 2014) filled with hate speech in 2014. Lastly, in Part III, the trilogy will bring the perceptions presented in Parts I and II together from the perspective of religious intolerance for immigrant faith systems and the potential this emotion has on violent extremism.

Effects of Immigration

This specific segment explores how the impact of immigration on the fabric of what comprises being American can lead to future homegrown terrorism. Regardless of how immigrants enter the country, the key to strengthening the nation's preparedness through immigration policies (Obama, 2011a) include the management of assimilation into Americanism (Meyers & Pitkin, 2010). Particularly salient in considering the breadth of assimilation are the anchor points of inclusion and exclusion. Mismanagement of the assimilation process (Kotkin, 2010), or establishing policies that deter assimilation (Aguila & Godges, 2013) could lead to violence as experienced in Europe with the non-European diaspora (Hoffman, Rosenau, Curiel & Zimmerman, 2007). Failure to recognize the overarching impact of immigration on terrorism is, once again, similar to concentrating on the burning of the fuse cord of an IED instead of concentrating on the explosive device.

Immigration is comprised of two significant sectors. The first is the process of entering America. Accomplishing entry can be through legal channels or through illegal methods. The latter includes entering America without proper documentation or by overstaying the authorized period of limited stay as dictated by specific VISA programs. Regardless of the manner in which a person enters the America, each person then has to undergo the process of acculturation into the diverse culture that makes America unique.

The current administration, like most administrations previously, practices immigration policies that do not please all of the nation's constituent political and social groups. President Obama draws criticism for being too soft by not enforcing immigration policies (Ferrechio, 2014), while at the same time, the National Council of La Raza declares Obama is the *"deporter-in-chief"* (Epstein,

2014). The pros and cons each find fault with the systemic policies and practices concerning immigration. The task of protecting the borders of America's
land area with Canada and Mexico, as well as the nautical approaches from the
Pacific and Atlantic Oceans is a challenge for the Department of Homeland
Security. The size of this area is too vast to guarantee, with certainty at all times
the safety of the nation (Boozman, 2014). To think differently, would be very
shallow in thought as well as in practice.

The goal of the Department of Homeland Security is for the immigration
program to allow visitors, students, professionals and returning citizens and
resident aliens to safely and efficiently enter the country, while keeping out
those people who are criminals or not desired by the government. However,
this task is never ending as evidenced by the numerous deportations of illegal
immigrants (Dade, 2012) during this and previous administrations. The twin
questions that need asking are, why do people want to come to America, as well
as, are the risks of illegal immigration worth the effort (Silsby, 2013)? The idea
of the opportunities contained within the American Dream (Kotkin, 2010)
best answer the first question. The second question, receives a definite yes,
though each person has a different reason for taking the risk (Silsby, 2013).
America is not alone in experiencing this phenomenon. Canada (Immigration Watch Canada, 2014), England (Basit, 2009; Boffey, 2013), Europe
(Dumalaon, Korolyov & Jones-Berry, 2014), and Japan (Dyloco, 2012) all
experience the same issues with immigration policies and enforcement. Moreover, in each of the countries previously mentioned, policies and implementation of those policies is a political hot potato as well (Papademetriou, 2005).
The controversy of immigration policy will continue to be a soapbox for both
pro and con supporters to lambast the administration in charge, regardless of
who is the president. While not a core issue in many immigration debates,
acculturation forms a significant factor immigrants face—regardless of which
generation they belong in the phenomenon—as they embark upon conquer-
ing the art of becoming an American.

Acculturation

Effective acculturation of immigrants into Americana is part of the government's responsibility. The other part falls to each individual immigrant
wishing to make America his or her adopted home. The government's goal,
as seen in Obama's 2013 Executive Order on immigration, is to reinforce
the country's abilities, across the spectrum of society, to fix and improve

the immigration system (Executive Office of the President, 2013) as well as supporting immigrant integration into the American culture (Vigdor, 2008). Without sustainable support, anti-immigration mindsets, and an inability to become American will be the fuel that has the potential to ignite the flame of homegrown terrorism and violent extremism. Similar development of terrorist beliefs has occurred with ethnic minorities in France ("A post-colonial France," 2014) and in China (Dynon, 2014). These challenges force American policy makers to ask what America can do differently with managing its immigrant populations. How does one make an immigrant feel at home in their new country?

An unintended consequence of immigration policy is how new immigrants are treated upon arrival. In an example of how policy can hamper assimilation, consider the example of a sponsored family member coming to America. In this example, like many immigrants who enter America as temporary registered aliens, their sponsorship is by an American citizen or another registered alien. The petitioner is required to receive financial support from their sponsoring citizen/registered alien for a specified period before they are eligible to work in the country. This practice results in many new immigrants settling, by a system default, into ethnic enclaves where they find the comfort and support of a familiar culture and language but not a true American experience. For those immigrants that do not leave these ethnic enclaves they fail to acclimate to their adopted American culture.

This separation of cultures adds to an identity complex that causes many immigrants to feel less than American as their ethnicity becomes a blemish on their status of being an American (Roediger, 2005). To many immigrants, the ultimate acceptance and perception of being an American is associated with becoming like a traditional American (Roediger, 2005) portrayed in movies—White, college educated, and financially successful. The Whiteness is a critical element of acculturation that is hard to put in policy, for obvious reasons. Understanding cultural differences from an American perspective is not always conducive to welcoming immigrants to America's shores (Shrestha, 2010), especially when the cultural differences heighten a demeaning posture toward foreign cultures (Condon, 2011).

The converse of becoming a traditional American is having an immigrant's ethnicity used as currency by friends and employers who see ethnicity as checking a box in the awareness and diversity boxes of being a tolerant and understanding American (Leong, 2013). This tokenism (Leong, 2013), while creating limited employment opportunities, does not really bridge the gap of meaningful diversity across the workforce (Aguila & Gidges, 2013). Highlighting this is the use of a hyphenated identification for those immigrants that have yet to fully assimilate into Americana. As an example, a person with a family name of Lopez is far more likely to find the label of Mexican-American attached to him than a person whose family name is Mueller receiving the label of German-American. This conviction supports the argument that Americanism is associated with Whiteness (Allen, 2004; Roediger, 2005). Though acculturation was a benefit for Europeans, the likelihood of a similar event transpiring is decades away if at all. What does it take to receive the recognition of simply being American? The answer to this question eludes current policymakers.

The feeling of nonacceptance has and will continue to foster discontentment among those immigrants that feel or know they are not part of the larger fabric of the culture in which they call home. The option left for people who do not acculturate into Americanism fall within two options. They can continue to live in their ethnic enclaves without ever becoming American or they can leave, even partially, the comfort of their enclaves and become part of the American fabric at the cost of forfeiting some of their unique ethnic identity. The riddle an immigrant would have to solve is in knowing how to balance their identity and purpose between two or more cultures.

Failure to Assimilate

For those immigrants that have difficulty in assimilating, they often become frustrated as American culture becomes prison walls they cannot pass. The threat of violence comes from these immigrants lashing out because of feelings of inferiority and inequality, along with a lack of identity, as they feel trapped between two unaccepting cultures. Again, violence manifests as the understood threat because that term lacks the muddled definitions of terrorism. Since September 11, 2001, the term terrorism has become subjective to the point where almost any act associated with any fear becomes terrorism. This tendency can cause problems for academics as well as the legal system as practitioners wrestle with differentiating terrorism dealing with national defense and terrorism dealing with a bully on the playground (Thompson, 2010). This trilogy is concerned with the former type of terrorism, those extreme acts of violence, which threaten the security of the homeland as demonstrated by the bombings at the 2013 Boston Marathon (Oliker, 2013) or the 2015 San Bernardino shootings (Gibbons-Neff, 2015).

Leaders, at all levels in America, need to devise policies that prevent the extremes of immigrant displeasure displayed in England (House of Commons, 2005) and Spain (Tures, 2009). Homegrown terrorism has a dual identity; those that commit violent acts within America's borders and those that commit acts outside American borders (Jenkins, 2011). For the latter classification, those people that join jihadi-terrorist causes overseas, join the internal threat spectrum because the fear is that they will return to America as veteran terrorists that could lead similar disenfranchised immigrants in violent acts within the nation (Jenkins, 2011). What is interesting in this assessment is the perception that picking up arms has rules of acceptable behavior. Primary is that a person can only fight for their home country, in this case America. Fighting for other nations or foreign causes was a common practice up to about the time of First World War, where it ended with the creation of standing national armies comprised of regular citizens (Lucassen, 2009). Currently however, this practice is very limited. What is telling about fighting for a country other than America is the acceptance of an American joining the French Foreign Service (Grimes, 2005), but not for an American joining a jihadi-based group, even a group that may be making claims of cultural preservation and sustainability (Jenkins, 2011).

Immigrant Power

Immigrants, inclusive of their following generations, have two ways to make their voice heard within society. One is through standardized political processes as governed by the American democratic system and the other is the use of illegal violence. The political parties in America have taken notice of the power of the ethnic minorities. In the elections of this century, both political parties have vied to win the Hispanic vote in order to maintain regime dominance. Drawing the attention of the growing Asian population will prove to be another goal for the political parties too (Ansolabehers, Persily & Stewart, 2010). The strategy of the current political parties is often to marginally support ethnic-based causes to attract votes by making it appear ethnic or immigrant issues are important. However, as the ethnic caucuses gain in influence it is not long before these minority populations start to flex their power in independent parochial endeavors that do not consider what the customary political parties desire ("Race and Higher Education," 2014). This shift in political influence will become more apparent as America enters its third civilization and the rise of non-Europeans and multihued (Krukenberg, 2008) people gain in political dominance.

The converse of making change through the accepted political pro-cess is when immigrants decide to use violence to pursue their objectives. Some examples of this are the Rajneeshees' food poisoning in Oregon that attempted to influence the outcome of an election in 1984 by poisoning the food at a restaurant in an effort to make potential voters too ill to vote (Bovsun, 2013). More recently, after 9/11, there have been immigrants charged with terrorist acts such as the attempted bombing in a New York subway in 2009 (Marzulli, 2013) and the Tsarnarev brothers at the Boston Marathon in 2013 (Oliker, 2013) and Tashfeen Farook in the 2015 San Ber-nardino shooting (Gibbons-Neff, 2015; Woodyard & Heath, 2015). While the latter incidents had links to Islamic-based terrorist causes, a deeper understanding of why these people living in America chose to pursue the use of violent extremism is yet unclear, at least as covered in the mainstream media. This again is an example of concentrating on responding to an IED after it explodes instead of deconstructing the explosive component parts of the IED before it explodes.

There are far more law abiding immigrants that support an American life-style than those few that cause violence in the name of anti-American causes. The inclusion of immigrants in the American lifestyle requires better image management (Camarota, 2004). Currently, it appears the government's lack of support facilitates media negativity of immigrant activities by concentrat-ing on the criminal element of immigration. Think of how quickly the media reported the bombing of the Murrah building in 1995 was likely an attack by Middle Eastern terrorists before the world learned of Timothy McVeigh as the bomber (Fuchs, 1995). After his arrest, concentration diverted from religion as a casual factor to McVeigh's faith in and following of the *Turner Diaries* as a reason for turning against America (Kifner, 1995).

Like most crimes committed in America, understanding the motivation for criminal activity is important in strengthening the deterrence capabil-ity of the nation. Quickly linking criminal activity solely to Islamic-based terrorism is often a convenient method to add shock to a news line. How-ever, it does not properly explore how current and future policies should be enforced or developed in order to prevent violence from occurring in the future.

In ending this first theme of this sectional trilogy on homegrown vio-lent extremism, it is clear that the homeland security enterprise reacts to the overall and complex arrangement that comprises the American immi-gration system. Due to the wave of social influence, immigration policies suffered circumvention by executive authority, more in the practice of acknowledging the eventuality of immigration reform than in an effort to dismiss the powers of American laws. Conversely, the same actions have created discontent among those that fear further immigration and the transformation of the American way of life to include other cultures and religious beliefs.

Immigrants have grown powerful, they have learned to navigate and control the democratic system that is the nation's pride and joy. However, as a political arm of minority groups becomes more formidable, it is not long before the minorities become the majority in census as well as political power. This power-shift has the potential to enact legislation on immigration more aligned to what is occurring within American borders rather than sustaining a system that is in the last years of its current focus and structure.

In the midst of the debates and political maneuvering is the immigrant that struggles to become acclimated to the American way of life. For a very select few, they have chosen to pursue paths of violence, acting out against America here at home or through the support of violent terrorist groups abroad. It is this last group of immigrants that the homeland security enterprise needs to be concerned with as the correlation with American policies and violent extremism further link in the future.

Part II—Anti-immigration Attitudes

This second composition in *Homegrown Violent Extremism as an IED* begins with a discussion of anti-immigrationists demonstrating in southern California. The 2014 demonstrations were against perceptions of Obama circumventing the current immigration laws in response to a mass immigration of children to America (Watson, 2014). This particular segment explores anti-immigration attitudes through the lens of how the perceived inconsistencies in contemporary immigration practices are drawing complaints from both sides of the immigration debate. These practices in turn, directly impact the security of America, as some might say by design of criminal elements south of the US-Mexico border (Beaubien, 2011). The change that will come in American immigration policies is a certainty. However, the outcome is pending the spin of a roulette wheel with few choices left on the game's face of chance.

The Right: Anti-immigrationism

Overall, contemporary anti-immigrationists are not against immigration as much as they are for the enforcement of current immigrations laws. Presidential actions to circumvent laws are what trouble this group of American citizens. Practices receiving exemptions from applicable laws in the name of humanitarianism link to perceptions of a nonstoppable erosion of border and national security.

Those people that believe Obama has circumvented the immigration process impeded the processing of a bus of immigrants in Murrieta, California in 2014 under the belief that the process would be a guise to release numerous illegal aliens into the community (Watson, 2014). The fear expressed by some of the demonstrators was that these illegal aliens would become pseudowards of the city since the federal government had no mechanism for reliable plans to house, care and feed for the illegal aliens (Rasley, 2014). The small and conservative town of Murrieta did not want to take on a burden that would aid in the entrenchment of illegal aliens into the community instead of deporting them as the demonstrators believe should be the only option for the federal government under applicable laws (Panza, 2014).

The preceding illustration materialized the disenfranchisement anti-immigrationists have in the federal government to protect its borders from illegal immigration. The actions of the demonstrators showed desperation with federal policy that resulted in their community being responsible for illegal aliens that had no connection with the people of Murrieta. Immigration officers could not provide a guarantee to the Murrieta residents that the illegal aliens would receive further federal assistance for food and shelter once they were processed.

For those immigrants that stayed in the town, they would most likely become the wards of proimmigration organizations (Lehrer, 2007) while their children potentially slow down other students in the public school system ("Illegal immigrants," 2008). The eventual prospect of the illegal immigrant children was a tendency for immigrant children joining gangs in lieu of integration into mainstream America (Mateu-Gelabert, 2002). There is also concern for the health risks many illegal immigrants bring to America (Carter, 2014b). These events provide anti-immigrationists with apprehension about the worst-case scenarios taking place with the growing illegal immigrant population. Supporting these fears is the 2015 outbreak of measles in California's Disneyland, which were traced to a suspected unvaccinated foreign visitor (CDC, 2015). Facilitating the measles outbreak is the belief that immigrants, who often do not receive the same preventive vaccination regime most Americans receive, will break down the protection (CIS, 2015) provided by an American herd approach (USDHHS, 2016) to medical safety and security. Of course, the outbreak's spread to other people was more from Americans that practiced nonvaccination for their children, a point left out of the immigration debate.

Adding to the anxiety of Obama's policies neglecting immigration law is the response from many people from Central America that swarmed to America in 2015 (Mascaro & Bennett, 2014). Prominent among the illegal aliens were children, many travelling on their own or in the custody of a mother or elder sibling (Mascaro & Bennett, 2014). Many traveled in a hurried fashion to America in the belief that an *el permiso*—a permit allowing entry to America—was being granted by Obama to all children who managed to cross the border (Cortes, 2014). For those immigrants detained, whether voluntarily or involuntarily, they have learned to declare in rehearsed English, statements about fearing for their lives and fleeing from gang violence; phrases that discontinue deportation proceedings (Carter, 2014a). This last tactic has provided focus for many a conservative radio talk show host as they fielded emotional rants on the air of a situation they claim is an exigent loss of sovereignty caused by a president that is circumventing federal law (Handel, 2014; O'Reilly, 2014).

The recent increase in illegal immigration is receiving help from drug cartels south of the border (Schladen, 2014). Besides paying for the trafficking fees, the illegal immigrants have the potential to serve as drug mules as the drug cartels take advantage of the political debate on immigration in America along with maximizing use of their established illegal supply chains (Gibson, 2013). The money they make is one benefit (Dickson, 2014). Another is the relationships they are making with officials south of the border as they gain tacit approval for their human trafficking enterprise (Walser, McNeill & Zukerman, 2011). Profit drives not only the actions of the cartels but it also serves as a motivator for those that see value in living in America.

The immediate threat to homeland security is in the shifting of resources from border operations to immigration processing (Cox, 2014). The absence of law enforcement officers on the border might have been an ulterior or primary motive of cartel strategists that gain an advantage in having officers stuck in offices processing the waves of illegal and legal immigrants (Heyes, 2014). Events like that in Murrieta heightened this advantage, which resulted in the unintended diversion of additional resources to another unprepared immigration facility in Chula Vista, a city thirty miles to the south, which had to process the illegal immigrants (Watson, 2014).

The anti-immigrationists believe that if immigrants overtake the United States, especially those of non-European extraction, the nation will become reflective of the third worlds, or developing worlds, they hail from ("Gohmert," 2014). Other fears find life in the belief that illegal immigrants will destroy the economic stability of America (Jones, 2011), beliefs that proimmigrationists campaign hard to call myths (Tone & Uwimana, 2013). While many of the claims are indeed myths, the underlying anxiety of anti-immigrationists is the fear of the change that comes with accepting to America new peoples and their cultural practices (Becerra, Androff & Ayon, 2012). They see the traditional American way of life giving way to inferior cultures, religions, and lifestyles.

The termination of immigration is not the primary goal of anti-immigrationists; it is the enforcement of current immigration laws, particularly the strengthening of the borders along with the immediate deporting of illegal immigrants (Lind, 2014). Instead, the perception is that the borders are unprotected ("Immigration facts," 2009). Furthermore, anti-immigrationists disagree in the belief of proimmigrationists that believe illegal immigrants have the expectation, if not a right, to stay in America at the expense of the American taxpayer ("Lewiston mayor," 2014). All this, while anti-immigrationists suppose the host governments of illegal immigrants encourage the migration of their people to the sanctuary of America (McKinley, 2005).

Border degradation facilitates the loss of taxes in nonstrategic band-aide remedies, which fail to secure the homeland (Vetter, 2013). The debate of a positive impact on the economy is another two-sided coin in immigration reform (Boozman, 2014). Anti-immigrationists stand by a claim that legalizing the current level of illegal immigrants would not bolster revenue through taxes as proimmigrationists tout (Davidson, 2013). Instead, some pundits claim the majority of the expected federal tax revenue to be collected may be unattainable because the anticipated income tax levels of the immigrants would place them outside the ability of the laws to collect and keep taxes in the national treasure, resulting in an overall deficit of billions of dollars. The tradeoff is in which taxes have the most benefit to a community, federal, state, or municipal purpose.

The Left: Proimmigrationism

Despite all the rhetoric from anti-immigrationists about Obama dismantling the immigration system, the proimmigrationists joined the 2014 Murrieta incident with demonstrations of their own (Sanchez & Cano, 2014). The banner they raised was one of humanitarianism. A duty they feel is the responsibility of the varied governments ranging from municipal to state and ultimately federal (Jeffers, Scroggin & Solis, 2014). The proimmigrationists claim for sanctuary ignores the legality of the situation that anti-immigrationists raise as their battle flag ("Gohmert," 2014). A significant question that the practice of sanctuary begs is; when does it stop? Will the current humanitarian efforts be jeopardized by people who will ultimately go down with a sinking ship as resources run out at all governmental levels?

In an effort to assist illegal aliens in the greater psychological debate on immigration, proimmigrationists won a decisive battle in practically eradicating the term of *illegal alien* and replacing it with the less criminally attributable term of *undocumented alien* (Haughney, 2013). This practice, has aided in the current modification of American immigration laws in preparation for an eventual permanent revision of the laws to allow illegal aliens to stay in America (Dinan, 2013a). Removing the semblance of criminality makes it easier to modify existing laws. The strength of public opinion is without a doubt a strong weapon wielded in the hands of proimmigrationists.

Anti-immigrationists (Snyder, 2013) do not recognize the argument proimmigrationists have that illegal aliens have a right to the protections of the U.S. Constitution. The anti-immigration logic would give other noncitizens around the world the unprecedented protections of the U.S. Constitution under an umbrella policy that they should not have, principally because they are not American citizens ("Citizenship,"2011; Snyder, 2013). As these arguments eventually make their way to the Supreme Court, it is definite that the breath of the U.S. Constitution will include more people under its definition since the term *people* has changed from that of the Founding Fathers.

Another theme in the debate for immigration reform is the recognized value of the immigrants once they receive legal residency in America (Patten & Lopez, 2013). The value is in controlling the votes that residential legitimacy of current illegal immigrants would add to the voting registry. This is an influence that both political parties view as powerful enough to direct the sovereignty of the nation (Camarota, Poston & Baumle, 2003). The strategy in action now, is in manipulating which party the immigrants will join once the immigration reform debate is over (Woodsome, 2013). From the media coverage, it appears that the democrats will gain power in the polls, as the illegal alien immigrant-turned-legal becomes American citizens (Gimpel, 2014). To the anti-immigrationists, this change in voting power may be the greatest threat they see with immigration reform. The one consideration both parties should have is that there is an eventuality for the differing immigrant populations to make their own political party. A party that will have a strong political effect on all levels of government while catering to their needs and not that of the well-worn issues of republicans and democrats whose main concern is political and regime continuity.

Analysis of Threats Now and in the Future

Regardless of the eventual changes to the immigration policies and/or laws, the current developments in immigration enforcement have affected homeland security. These include drug enforcement, criminal, and or terrorist access and economic degradation. Of course, immigration enforcement is the umbrella covering all of these areas.

The first vulnerability in the security of the homeland comes from the continuance of the illegal drug trade across American borders. Besides drugs crossing the border undetected over land and through waterways, the diversion of officers to the recent flood of immigrants will take officers off the front lines of the border. The current confusion is ripe for use by cartels, and others with nefarious intent, for the construction of more tunnels that could not only serve as a conduit for drugs but also for weapons and terrorists ("How cartels," 2014).

This statement is not farfetched, as the presence of jihadi terrorist cells exist south of the America's borders (Ibrahim, 2012). Whether for profit or ideological reasons, the merging of cartel and terrorist capabilities can pose a significant threat to the American homeland as many of their motivations directly conflict with the Department of Homeland Security's strategic plan (Napolitano, 2012). The cartel's quest for money marries well with the jihadi's quest to destroy the contemporary government in America. Along with the illegal immigrants, who are looking for a new life in America, there are also many criminals that see the benefit of extending their illicit activities in America (Riddell, 2014).

Another consequence of weakened borders is the increase of sex crimes (O'Connor, 2011). Using ulterior schemes to get women to America to support criminal sex rings is not new (Rice, 2007). The trafficking of children today could prove to be a monetary source for criminals as they locate trafficked women in the future to serve their needs. This eventuality can become realism, regardless of the legal or illegal status these women have in America. This scheme is not new. Korean gangs routinely marry women to American service members only to have them work as prostitutes once they are in America (Hughes, Chon & Ellerman, 2007). What if those trafficked to America eventually form a fifth column in a war against America? Consider the circumstances surrounding the Syed and Tashfeen Farook. Detecting someone who does not exist would prove difficult in preventing acts of violent extremism.

Relaxing immigration, not just at the southern borders, but also through all pathways into America will bring in more terrorists. Some of these terrorists could even be American citizens that violate national laws on supporting terrorism overseas (Lake, 2013). Many of these *Americans* come from immigrant families and communities that anti-immigrationists say is a problem with undisciplined immigration. The northern border with Canada experiences the same challenges with border control (Toews, 2013). The homegrown terrorists within the Americas often find support from their ethnic communities (Beutel, 2007). The threat is from seasoned veterans returning from jihadi wars overseas and bringing back their skills for eventual use against the American homeland.

In closing this section, a significant threat of the future is in the realization of the harshest of anti-immigration desires; the expelling of all illegal immigrants and their families (Bocanegra, n.d.). Curbing or ceasing of immigration to America, and the maintaining at all costs of a European- and Christian-based vision of America, could prove to be the largest and worst threat to the homeland ("Anti-immigration groups," 2001). A divided America, based on race and religion, is not what America needs at this time in its history. The key is in finding a balance in immigration policies in America while encouraging other countries to better their own social systems, keeping their people home by providing opportunities that are currently are nonexistent.

Inferences

A solution to address the flood of children from South America was out of reach for lawmakers. In Congress, both parties came to a compromise to as they hold on to their deeply rooted political beliefs of self-preservation (Werner & Caldwell, 2014). At the center of the debate was if the $3.7 billion directed to the issue was for protecting the border or a continuation of federal daycare ("Homeland Secretary," 2014; Werner & Caldwell, 2014). Again, national security and humanitarianism takes opposing sides in the continuing gladiatorial debate. Republicans wanted some of the emergency funding to enforce laws at the border, a point not included in the democratic proposal (Werner & Caldwell, 2014). Interesting in the media was a comment by the Secretary of Homeland Security, Jeh Johnson, which linked the funding request with an ability to have more discretion in performing his mission (Chang, 2014). Was the discretion referring to ignoring current laws and policies to process children from other than Mexico differently (Hennessy-Fiske, Bennett & Carcamo, 2014), or to use critical homeland security resources to process the influx of children? An eventual outcome was that the rumors were true—authorities will care for and retain illegal immigrant children in America, though, only while people are paying attention.

Part III—Immigration and Religious Intolerance

Overview

This is the final composition in the trilogy, *Violent Extremism as an IED*. In this segment, the first two essays of U.S. Immigration Policy and anti-immigration attitudes combine through the lens of religious intolerance to complete the analogy for constructing an IED. This subject is important because immigration brings to America different cultures, beliefs, and family practices (Griswold, 2002). The inability of current residents and those of the immigrants to be tolerant of differing faiths and customs can mirror what has occurred in Europe with their diaspora and violent extremism (Hoffman, et al., 2007). This segment will primarily concentrate on the religions of Christianity and Islam as a discussion including all religions is beyond the scope of this book.

Homegrown Terrorism as Violent Extremism

Overused in the contemporary lexicon of public safety professionals, academics, and politicians is the term *terrorism* (Huxley, 2013). At the core of the definition is the use of fear against other people. This includes killing, maiming, poisoning, and creating fear within the population. Since 9/11, various governments used the idea of terrorism to provide a license for governments to take excessive actions against its people, imprison people with little cause and to use violence as a preemptive action within the international community (Stern, 2000; Hoffman, 2006).

Violent extremism represents the use of aggression by terrorists, criminals, and governments alike. As the world grows smaller, previous delineation of terrorism being different from criminal activity or governmental oppression is giving way to an internationalism that is eroding the territorial barriers of defining terrorism (Caulderwood, 2014).

Violent extremism has long been part of the political and expansionist experience in America (Kumamoto, 2006). Violent extremism was not new to Americans with the events of September 11, 2001 (9/11 Commission, 2004). Historically there were the conquistadors and English colonists that decimated America's native peoples in the names of their respective governments and faith systems. Contemporarily there was Timothy McVeigh, a person excused from the full label of being a terrorist (Kifner, 1995), maybe because he was not a Muslim. Since then, other Americans have joined terrorist causes around the world (Alter, 2013). The surprise in quantifying a presumed rise in homegrown terrorism is that for many years, people believe Americans cannot be terrorists, particularly against their home nation. For those few that are terrorists (CNN, 2010), the media is quick to link their actions to Islamic extremism in the belief that all Muslims are terrorists (Rustom, 2012)—according to a rising Islamophobia that dictates Muslims are incapable of being true Americans.

This is interesting since American revolutionary actions are commensurate with contemporary definitions of terrorism (Owens, 2012). Another theme in Americans fighting for other countries or entities mirror the biases that echo the concerns of intolerance for practices perceived as non-American. It appears that Americans who support their Islamic ideology of religious freedom can only be terrorists in the American mindset (Hoffman, et al., 2007). Conversely, Americans who fight with similar religious ideology become heroes in their sacrifice when killed fighting for their American-approved causes (Lovett & Montgomery, 2014). This dualistic perception of supporting personal religious beliefs is victim to an American tendency to default to European Judeo-Christian-based causes above all else. This biased principle is a disservice to the Muslims—and all other non-Christians—that honorably serve or served in the U.S. armed forces, as well as being part of America's history since the nation's inception (Considine, 2013). This comparison is not an excuse for terrorism; it serves to acknowledge the wedge of intolerance that is dividing Americans, a phenomenon that could lead to future Americans using violent extremism to place their personal ideology into practice (Castagnera, 2009). Consider the killing of five police officers in Dallas, Texas by Micah Johnson in July of 2016 (Achenbach, Wan, Berman & Balingit, 2016). The motive for the killings was in retaliation against White police officers (Fernandez, Perez-Pena & Bromwich, 2016), reasoning grounded in the model of hegemonically provoked violent extremism. Part of Johnson's grievance against White officers is the fact that over 100 unarmed black people have been killed in 2015 (Mapping Police Violence, 2017). These numbers continue to rise in 2016 with the killing by Baton Rouge police officers of Alton Sterling (Balko, 2016). Despite these killings, the Black Lives Matter movement (Cullors, Tometi & Garza, 2016) still is seen as dangerous to the overall American society (Rodgers, 2015).

Islamic Extremists

Unfortunately, terrorism is practically synonymous with Islam to many Americans; lawmakers and academicians included (Rustom, 2012). This perception results from the words and actions of many Muslim, or jihadi extremists that have proclaimed their intent is to spread Islam throughout the world so that eventually all people would follow their way of Islam (Qutb, 1991). To extremists, this grand strategy (Crenshaw, 1998) includes the use of violence as part of the conversion process of non-Muslims to Islam (Lawrence, 2005). Divorcing the jihadists from the question of religious expansion, why is it that the spread of Islam is a crime? Is not conversion of nonbelievers a goal of many religions?

Islamic extremists took advantage of the U.S.' open culture to accomplish some of the most notable terrorist attacks within the nation's borders. These include the first attack on the World Trade Center in 1993. The planning and coordination for this event took place within the United States (Lance, 2013). Sheikh Abdel-Rahman, though in an American prison, is still managing to influence anti-American attitudes throughout the world (Lance, 2013). Extremism in America is not limited to antigovernment actions against America. Fethullah Gulen, a very influential spiritual leader resides in the Poconos and causes concern for Turkish leaders who consider him a terrorist (Taraby, 2013). Blamed for the failed military coup in Turkey in July 2016, Gulen's (Arango & Yeginsu, 2016) alleged coup (Fortanella-Khan, 2016) showed the power of social media (Snowden, 2014) in commencing and terminating violent extremism.

America's diverse culture is capable of producing terrorists that can export their unique leadership to wars on foreign shores. Notable among these Americans turned jihadi terrorists are Anwar Al-Awlaki (Savage, 2014) of Al Qaeda and Omar Hammami al-Amriki formally of Al Qaeda and Al Shabaab (Al

Jazeera, 2013). Both of these leaders have attracted other Americans to follow extremist ways (Straziuso, Forliti & Watson, 2012) particularly Al-Awlaki, who influenced Major Nidal Hasan before his shooting spree at Fort Hood in 2009 (Kenber, 2013).

The theme in the conversion of normal Americans to Islamic extremism is an individual Islamic identity that does not merge with traditional American values (Hoffman, et al., 2007; Akers, 2013; Hoffman, 2013). This question becomes victim to misunderstanding, as Americans do not want to look at why a person becomes a terrorist. The need to do something for a greater purpose becomes a driving force in some converted to Islamic extremism. This includes people like Moner Mohammad Abusalha, who become a suicide bomber in Syria (Ferran, 2014) or the Tsarnarev brothers, who were committed to dying in the act of bombing the Boston Marathon (Dawsey, Perez & Barrett, 2013).

The fear security specialists have concerning Western jihadists are the skills and knowledge they bring back to the homeland. As war veterans, these hometown boys and girls turned terrorists, could easily mobilize like-minded extremists for similar operations in and against America (Jenkins, 2014). This is not to mention the creation of a new type of hero that uses deeds and practices to show their defiance toward their perception of an oppressive government.

Christian Extremists

Christianity is not immune to extremism. The actions of Timothy McVeigh and Clive Bundy are examples of Christians that endorse extreme violence to preserve, protect, and project their belief system. Of the top ten White terrorists in the world, nine are Americans (McCalla, 2011). Of the nine terrorists, eight practiced extreme versions of Christianity, attacking government officials (Shapira, 2010), African Americans (Robbins & Hamill, 2009), and Jewish Americans (Wilber, 2010).

Like many who do not know what they hate, so are many Christian extremists. It is easier to hate the difference in people than it is to learn about diversity. Often relying on stereotypical perceptions, Christian extremists lash out at innocent people in the belief they look like the enemy of their minds (Singh, 2014). In 2014, Jon Stewart illustrated the comedy in the fallacies of such perceptions by scoffing at the differences between the beards on Bob Bergdhal, father of U.S. Army Deserter and prisoner of the Taliban Bowe

Bergdhal and the stars of Duck Dynasty (Campbell, 2014). While entertaining, Stewart's assessment cut to the core of Christian extremism—*they are not us*. Bob Bergdhal received criticism in mainstream American media because he learned to speak Pashto and studied Islam in an effort to communicate with the Taliban (Campbell, 2014). Bergdhal's beard, perceived as Muslimism, therefore became directly associated with terrorism, while the beards of the Duck Dynasty reality stars reflected the trait of being truly American.

Extremism among White supremacists in America is growing. Witness the rancher Clive Bundy, who took on the federal government in Nevada. His stand against the federal government attracted an impromptu militia to support his extremist views, including the will to use firearms against federal officers (Sonner, 2014). The extremist-based support should not have been a surprise to government leaders. Pundits claim membership in extremist hate groups increased by over fifty-four percent in the previous decade (SPLC, 2009). The correlation between the rise in White extremism and immigration is growing. Supported by anti-immigration causes, White extremism provides a means of protecting the fabric of a traditional White America ("Citizenship in balance," 2011). Consider how immigration issues are driving people to vote on both sides of the 2016 presidential campaign (Sakuma, 2015; Levy, 2016).

An often-overlooked perspective in highlighting Islamic violence is a comparison to Christian violence (Hagerty, 2010). The National Public Radio's, All Things Considered broadcast, reported in "Is the Bible More Violent than the Quran?" that Christians have been more violent than Muslims throughout history (Rudolph, 2013). Adding to this confusion is how most news reports label the actions of people with European and Middle Eastern extraction. An example of this is how the American media branded Timothy McVeigh (Kifner, 1995) compared to Dzhokhar Tsarnarev (Dawsey, Perez & Barrett, 2013) in reference to how their respective religions became part of their crime.

The attitude of Christians being infallible fuels a fear of America becoming more diverse (Tashman, 2011). The freedom and security Christian extremists want is commensurate with their ideas of what the Founding Fathers believed, particularly where slaves were considered 3/5 of a *real* citizen. This is interesting because David Holmes (2006) discussed in *The Faiths of the Founding Fathers*, how Deism played a significant role in the beliefs of the Founding Fathers. This however, did not stop early government and religious leaders forcing Native Americans to convert to Christianity (Nebraska

Studies, 2014). An America comprised of different colored peoples, religions, and customs that are equal, is a society Christian extremists want to avoid (Parikh, 2006; Wellman, 2013).

Fearing Change

A motivator in being intolerant is that people do not normally accept change, particularly that of their basic culture and belief system. For many Americans of European extraction, they have forgotten or do not realize the kinds of violence that occurred in the name of their religion in colonizing America (Nebraska Studies, 2014). The fear the Native Americans had during colonization is what White extremists fear from Islam and the other religions that are spreading across the nation (Brown, 2011). Just as dearly, as the Native Americans held on to their cultures (Utley & Washburn, 2002), so to do the contemporary people of the United States want to preserve their American culture from contamination (Cohen, 2013). They do not want their way of life threatened in the name of an ideology different from their own.

Change is coming to the way of life Americans know of today. Besides the fear of changing the religious construct of America, the current political parties fear losing control of the government to an immigrant, non-White population (Wolgin & Garcia, 2013). Congressman Virgil Goode proved this point when he called Keith Ellison's use of a Quran to take his oath of office as a threat to the American way of life (Argetsinger & Roberts, 2007). Validity for using the Quran seemed to come from the Islamic Holy Book being that of Thomas Jefferson and not on the word, the Quran contained. However, this asks the question of: does one have to be a Christian to govern adequately in America? Theoretically, the design of America's government was to be a secular form of government; however, that perspective draws criticism from Atheistic and non-Christian points of view.

Throughout history, rarely has religion spread without the complementary use of extreme violence (De Vries, 2002). Think of some of the contemporary religions that exist throughout the world today, Christianity (McCalla, 2011), Islam (Savage, 2014), Judaism (Casey, 2014), Buddhism (McCartney, 2013), Mormonism (Lebaron, 1995), Hinduism (HRW, 1999), Sikhism (Marszal, 2014), and Atheism (Oakes, 2008); all have experienced violence in the spread, protection and maintenance of their respective faiths and beliefs. Extreme faith-based movements directly link to genocide as experienced with the spread of Christianity in the new world (Nebraska Studies, 2014), Islam in the Fertile Crescent (Sizgorich, 2008), Judaism when colonizing Israel in its early history (Lipovsky, 2012), Hinduism in the disaggregating of the sub-continent (Khan, 2008), and Atheism in France during their revolution (Fife, 2004).

The technological innovations of the twenty-first century have not alle-viated the use of violent extremism as evidenced by the ideological wars in Africa (Sergie & Johnson, 2014), the Middle East (Lister, 2014), and Europe (Menon & Fuller, 2000). At the root of the fear of change is the person or persons that control the differing belief systems. To these people, the spread of their faiths is the spread of their power. Politically, economically, and ideo-logically, power is what drives people to violence. Maintaining power is a concept that provides justification for wielding violence, regardless of the extremity of the violence used. The causes and people wielding the violence validate the use of violence by dehumanizing the victims. In the end, the victor will always have the sovereignty over writing history to make the use of violence as a noble cause.

The Decay of Religious Tolerance

The social divides occurring around the world are taking place within Amer-ica as immigration creates enclaves of lesser Americans (Gonzalez, 2013). Adding to the question of normalized immigration is the impact refugeeism will have on the social construct of America as the Syrian Civil War/Islamic State expansion and other growing issues of survivability in the world increase. Social mobility through education, employment opportunities, access to the internet, and land ownership is growing as fast as technology is advancing. The divergence between the *haves* and *have nots* did not disappear ("Mobility measured," 2014) as many social scientists thought in the last century (Lerche, 1998). The reality is that immigration is bringing to the United States not only different people but different religions and lifestyles (US Census Bureau, 2012). This phenomenon is not new to Western countries. Non-Christians have long worn out their welcome in Europe. This includes Chinese (Squires, 2008), Muslims (Nelson, 2013), and Jewish (Algemeiner, 2014) people alike.

In America, similar attacks are on the rise. The aptitude for tolerance in America changed with the events of 9/11 (Blake, 2011). Lines of demarcation in Americans accepting non-Americans resemble the definition of Samuel Huntington's (1999) future in which civilizations collide in an effort to sur-vive. Culture became as important as country after 9/11 as people sought to identify with the right causes and purposes to preserve Americanism. Being an American has to include the diversity of America's citizens or the conflicts of the world will seep into the daily lives of being American (Hsu, 2009).

After the Boston Marathon bombings, an innocent Muslim woman in Boston suffered an attack from a resentful man, because she looked like the perceived enemy based on religious symbolism (NewsOne, 2013). Not all confrontations are this violent. Adding to misdirected violence, many Christians debate whether it is of value to have non-Christian friends as the divide between religious tolerances widens (Wellman, 2013). This proposes an argument that non-Christians somehow taint the lives of Christians. This rational is on a cosmic level that disregards the norms of an enlightened society as civilizational preferences based on narrow readings of culture becomes justification for any acts to ensure preservation. The underlying distain for non-Christians is often subtle and packaged in the practice of unconscious bias, an excuse for overtly supporting a preferred traditional American society. There is a belief among many immigrants, particularly those of non-Christian faiths, that Christians exercise a system of privilege that is exclusive as well as tiered (Killerman, 2014). At the top of the hierarchy is, of course, Christians of European extraction (CARM, 2014).

Attempts to address the tolerance debate in America are even hidden behind a thin veil of all people are equal, just not as equal as the hegemonic faith in power (Fanon, 1961/2004). The intent of messages like this, only serve to erode the tolerance of other faiths, people, and cultures in America. Those subjected to these various forms of oppression have a limit on how much oppression they can withstand (Fanon, 1952/2008; Freire, 1970/2000). This sentiment, though often overlooked as non-European-based Christians receive limited consideration for their customs and practices (Said, 1993). The extremist perception is that non-Christians are less than human. While dehumanization does not find currency openly, the actions and deeds of extremists speak volumes on their inner perceptions of humanness.

The Future of Extreme Violence

When the varied causes explored in this book come together, a window to the potential for future violent extremism in America opens up. The violent crime rate is going up across America (Saad, 2013). Violence extremism, as used in this trilogy on *Homegrown Terrorism as an IED*, has increased in America since 9/11 (Myre, 2013). Perpetrators of violence include people from differing cultures; both for and against American values. The homegrown aspect of violent extremism is likely to increase in consequence as America transforms its identity to a non-European-based population to one that is multihued (Krukenberg, 2008). The new face of America includes Asians, Hispanics, Middle Easterners and, the mixture of inter-racial marriages that are becoming more common among Americans (Associated Press, 2012). Besides the concern of religious change, there are different languages, customs, and lifestyles that are coming to the American shores. For those people that do not assimilate to Americanism, they often find themselves in the lower social economic levels of the population. This disparity in economic status, along with the highlighted differences in religion, can alienate a person to the point where frustration with society can morph into violent extremism.

Learning from the lessons of Europe can prevent America from experiencing a growth in homegrown violent extremism. Leaders in America need to take advantage of the belief many immigrants have in the American dream (Braukis, 2014). Unlike Europe, immigrants in America are more likely to assimilate into the American culture (Venugopal, 2011; Myers, 2015). Assimilation to Americanism will not prevent all people from becoming terrorists; however, it can aid in immigrant community leaders identifying potential terrorists in the making (Schanzer, Kurzman & Moosa, 2010). Inclusion of immigrants to Americana is the best mitigation to an increase in homegrown violent extremism.

References

9/11 Commission. (2004). The 9/11 commission report; Final report to the national commission on terrorist attacks upon the United States. Harrisonburg: W.W. Norton & Company.

"A post-colonial France: A chronicle of years of fire, France's relationship with its Arab population is defined by hatred and hurt." (2014, March 1). *The Economist.*

Achenbach, J., Wan, W., Berman, M., & Balingit, M. (2016, July 8). Five Dallas police officers were killed by a lone attacker; authorities say. *The Washington Post.* Retrieved from https://www.washingtonpost.com/news/morning-mix/wp/2016/07/08/like-a-little-war-snipers-shoot-11-police-officers-during-dallas-protest-march-killing-five/.

Aguila, E., & Godges, J. (2013). *Heavy lift: Truly comprehensive immigration reform would span the migrant labor lifecycle.* Rand Review, pp. 18–26.

Akers, S. (2013, October 2). Muslim man wakes from coma, converts to Christianity. *Charisma News.* Retrieved from http://www.charismanews.com/culture/41212-muslim-man-wakes-from-coma-converts-to-christianity.

Al Jazeera America. (2013, September 12). Somalia's al-Shabaab kills US fighter: Omar Hammami, known as al-Amriki or the American, killed in an ambush after falling out with group's leader. *Al Jazeera America*. Retrieved from http://www.aljazeera.com/news/africa/2 013/09/201391293315761506.html.

Algemeiner. (2014, January 27). Hate-filled protest in France attracts thousands: Crowd chants 'Jew, France is not for you!' *The Algemeiner*. Retrieved from http://www.algemeiner. com/2014/01/27/hate-filled-protest-in-france-attracts-thousands-crowd-chants-jew-france-is-not-for-you-video/.

Allen, R. L. (2004). Whiteness and critical pedagogy. *Educational Philosophy and Theory*. Vol. 36/2.

Alter, C. (2013, September 24). Born in the USA: 5 American terrorists: If Americans were among the Kenya mall attackers as claimed, they'll join a growing list of home-grown terrorism. *Time*. Retrieved from http://world.time.com/2013/09/24/born-in-the-usa-5-ameri can-terrorists/.

Ansolabehers, S., Persily, N., & Stewart, C. III. (2010, April). Race, region, and vote choice in the 2008 election: Implications for the future of Voting Rights Act. *Harvard Law Review*, Vol. 123, No. 6, pp. 1386–1436.

"Anti-immigration groups." (2001). *Southern Poverty Law Center*. Retrieved from http://www. splcenter.org/get-informed/intelligence-report/browse-all-issues/2001/spring/blood-on-the-border/anti-immigration-.

Argetsinger, A., & Roberts, R. (2007, January 2007). But it's Thomas Jefferson's Koran! *The Washington Post*. Retrieved from http://www.washingtonpost.com/wp-dyn/content/arti cle/2007/01/03/AR2007010300075.html.

Arango, T., & Yeginsu, C. (2016, July 16). Turkey detains thousands in military in bid to regain control. *The New York Times*. Retrieved from http://www.nytimes.com/2016/07/17/world/ europe/turkey-attempted-coup-erdogan.html.

Associated Press. (2012, February 16). Interracial marriages in the U.S. hit all-time high 4.8 million: 1 in 12 involved in interracial union, rise pegged to steadily flow of Asian and Hispanic immigrants. *Daily news*. Retrieved from http://www.nydailynews.com/life-style/ interracial-marriages-u-s-hit-all-time-high-4-8-million-article-1.1023643.

Basit, T. N. (2009). White British; dual heritages; British Muslim: Young Britons' conceptualization of identity and citizenship. *British Educational Research Journal*. October, Vol. 35/5, pp. 723–743.

Beaubien, J. (2011, July 7). Drug cartels prey on migrants crossing Mexico. *National Public Radio*. Retrieved from http://www.npr.org/2011/07/07/137626383/drug-cartels-prey-on-migrants-crossing-mexico.

Becerra, D., Androff, D. K., Ayon, C., & Castillo, J. T. (2012). Fear vs. facts: Examining the economic impact of undocumented immigrants in the U.S. *Journal of Sociology & Social Welfare*, December, Vol. 39, No. 4, pp. 111–135. Retrieved from http://www.google.com/url?sa=t&rct=-j&q=&esrc=s&source=web&cd=2&ved=0CCcQFjAB&url=http%3A%2F%2Fwww. wmich.edu%2Fhhs%2Fnewsletters_journals%2Fjssw_institutional%2Finstitutional_sub scribers%2F39.4.Becerra.pdf&ei=m2y3U_GXN9TboATn1oKAAQ&usg=AFQjCNH0iexe GuoXJbQQ7yyVFdYImbOsUQ.

Beutel, A. J. (2007). Radicalization and homegrown terrorism in western Muslim communities: Lessons learned for America. *Minaret of Freedom Institute: Calling the faithful to Freedom.* Retrieved from http://www.google.com/url?sa=t&rct=j&q=&esrc=s&source=web&cd=5&ved=0CDsQFjAE&url=http%3A%2F%2Fwww.minaret.org%2FMPAC%2520Backgrounder.pdf&ei=6mC4U770MoffoAT004CQDA&usg=AFQjCNF1D79j_vew_HEP3EFDzZYxdzfdqA.

Blake, J. (2011, September 11). Four ways 9/11 changed America's attitude toward religion. *CNN.* Retrieved from http://religion.blogs.cnn.com/2011/09/03/four-ways-911-changed-americas-attitude-toward-religion/.

Bocanegra, M. (n.d.). Homegrown terrorism in the United States. *Michael Bocanegra: Political and social issues.* Retrieved from http://mikebocanegra.hubpages.com/hub/Homegrown-Terrorism-in-the-United-States.

Boffey, D. (2013, January 12). Immigration is British society's biggest problem, shows survey to public. *The Guardian.* Retrieved from http://www.theguardian.com/uk/2013/jan/13/immigration-british-society-biggest-problem.

Boozman, J. (2014). Immigration reform & border security. On John Boozman US Senator for Arkansas website. Retrieved from http://www.boozman.senate.gov/public/index.cfm/immigration-reform-border-security.

Bovsun, M. (2013, June 15). 750 sickened in Oregon restaurants as cult known as the Rajneeshees spread salmonella in the town of The Dalles. *Daily News.* Retrieved from http://www.nydailynews.com/news/justice-story/guru-poison-bioterrorrists-spread-salmonella-oregon-article-1.1373864.

Braukis, H. (2014, April 14). Europe, U.S. immigration issues are worlds apart. *AZ Central.* Retrieved from http://www.azcentral.com/story/opinion/op-ed/2014/04/13/europe-us-immigration-issues-different/7685611/.

Brown, M. (2011, December 6). Do American Muslims want to take over our country? *Town Hall.com.* Retrieved from http://townhall.com/columnists/michaelbrown/2011/12/06/do_american_muslims_want_to_take_over_our_country/page/full.

Camarota, S. A. (2004). The high cost of cheap labor: Illegal immigration and the federal budget. *Center for Immigration Studies.* Retrieved from http://cis.org/High-Cost-of-Cheap-Labor.

Camarota, A. A., Poston, D. L. Jr., & Baumle, A. K. (2003, October). Remaking the political landscape: The impact of illegal and legal immigration on Congressional apportionment. *Center for Immigration Studies.* Retrieved from http://cis.org/ImmigrationEffectCongressionalApportionment.

Campbell, C. (2014, June 4). Jon Stewart mocks Fox News for 'hatred of facial hair.' *Business Insider.* Retrieved from http://www.businessinsider.com/jon-stewart-mocks-fox-news-for-hatred-of-facial-hair-2014-6.

Canble Network News (CNN). (2010, January 6). Study: Threat of Muslim-American terrorism in U.S. exaggerated. *CNN.* Retrieved from http://edition.cnn.com/2010/US/01/06/muslim.radicalization.study/.

Casey, N. (2014, July 30). U.N. blames Israel for shelter attack. *The Wall Street Journal.* Retrieved from http://online.wsj.com/articles/gaza-health-ministry-explosions-at-school-kill-15-1406705906?mod=wsj_india_main.

Castagnera, J. O. (2009, June). America's homegrown terrorists of the 21st Century: The disgruntled, the obsessed, and the mad three types, one challenge? *Homeland Security Review.* Vol. 3, No. 2, p. 75-100.

Carter, S. (2014a, Jun 16). 'They keep coming': The 'rehearsed' answers illegal immigrants are using at the border to gain entry into the U.S. *The Blaze.* Retrieved from http://www.theblaze.com/stories/2014/06/16/they-keep-coming-the-rehearsed-answers-illegal-immigrants-are-using-at-the-border-to-gain-entry-into-the-u-s/.

Carter, S. (2014b, June 24). 'Potential for a public health disaster': Illegal immigrant surge leaves officials with 'no idea' which diseases are coming across. *The Blaze.* Retrieved from http://www.theblaze.com/stories/2014/06/24/potential-for-a-public-health-disaster-illegal-immigrant-surge-leaves-officials-with-no-idea-which-diseases-are-coming-across/.

Caulderwood, K. (2014, June 17). Different ends same means: Research shows what terrorists and crime syndicates have in common. *International Business Times.* Retrieved from http://www.ibtimes.com/different-ends-same-means-research-shows-what-terrorists-crime-syndicates-have-common-1603628.

Center for Disease Control (CDC). (2015, February 20). Measles Outbreak—California December 2014–February 2015. *Center for Disease Control.* Retrieved from https://www.cdc.gov/mmwr/preview/mmwrhtml/mm6406a5.htm.

Center for Immigration Studies (CIS). (2015, February, 9). Vaccination rates among immigrants are a legitimate concern. *Center for Immigration Studies.* Retrieved from http://cis.org/cis/vaccination-rates-among-immigrants-are-legitimate-concern.

Chang, A. (2014, July 11). Morning Edition: Administration officials defend funding request to stem border crisis. *National Public Radio.* Sound recording available at http://www.npr.org/2014/07/11/330631664/administration-officials-defend-funding-request-to-stem-border-crisis.

Christian Apologetics & Research Ministry (CARM). (2014). CARM, retrieved on August 3, 2014 from http://carm.org/more-stuff/features/religious-tolerance-america.

Citizenship in the Balance: How anti-immigration activists twist the facts, ignore history, and flout the Constitution. (2011, February). *People for the American Way,* retrieved on July 5, 2014 from http://www.pfaw.org/rww-in-focus/citizenship-the-balance-how-anti-immigrant-activists-twist-the-facts-ignore-history-and.

Cohen, L. (2013, October 14). Shutdown power play: Stroking racism, fear of culture change to push anti-government agenda. *Forbes.* Retrieved from http://www.forbes.com/sites/robwaters/2013/10/14/shutdown-power-play-stoking-racism-fear-of-culture-change-to-push-anti-government-agenda/.

Condon, S. (2011, November 18). Americans split on American exceptionalism, poll shows. *CBS news Online.* Retrieved from http://www.cbsnews.com/news/americans-split-on-american-exceptionalism-poll-shows/.

Considine, C. (2013, May 26). Honoring Muslim American veterans on memorial Day. *The Huffington Post.* Retrieved from http://www.huffingtonpost.com/craig-considine/lets-honor-muslim-america_b_3339838.html.

Cortes, J. (2014, June 25). Honduran kids flee terror at home, hope for opportunity in U.S. *Reuters*. Retrieved from http://uk.reuters.com/article/2014/06/25/uk-usa-immigration-mexi co-idUKKBN0F00CS20140625.

Cox, J. D. (2014, July 10). The unsung heroes in the immigration crises. *National Border Patrol Council Local 2554*. Retrieved from http://www.nbpc2554.org/.

Crenshaw, M. (1998). Logic of terrorism: Terrorist behavior as a product of strategic choice. *Origins of terrorism*. (Reich, Walter, ed.), pp. 7–17. Baltimore: John Hopkins University.

Cullors, P., Tometi, O., & Garza, A. (2016). Black lives matter. Official Website. Retrieved from http://blacklivesmatter.com/about/.

Dade, C. (2012, December 24). Obama administration deported record 1.5 million people. *National Public Radio (NPR)*. Retrieved from http://www.npr.org/blogs/itsallpolitics/2012/12/24/167970002/ obama-administration-deported-record-1-5-million-people.

Davidson, A. (2013, February 12). Do illegal immigrants actually hurt the U.S. economy? *The New York Times*. Retrieved from http://www.nytimes.com/2013/02/17/magazine/do-illegal-immi grants-actually-hurt-the-us-economy.html?pagewanted=all&_r=0.

Dawsey, J., Perez, E., & Barrett, D. (2013, May 8). Manhunt ends with capture of Boston bombing suspect. *The Wall Street Journal*. Retrieved from http://online.wsj.com/news/articles/ SB10001424127887324493704578432030609754740.

De Vries, H. (2002). *Religion and violence: Philosophical perspectives from Kant to Derrida*. Baltimore: The John Hopkins University Press.

Dickson, C. (2014, June 23). How Mexico's cartels are behind the border kid crises. *The Daily Beast*. Retrieved from http://www.thedailybeast.com/articles/2014/06/23/how-mexico-s-cartels-are-behind-the-border-kid-crisis.html.

Dinan, S. (2013a, February 5). Top democrat warns against using the term 'illegal immigrants.' *The Washington Times*. Retrieved from http://www.washingtontimes.com/blog/inside-poli tics/2013/feb/5/top-democrat-warns-against-using-term-illegal-immi/.

Dinan, S. (2013b, August 23). Obama adds to list of illegal immigrants not to deport: Parents. *The Washington Times*. Retrieved from http://www.washingtontimes.com/news/2013/ aug/23/new-obama-policy-warns-agents-not-detain-illegal-i/?page=all.

Dumalaon, J., Korolyov, A., & Jones-berry, S. (2014, March 31). Immigration backlash is on the rise in Europe. *USA Today*. Retrieved from http://www.usatoday.com/story/news/ world/2014/03/31/europe-anti-immigration/5706575/.

Dyloco, P. (2012, January 6). What are Japanese averse to immigration? *Japan Today*. Retrieved from http://www.japantoday.com/category/opinions/view/why-are-japanese-averse-to-immi gration.

Epstein, R. (2014, March 4). National council of La Raza leader calls Barak Obama 'deporter-in-chief.' *Politico*. Retrieved from http://www.politico.com/story/2014/03/national-council-of-la-raza-janet-murguia-barack-obama-deporter-in-chief-immigration-104217.html.

Executive Office of the President. (2010). *Remarks by the President on comprehensive immigration reform*. Washington, DC: Office of the Press Secretary. Retrieved from https://www.white house.gov/the-press-office/remarks-president-comprehensive-immigration-reform.

Executive Office of the President. (2013). *The economic benefits of fixing our broken immigration system*. Washington, DC: Government Printing Office.

Fanon, F. (1952/2008). *Black skin: white masks: Get political.* London: Grove Press.

Fanon, F. (1961/2004). *The wretched of the earth.* (R. Philcox, Trans.). New York: Grove Press.

Fernandez, M., Perez-Pena, R., & Bromwich, J. (2016, July 8). Five Dallas officers were killed as payback, police chief says. *The New York Times.* Retrieved from http://www.nytimes.com/2016/07/09/us/dallas-police-shooting.html.

Ferran, L. (2014, July 31). 'Troubling': Suicide bomber hung out in US after terror training. *ABC News.* Retrieved from http://abcnews.go.com/Blotter/troubling-suicide-bomber-hung-us-terror-training/story?id=24790407.

Ferrechio, S. (2014, February 6). House republicans hit wall on immigration reform. *Washington Examiner,* as linked to "GOP leaders face wave of Opposition on immigration reform" on the Tea Party website at http://www.teaparty.org/gop-leaders-face-wave-opposition-immigration-reform-34247/.

Fontanella-Khan, A. (2016, July 16). Fetullah Gulen: Turkey coup may have been 'staged' by Erdogan regime. *The Guardian.* Retrieved from https://www.theguardian.com/world/2016/jul/16/fethullah-gulen-turkey-coup-erdogan.

Freudenrich, C. (2015). How IEDs work. *How Stuff works.* Retrieved from http://science.howstuffworks.com/ied1.htm.

Fuchs, P. (1995, June). Jumping to Conclusions in Oklahoma City? *American Journalism Review.* Retrieved from http://ajrarchive.org/article.asp?id=1980.

Gibbons-Neff, T. (2015, December 4). The striking militarization of the San Bernardino shooters. *The Washington Post.* Retrieved from https://www.washingtonpost.com/news/checkpoint/wp/2015/12/04/the-weapons-used-by-the-san-bernardino-shooters-were-strikingly-militarized/.

Gibson, G. (2013, July 24). Steve King doubles down on 'drug mules' comment. *Politico.* Retrieved from http://www.kfiam640.com/media/podcast-handel-on-demand-BillHandel/immigration-crisis-7a-0703-24985857/.

Gimpel, J. G. (2014, April 24). Immigration's impact on republican prospects, 1980 to 2012. *Center for Immigration Studies.* Retrieved from http://cis.org/immigration-impacts-on-republican-prospects-1980-2012.

Gohmert: US will become 'third world nation' if feds cont. enforce immigration laws. (2014, July 1). *CBS, DC.* Retrieved from http://washington.cbslocal.com/2014/07/01/gohmert-us-will-become-third-world-nation-if-feds-dont-enforce-immigration-laws/.

Grimes, W. (2005, September 2). Legion of the lost: The true experience of an American in the French Foreign Legion. *The New York Times.* Retrieved from http://www.nytimes.com/2005/09/01/arts/01iht-bookfri.html?_r=0.

Griswold, D. (2002, February 8). Immigrants have enriched American culture and enhanced our influence in the world. CATO Institute, originally appeared in *Insight* magazine. Retrieved from http://www.cato.org/publications/commentary/immigrants-have-enriched-american-culture-enhanced-our-influence-world.

Hagerty, B. B. (2010, March 18). Is the Bible more violent than the Quran? *National Public Radio, All things Considered.* Retrieved from http://www.npr.org/templates/story/story.php?storyId=124494788.

Handel, B. (2014, July 3). Immigration crises 7A. *KFI AM Radio*, podcast available at http://www.kfiam640.com/media/podcast-handel-on-demand-BillHandel/immigration-crisis-7a-0703-24985857/.

Haughney, C. (2013, April 23). The Times shifts on "illegal immigrant," but doesn't ban the use. *The New York Times*. Retrieved from http://www.nytimes.com/2013/04/24/business/media/the-times-shifts-on-illegal-immigrant-but-doesnt-ban-the-use.html?pagewanted=all.

Hennessy-Fiske, M., Bennett, B., & Carcamo, C. (2014, June 20). Obama administration acts to ease immigration legal crunch at border. *Los Angeles Times*. Retrieved from http://www.latimes.com/nation/nationnow/la-na-nn-border-migrants-white-house-20140620-story.html#page=1.

Heyes, J. D. (2014, July 2). Mexican drug cartels using illegal immigration flood as cover to smuggle operatives and hard drugs into the U.S. *Natural News*. Retrieved from http://www.naturalnews.com/045822_illegal_immigration_Mexican_cartels_drug_smuggling.html.

Hoffman, B. (2006). *Inside terrorism*. New York: Columbia University Press.

Hoffman, B. (2013, April 27). Answers to why people become terrorists. *The Daily Beast*. Retrieved from http://www.thedailybeast.com/articles/2013/04/27/answers-to-why-people-become-terrorists.html.

Hoffman, B., Rosenau, W., Curiel, A., & Zimmermann, D. (2007). *The radicalization of Diasporas and terrorism: A joint conference by RAND corporation and the Center for Security Studies, ETH Zurich*. Santa Monica: RAND.

Holmes, D. L. (2006). The faiths of the Founding Fathers. New York: Oxford University Press.

Homeland Secretary: Agency that removes immigrants will be out of money by mid-September at 'current burn rate.' (2014, July 11). *CBS Local*. Retrieved from http://washington.cbslocal.com/2014/07/11/homeland-secretary-agency-that-removes-immigrants-will-be-out-of-money-by-mid-september-at-current-burn-rate/.

House of Commons. (2005). *Report of the official account of the bombings in London on 7th July 2005*. London: The Stationary Office.

"How cartels use tunnels to send drugs into US." *New York Post*, Associated Press. Retrieved from http://nypost.com/2014/01/14/how-smuggling-tunnels-are-built-used-along-us-border/.

Hsu, H. (2009, January 1). The end of white America? *The Atlantic*. Retrieved from http://www.theatlantic.com/magazine/archive/2009/01/the-end-of-white-america/307208/.

Hughes, D. M., Chon, K. Y., & Ellerman, D. P. (2007, September). Modern-day comfort women: The U.S. military, transnational crime, and the trafficking of women. *The University of Rhode Island*. Retrieved from http://www.google.com/url?sa=t&rct=j&q=&esrc=s&source=web&cd=8&ved=0CFIQFjAH&url=http%3A%2F%2Fwww.cops.usdoj.gov%2Fhtml%2Fcd_rom%2Fsolution_gang_crime%2Fpubs%2FDreamsGangsandGunsTheInterplayBetweenAdolescent.pdf&ei=DJ24U4mMCJCgogTmz4LYBg&usg=AFQjCNHLNY5ET9OFEDvqEBMFl48J90EJAg&bvm=bv.70138588,d.cGU.

Human Rights Watch (HRW). (1999, October 1). Anti-Christian violence on the rise in India: New report details behind extremist Hindu attacks. *Human Rights Watch*. Retrieved from http://www.hrw.org/en/news/1999/09/29/anti-christian-violence-rise-india.

Huntington, S. P. (1996). *The clash of civilizations and the remaking of world order.* New York: Touchstone.

Huxley, A. (2013, January 25). It's official: "Terrorist" is the most inappropriately over-used word in American English. *Forming the Thread.* Retrieved from http://formingthethread.wordpress. com/2013/01/25/its-official-terrorist-is-the-most-inappropriately-over-used-word-in-ameri can-english/.

Ibrahim, R. (2012, May 15). Mexican jihad. *Front Page Mag.* Retrieved from http://www.front pagemag.com/2012/raymond-ibrahim/mexican-jihad/.

"Immigration facts: Immigration and terrorism polls." (2009). *Federation for American Immigra- tion Reform.* Retrieved from http://www.fairus.org/facts/immigration-and-terrorism-polls.

Immigration Watch Canada. (2014). Homepage at http://www.immigrationwatchcanada.org/.

Jeffers, G. Jr., Scoggin, A., & Solis, D. (2014, June 28). Clay Jenkins wants Dallas County to house children. *Dallas News.* Retrieved from http://www.desertsun.com/story/news/ local/2014/07/04/murrieta-california-border-patrol-immigration-protests-undocument ed-immigrants-july-fourth/12217279/.

Jenkins, B. M. (2011). *Stray dogs and virtual armies: Radicalization and recruitment to jihadist ter- rorism in the United States since 9/11.* Santa Monica: RAND.

Jenkins, B. M. (2014, July 30). An evil wind. *The RAND Blog* at http://www.rand.org/ blog/2014/07/an-evil-wind.html.

Johnson, J. (2014). *Quadrennial Homeland Security Review Report (QHSR).* Washington, DC: Government Printing Office.

Jones, A. (2011, May 11). 18 facts prove illegal immigration is absolute nightmare for U.S. economy. *Infowars.* Retrieved from http://www.infowars.com/18-facts-prove-illegal-immi gration-is-absolute-nightmare-for-u-s-economy/.

Kenber, B. (2013, August 28). Nidal Hassan sentenced to death for Fort Hood shooting ram- page. *The Washington Post.* Retrieved from http://www.washingtonpost.com/world/nation al-security/nidal-hasan-sentenced-to-death-for-fort-hood-shooting-rampage/2013/08/28/ aad28de2-0ffa-11e3-bdf6-e4fc677d94a1_story.html.

Khan, Y. (2008). *The great partition: The making of India and Pakistan.* New Haven: Yale Uni- versity Press.

Kifner, J. (1995, December 31). McVeigh's mind: A special report; Oklahoma bombing sus- pect: Unraveling of a frayed life. *The New York Times.* Retrieved from http://www.nytimes. com/1995/12/31/us/mcveigh-s-mind-special-report-oklahoma-bombing-suspect-unravel ing-frayed-life.html.

Killerman, S. (2014). 30+ examples of Christian privilege. Its Pronounced Metrosexual. Retrieved from http://itspronouncedmetrosexual.com/2012/05/list-of-examples-of-christian-privileg/.

Kotkin, J. (2010, August). The changing demographics of America: The United States popu- lation will expand by 100 million over the next 40 years. Is this a reason to worry? *Smith- sonian Magazine.* Retrieved from http://www.smithsonianmag.com/40th-anniversary/ the-changing-demographics-of-america-538284/.

Krukenberg, K. A. (2008, April). *Multi-hued America: The case for the civil rights movement's embrace of multiethnic identity.* From the selected works of Kamaria A. Kruckenberg.

Retrieved from http://works.bepress.com/cgi/viewcontent.cgi?article=1000&context=ka maria_kruckenberg.

Lake, E. (2013, September 12). Americans join Syrian jihad, sparking U.S. intelligence fears. *The Daily Beast*. Retrieved from http://www.thedailybeast.com/articles/2013/09/12/ameri cans-join-syrian-jihad-sparking-u-s-intelligence-fears.html.

Lance, P. (2013, February 26). The blind sheikh: A flashpoint for terror 20 years after the World Trade Center bombing: Just how dangerous is the blind sheikh? *Alternet*. Retrieved from http://www.alternet.org/blind-sheikh-flashpoint-terror-20-years-after-world-trade-center-bombing.

Lawrence, B. (Ed.) (2005). *Messages to the world: The statements of Osama bin laden*. New York: Verso.

LeBaron, G. Jr. (1995). Mormon fundamentalism and violence: A historical analysis. *ExMormon*. Retrieved from http://www.exmormon.org/violence.htm.

Lehrer, J. (2007, June 18). Churches providing sanctuary for illegal immigrants. *Public Broadcasting System*, podcast transcript available at http://www.pbs.org/newshour/bb/social_issues-jan-june07-sanctuary_06-18/.

Leong, N. (2013, June). Racial capitalism. *Harvard Law Review*, Vol. 126, No. 8, pp. 2152–2226.

Lerche, C. O. III. (1998). The conflicts of globalization. *The International Journal of Peace Studies*. Vol. 3, No, 1. Retrieved from http://www.gmu.edu/programs/icar/ijps/vol3_1/learch.htm.

Levy, G. (2016, March 10). Immigration dominates democratic debate. *U.S. News & World Report*. Retrieved from http://www.usnews.com/news/articles/2016-03-10/immigration-dom inates-democratic-debate.

Lewiston mayor reacts to immigrants' protest. (2014, July 2). *Lewiston-Auburn Sun Journal*. Retrieved from http://www.sunjournal.com/news/lewiston-auburn/2014/07/02/lewiston-may or-reacts-immigrants-protest/1556623#.

Lind, D. (2014, May 9). What do pro-enforcement groups want out of the deportation review? *Vox*. Retrieved from http://www.vox.com/2014/5/9/5699288/what-do-pro-enforcement-groups-want-out-of-the-deportation-review.

Lipovsky, I. P. (2012). *Early Israelites: Two peoples, one history: Rediscovery of the origins of Biblical Israel*. Igor P. Lipovsky.

Lister, T. (2014, June 13). ISIS: The first terror group to build an Islamic state? *CNN*. Retrieved from http://edition.cnn.com/2014/06/12/world/meast/who-is-the-isis/.

Lovett, I., & Montgomery, D. (2014, July 21). For two slain Americans, commitment came early. *The New York Times*. Retrieved from http://www.nytimes.com/2014/07/22/world/middleeast/2-americans-among-israeli-soldiers-killed-in-gaza.html?_r=0.

Lucassen, J. (2009). The mobility transition revisited, 1500–1900: What the case of Europe can offer to global history. *Journal of Global History*, 4, Issue 3, p. 347-377.

McCalla, C. (2011). The top ten white terrorists of all-time. *NewsOne*. Retrieved from http://newsone.com/1417755/top-10-white-christian-terrorists/.

Mapping Police Violence. (2017, January 1). Unarmed black people were killed by police at 5X the rate of unarmed whites in 2015. *Mapping Police Violence*. Retrieved from http://mappingpoliceviolence.org/unarmed/.

Marszal, A. (2014, June 6). Sword fight at India's Golden temple on raid anniversary. *The Telegraph*. Retrieved from http://www.telegraph.co.uk/news/worldnews/asia/india/10880015/Sword-fight-at-Indias-Golden-Temple-on-raid-anniversary.html.

Marzulli, J. (2013, May 27). Adis medunjanin, terrorist foiled in 2009 bomb plot on New York subway, to serve life sentence in notorious Colo. Prison: 'Cleaner version of hell.' *Daily News*. Retrieved from http://www.nydailynews.com/news/national/foiled-terrorist-serve-life-notorious-colo-prison-article-1.1355289.

Mascaro, L., & Bennett, B. (2014, June 29). Obama's bid to deport children complicates immigration reform effort. *Los Angeles Times*. Retrieved from http://www.latimes.com/nation/la-na-obama-immigration-reform-20140630-story.html#page=1.

Mateu-Gelabert, P. (2002). Dreams, gangs, and guns: The interplay between adolescent violence and immigration in a New York City neighborhood. *Vera Institute of Justice*. Retrieved from http://www.google.com/url?sa=t&rct=j&q=&esrc=s&source=web&cd=8&ved=0CFIQFjAH&url=http%3A%2F%2Fwww.cops.usdoj.gov%2Fhtml%2Fcd_rom%2Fsolution_gang_crime%2Fpubs%2FDreamsGangsandGunsTheInterplayBetweenAdolescent.pdf&ei=DJ24U4mMCJCgogTmz4LYBg&usg=AFQjCNHLNY5ET9OFEDvqEBMFl48J90EJAg&bvm=bv.70138588,d.cGU.

McCartney, C. (2013, August 26). Mob of 1,000 Buddhists burns down Muslim homes and shops in Myanmar. *The Global Post*. Retrieved from http://www.globalpost.com/dispatches/globalpost-blogs/belief/mob-1000-buddhist-burn-down-muslim-homes-and-shops-myanmar.

McKinley, J. C. Jr., (2005, January 6). A Mexican manual for illegal migrants upsets some in U.S. *The New York Times*. Retrieved from http://www.nytimes.com/2005/01/06/international/americas/06mexico.html?_r=0.

Menon, R., & Fuller, G. E. (2000, March/April). Russia's ruinous Chechen war. *Foreign Affairs*. Retrieved from http://www.foreignaffairs.com/articles/55844/rajan-menon-and-graham-e-fuller/russias-ruinous-chechen-war.

Meyers, D., & Pitkin, J. (2010). *Assimilation today: Evidence shows the latest immigrants to America are following in our history's footsteps*. Washington, DC: Center for American Progress.

Myre, G. (2013, April 20). Boston bombings point to growing threat of homegrown terrorism. *National Public Radio*. Retrieved from http://www.npr.org/blogs/thetwo-way/2013/04/20/177958045/boston-bombings-point-to-growing-threat-of-homegrown-terrorism.

Napolitano, J. (2010). *Quadrennial Homeland Security Review Report (QHSR)*. Washington, DC: Government Printing Office.

Napolitano, J. (2012). *Department of Homeland Security Strategic Plan: Fiscal years 2012–2016*. Washington, DC: US Government Printing Office.

Nebraska Studies. The missionary spirit: The conversion struggle. *Nebraska Studies*. Retrieved from http://www.nebraskastudies.org/0400/frameset_reset.html?http://www.nebraskastudies.org/0400/stories/0401_0129.html.

Nelson, R., & Bodurian, B. (2010, March). A growing terrorist threat? Assessing "Homegrown" extremism in the United States. *Center for Strategic & International Studies A report of the CSIS homeland security and counterterrorism program*. Washington, DC. Retrieved from http://csis.org/files/publication/100304_Nelson_GrowingTerroristThreat_Web.pdf.

Nelson, S. S. (2013, September 16). German nationalists protest against Muslim immigration. *National Public Radio.* Retrieved from http://www.dailystormer.com/german-nation alists-protest-against-muslim-immigration/.

NewsOne. (2013, April 19). Muslim woman attacked after Boston Marathon bombings. *NewsOne.* Retrieved from http://newsone.com/2396424/heba-abolaban-boston-marathon-bombings-ter rorist/.

Oakes, E. T. (2008, January 29). Atheism and violence. *First Things.* Retrieved from http:// www.firstthings.com/web-exclusives/2008/01/atheism-and-violence.

Obama, B. (2011a). *Presidential Policy directive—8: National Preparedness.* Washington, DC: Government Printing Office.

Obama, B. (2011b). *Empowering local partners to prevent violent extremism in the United States.* Washington, DC: Government Printing Office.

O'Connor, A. (2011, July 27). Mexican cartels move into human trafficking. *The Washington Post.* Retrieved from http://www.washingtonpost.com/world/americas/mexican-car tels-move-into-human-trafficking/2011/07/22/gIQArmPVcI_story.html.

Oliker, O. (2013, May 6). Searching for clues on the brothers Tsarnarev. *Rand.* Retrieved from http://www.rand.org/blog/2013/05/searching-for-clues-on-the-brotherstsarnarev.html.

O'Reilly, B. (2014, July 2). Talking points: America growing angrier at the federal government. *Fox News,* video available at http://www.foxnews.com/on-air/oreilly/index.html.

Owens, E. (2012, November 26). Texas school teach Boston tea party as act of terrorism. *The Daily Caller.* Retrieved from http://dailycaller.com/2012/11/26/texas-schools-teach-boston-tea-party-as-act-of-terrorism/.

Panza, S. (2014, July 2). Furious California citizens block buses carrying illegal immigrants, force them to turn around. *IJReview.* Retrieved from http://www.ijreview.com/2014/07/152958-even-california-citizens-are-angrily-protesting-against-obamas-plan-to-bus-illegal-aliens-all-over-america/.

Papademetriou, D. (2005, September 1). The global struggle with illegal migration: No end in sight. *Migration Information* Source, Migration Policy Institute. Retrieved from http:// www.migrationpolicy.org/article/global-struggle-illegal-migration-no-end-sight.

Parikh, R. (2006). White males, racism and Christian fundamentalism in American politics. *Sulekha.com.* Retrieved from http://creative.sulekha.com/white-males-racism-and-christian-fundamentalism-in-american-politics_190267_blog.

Patten, E., & Lopez, M. H. (2013, July 22). Are unauthorized immigrants overwhelmingly democrats? *Pew Research Center.* Retrieved from http://www.pewresearch.org/fact-tank/2013/07/22/are-unauthorized-immigrants-overwhelmingly-democrats/.

Preston, J. (2013, September 23). Number of illegal immigrants in U.S. may be on rise again, estimates say. *The New York Times.* Retrieved from http://www.nytimes.com/2013/09/24/us/immigrant-population-shows-signs-of-growth-estimates-show.html?_r=0.

Qutb, S. (1991). *The Islamic concept and its characteristics.* (Mohammed Moinuddin Siddiqui, Trans.). Plainfield: American Trust Publications.

Rasley, G. (2014, July 3). Murrieta shows citizens can strike back against illegal alien invasion. *Conservative HQ*. Retrieved from http://www.conservativehq.com/article/17653-murrie ta-shows-citizens-can-strike-back-against-illegal-alien-invasion.

Rice, C. (2007). *Trafficking in persons reports*. Washington, DC: US Government Printing Office.

Riddell, K. (2014, April 9). Sheriffs warn of violence from Mexican cartels deep into interior of U.S. *The Washington Times*. Retrieved from http://www.washingtontimes.com/news/2014/ apr/9/sheriffs-warn-of-violence-from-mexican-cartels-dee/?page=all.

Robbins, L., & Hamill, S. D. (2009, April 4). Gunman kills 3 police officers in Pittsburgh. *The New York Times*. Retrieved from http://www.nytimes.com/2009/04/05/us/05pittsburgh. html.

Roediger, D. (2005). *Working toward whiteness: How America's immigrants became white: The strange journey from Ellis Island to the suburbs*. New York: The Perseus Books Group.

Rudolph, E. (2013, April 24). Are Christians more violent than Muslims? *Abagond*. Retrieved from http://abagond.wordpress.com/2013/04/24/are-christians-more-violent-than-muslims/.

Rustom, R. (2012, September 15). Why most terrorists are Muslims. *Islam Watch*. Retrieved from http://www.islam-watch.org/authors/142-rami/1145-why-most-terrorists-are-muslims.html.

Saad, L. (2013, October 31). U.S. crime is up, but Americans don't seem to have noticed. *Gallup*. Retrieved from http://www.theatlantic.com/magazine/archive/2009/01/the-end-of-white-america/307208/.

Said, E. W. (1993). *Cultural imperialism*. New York: Vintage Books.

Sanchez, T, & Cano, R. (2014, July 5). Dueling immigration rallies in Calif. Town: 6 arrested. *The Desert Sun*. Retrieved from http://www.desertsun.com/story/news/local/2014/07/04/ murrieta-california-border-patrol-immigration-protests-undocumented-immigrants-ju ly-fourth/12217279/.

Sakuma, A. (2015, August 6). Immigration issues dominate opening of GOP presidential debate. *MSNBC*. Retrieved from http://www.msnbc.com/msnbc/immigration-issues-dom inate-opening-gop-presidential-debate.

Savage, C. (2014, June 23). Court releases large parts of memo approving killing of American in Yemen. *The New York Times*. Retrieved from http://www.nytimes.com/2014/06/24/us/ justice-department-found-it-lawful-to-target-anwar-al-awlaki.html?_r=0.

Schanzer, D., Kurzman, C., & Moosa, E. (2010). Anti-terror lessons of Muslim-Ameri-cans. *Duke University*. Retrieved from http://www.google.com/url?sa=t&rct=j&q=&es rc=s&source=web&cd=1&ved=0CB0QFjAA&url=http%3A%2F%2Fsites.duke. edu%2Ftcths%2Ffiles%2F2013%2F06%2FSchanzer_Kurzman_Moosa_Anti-Terror_Les sons1.pdf&ei=ZqneU6uTL9PooATEiIHQBA&usg=AFQjCNETb-hEGBweLfZYZMk mPkqYfv_xpw&bvm=bv.72197243,d.cGU.

Schladen, M. (2014, July 2). DPS: Cartels helping immigrant children enter US illegally. *El Paso Times*. Retrieved from http://www.kfiam640.com/media/podcast-handel-on-demand-Bill Handel/immigration-crisis-7a-0703-24985857/.

Sergie, M. A., & Johnson, T. (2015, March 5). Boko Haram. *Council on Foreign Relations*. Retrieved from http://www.cfr.org/nigeria/boko-haram/p25739.

Shapira, I. (2010, March 7). Pentagon shooter's spiral from early promise to madness. *The Washington Post*. Retrieved from http://www.washingtonpost.com/wp-dyn/content/article/2010/03/06/AR2010030602537.html.

Shrestha, N. (2010, September 29). Explore other cultures to understand your own. *Collegiate Times*. Retrieved from http://www.collegiatetimes.com/opinion/columnists/article_8c7d-4da2-8ff9-548f-857e-03b9384e2193.html.

Silsby, G. (2013, August 7). Why people take the risk of illegal immigration. *Futurity*: University of Southern California Study. Retrieved from http://www.futurity.org/why-people-take-the-risk-of-illegal-immigration/.

Singh, J. (2014, June 16). Robert Bergdhal's beard is not the threat. *Huffington Post*. Retrieved from http://www.huffingtonpost.com/jasjit-singh/robert-bergdahls-beard-is_b_5500749.html.

Sizgorich, T. (2008). *Violence and belief in late antiquity: Militant devotion in Christianity and Islam (Divinations: Rereading late ancient religion)*. Philadelphia: University of Pennsylvania Press.

Snowden, P. (2014). The revolution will be uploaded: Vernacular video and the Arab Spring. *Culture Unbound*, Vol. 6, pp. 401–429.

Snyder, M. (2013, August 10). 19 very disturbing facts on illegal immigration every American should know. *Right Side News*. Retrieved from http://www.rightsidenews.com/2013081033026/us/homeland-security/19-very-disturbing-facts-on-illegal-immigration-every-american-should-know.html.

Southern Poverty Law Center (SPLC). (2009, February 26). Hate group numbers up by 54% since 2000. *Southern Poverty Law Center*. Retrieved from http://www.splcenter.org/get-informed/news/hate-group-numbers-up.

Sonner, S. (2014, July 10). Report shows how Cliven Bundy has emboldened right-wing extremists. *Huffington Post*. Retrieved from http://www.huffingtonpost.com/2014/07/10/cliven-bundy-report_n_5574512.html.

Squires, N. (2008, October 5). Protests in Italy against escalating racism. *The Telegraph*. Retrieved from http://www.telegraph.co.uk/news/worldnews/europe/italy/3141066/Protests-in-Italy-against-escalating-racism.html.

Stern, J. (2000). *The ultimate terrorists*. Boston: Harvard University Press.

Straziuso, J., Forliti, A., & Watson, J. (2012, January 14). Al Shabaab's American recruits in Somalia. *Huffington Post*. Retrieved from http://www.huffingtonpost.com/2012/01/14/americans-al-shabaab_n_1206279.html.

Taraby, J. (2013, August 14). A rare meeting with reclusive Turkish spiritual leader Fethullah Gulen. *The Atlantic*. Retrieved from http://www.theatlantic.com/international/archive/2013/08/a-rare-meeting-with-reclusive-turkish-spiritual-leader-fethullah-gulen/278662/.

Tashman, B. (2011, March 29). Tea party group warns of white "extinction" in America. *Right Wing Watch*. Retrieved from http://www.rightwingwatch.org/content/tea-party-group-warns-white-extinction-america.

Thompson, P. (2010). Autistic child charged with terrorism over school drawing. *The Telegraph*, May 16. Retrieved from http://www.telegraph.co.uk/news/worldnews/northamerica/usa/7731513/Autistic-boy-charged-with-terrorist-offence.html.

Toews, V. (2013). *2013 public report on the terrorist threat to Canada*. Canada; Ministry of Public Safety.

Tone, H., & Uwimana, S. (2013, February 1). 10 myths conservative media will use against immigration reform. *Media Matters for America*. Retrieved from http://mediamatters.org/research/2013/02/01/10-myths-conservative-media-will-use-against-im/192494.

Tures, J. (2009, September). Do terrorists win elections? *Homeland Security Affairs*. Vol. V, No. 3, p. 1-10. Retrieved from http://www.hsaj.org/?fullarticle=5.3.5.

U.S. Census Bureau. (2012). Statistical abstract of the United States: 2012. U.S. Census Bureau. Retrieved from http://www.google.com/url?sa=t&rct=j&q=&esrc=s&source=web&cd=1&ved=0CB0QFjAA&url=http%3A%2F%2Fwww.census.gov%2Fprod%2F2011pubs%2F12statab%2Fpop.pdf&ei=UHDeU8n9F8XaoATLr4D4DQ&usg=AFQjCNHabHgDXuO-kS1UMDIUFyYAbw8CSQ&bvm=bv.72197243,d.cGU.

U.S. Department of Health and Human Services (USDHHS). (2016, June 23). Community immunity. Retrieved from http://www.vaccines.gov/basics/protection/.

Utley, R. M., & Washburn, W. E. (2002). *Indian wars*. New York: American Heritage Press.

Venugopal, A. (2011, May 24). Immigrants assimilate more successfully in the U.S. than in Europe: Report. *WNYC*. Retrieved from http://www.wnyc.org/story/136690-immigrants-assimilate-more-successfully-us-europe-according-report/.

Vetter, R. (2013, August 5). Border security costs taxpayers $12 Billion. *IVN*. Retrieved from http://ivn.us/2013/08/05/border-security-costs-taxpayers-12-billion-2/.

Vigdor, J. (2008). *Measuring immigrant assimilation in the United States*. Manhattan: Center for Civic Innovation.

Walser, R., McNeill, J. B., & Zuckerman. (2011). The human tragedy of illegal immigration: Greater efforts needed to combat smuggling and violence. *The Heritage Foundation*. Retrieved from http://www.heritage.org/research/reports/2011/06/the-human-tragedy-of-illegal-immigration-greater-efforts-needed-to-combat-smuggling-and-violence.

Watson, J. (2014, July 2). Buses with migrant families rerouted amid protest. *Associated Press*. Retrieved from http://talkingpointsmemo.com/news/buses-with-migrant-families-rerouted-protests.

Wellman, J. (2013, July 7). Should Christians have non Christian friends? *What Christians Want to Know*. Retrieved from http://www.whatchristianswanttoknow.com/should-christians-have-non-christian-friends/.

Werner, E., & Caldwell, A. A. (2014, July 14). Possible compromise emerges on border security. *Associated Press*. Retrieved from http://www.aol.com/article/2014/07/10/possible-compromise-emerges-on-border-request/20928845/?icid=maing-grid7 | main5 | dl17 | sec1_lnk2%26pLid%3D500053.

Wilber, D. Q. (2010, January 7). Von Brunn, white supremacist Holocaust museum shooter, dies. *The Washington Post*. Retrieved from http://www.washingtonpost.com/wp-dyn/content/article/2010/01/06/AR2010010604095.html.

Wolgin, P. E., & Garcia, A. (2013, August, 8). Immigration is changing the political landscape in key states. *Center for American Progress*. Retrieved from https://www.americanprogress.org/wp-content/uploads/2013/04/ImmigrationPolitics.pdf.

Woodyard, C., & Heath, B. (2015, December 3). San Bernardino shooters lived a double life. *USA Today*. Retrieved from http://www.usatoday.com/story/news/2015/12/03/san-bernardi no-shooter/76710658/.

Woodsome, K. (2013, April 26). Immigration shapes US political parties as much as demograph-ics. *Voice of America*. Retrieved from http://www.voanews.com/content/immigration-shapes-us-parties-as-much-as-demographics/1649600.html.

· 4 ·

ADVANCE AND TRANSFER

Naval Shiphandling and Violent Extremism

In this last book, the discussion concentrates on how hegemonically provoked violent extremism is a realization of past warning through a concept used in naval shiphandling known as *advance and transfer* (Crenshaw,
1974). Advance and transfer is a term shiphandlers use to identify turning
points when maneuvering at sea. Advance is the distance a ship continues
on its original course from the time a shiphandler puts over the rudder until
the ship comes to its new course. Complementing advance is transfer; the
movement a ship travels perpendicular to the ship's original course prior
to putting the rudder over. Working with a ship's inertia in the physics
of advance and transfer are the characteristics of the wind and sea. The
strength of the wind and sea against a ship are the properties of set and
drift. In shiphandling, set and drift are natural features of the sea's current
and winds working against a ship's motion. Set is the bearing of the sea's
current. Drift is the speed of the current and the force of the wind working
on a ship's sail area.

Shiphandling fits into an analogy on violent extremism because a ship represents a large entity in motion that cannot control for all the variables working against its exterior. Figure 4.1 illustrates how advance and transfer and set and drift relate to violent extremism. Essentially, shiphandling is an art that takes years to master (Stavridis & Girrier, 2007). A ship is thousands of tons of steel in forward motion on a surface that is also moving. Stopping a ship takes great distances. Stopping on a dime is impossible. Therefore, controlling the movement of a ship is as challenging as managing the current challenges of violent extremism. So far, declaring a war on terrorism (Moeller, 2004) and claiming victory over Al Qaeda (Habeck, 2012) have not stopped the inertia of violent extremism or terrorism (Lee-Ashley, 2016; Sewall, 2016).

Shiphandling is analogous to the current challenges facing America in its war on terrorism. Figure 4.1 is a simple drawing for the course a ship is following. The ship is commensurate with contemporary American society. As the ship turns it rudder over to start a right turn, the dynamics of advance and transfer work on the ship as making an immediate right turn at sea is impossible. Advance is the direction intended of the current policy on violent extremism. Transfer is the distance America will travel until it reaches its final course; or implementation of the strategy to combat terrorism.

A seasoned shiphandler is aware that there are other forces working on a ship as it goes through the physics associated with advance and transfer. One set of factors working along with a ship turning is set and drift. In this analogy, set and drift represents the violent extremism of terrorism. In Figure 4.1, violent extremism is working on American policy heading in the general direction of the ship's turn. This illustration represents that America, in its current approach to countering violent extremism, is actually plotting a course that will take the nation into the rocks and shoals of violent extremism practiced by both dissenters of American policy as much as by America, the state wielding hegemonic authority. This is an illustration of violence causing more violence.

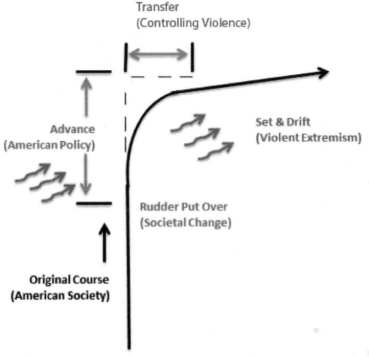

Figure 4.1: Advance and Transfer Model.
Source: Author, Copyright 2015

The current policy America has in combating violent extremism is taking a course many extremists desire (Chomsky, 2016). On one side, White supremacists see the American government giving too much away to foreigners (Rice, 2016) while Islamists gain currency by having the might of America thrown against them (Ross & Ferran, 2011). America needs to shift its rudder 180 degrees in the opposite direction. The question facing America is how far will the nation's captain put the rudder over? That is, if the order is ever given. The more the rudder moves, the more it will cause short-term pressure on America's hull as it comes to a new course. The sociopolitical seas facing America are rough and require good shiphandling for America to find a course that has fair winds and following seas. This will take time as any movement America makes has to follow a process based on time. America needs to approach the prevention of violent extremism from the mindset of doing it right, not right away.

The Farsighted: Voices of Thunder

Freire's (1970/2000) view of pedagogy goes far beyond the interactions of a teacher and student and enters social, political, and educational domains that still have merit years after his passing. Yet, Freire is not alone in critically identifying the faults of hegemonic societies over those they oppress in the name of sustaining hegemony. Unfortunately, many of the voices suffered dismissal and criticism because their messages did not bank American hegemony. Despite the fact Freire (1970/2000), Ivan Illich (1968), and Frantz Fanon (1952/2008; 1961/2004) discussed countries other than America in their descriptions of oppression, the root of their lessons and warning ring true today as the variables of subjugation are cause for contemporary violent extremism. In studying the history of oppression, why has the Western world not learned from the past? The answer is that hegemonic banking makes an enemy of dissention.

The fault with hegemonic oppressiveness is that the oppressors often fail to recognize the consequences of their actions. Fanon (1952/2008; 1961/2004) saw race and culture as instruments to oppress people colonized by Western powers. He also spoke out against the perceived pathway to success was to be as White as possible. Fanon valued the diversity of modern societies. Unfortunately, hegemonic characterizations of the value in diversity differ from those experiencing oppression.

A discussion of voices that gave warning to practicing hegemonic oppression would not be complete without hearing from those the hegemonic authorities call the enemy. Bringing into this dialectical dissertation the voices of terrorists and White supremacists is not showing cause in support of their ideologies, rather providing an outlet for their voice to cast light on to the shadow ignored or misrepresented by many in the security professionals and academia in the West. How else can America know what motivates its enemies if America does not know their enemy. Sharing knowledge of the enemy with the general population is mandatory if dissention within society is the goal of the government.

The pedagogy of violent extremism will take generations to develop a counter pedagogical approach to the learning of hate that has been the banner of Western hegemony. Currently, the demographic shift (Hobbs & Stoops, 2002) points to a storm on the horizon of intercivilizational relationships. Many issues will resolve themselves through the normal political processes in the West. The resultant society will however not be dominated by traditional Americanism. The danger facing the new face of America, whenever that eventuality occurs, is in falling into the same pattern of oppressors controlling the oppressed. If this happens, then the cyclical phenomenon of violent extremism will continue to exist—changing only who is master and who is servant. The peace that nearsighted leaders seek needs to consider the long-term outcomes of preserving the status quo.

Violent extremism will continue to be the product of, or the cause for future wars. The more violence society experiences, the more the unexpected becomes the expected. Many in the oppressed regions of the world currently live under this model. Is America ready to see violence as part of a daily routine? The approach to reducing violent extremism obliges society to take a multilayered approach to valuing diversity in a mixed society. This must begin in the high chair as part of an educational process that envelops social development, the economy, and most importantly the use of government-sanctioned violence using military and law enforcement as judge and jury. The current pedagogical approach to an inclusive society has created the foundation for the growing use of violent extremism. The systemic curriculum used to raise a society requires transformation.

A delicate area of transformation will be in personal liberties, especially in using the internet as a source of learning. Transforming the systemic pedagogical machine that educates America needs to include the autodidactic learning that takes place in the confines of a person's house or private zone. A national dialectic on violent extremism supported with meaningful praxis by prominent leaders will set the example for revealing to the citizenry, options other than the use of violent extremism as the primary source of communication.

Conclusions

Chomsky (2007) has provided an easy answer to ceasing many of the world's woes, like violent extremism, which is stop participating in the acts of violent extremism. The simplicity of this solution, is regrettably, not as simple as the four words in the answer. Reality must answer to the inertia of past political decisions. Change is generational. Violent extremism, as detailed in this book, is difficult to understand since there are many simultaneous equations that can represent the dynamics of the phenomenon. There are also too many events currently set in action, that have to answer to the inertia of their antecedent factors before violent extremism is reduced.

Governments have long had to deal with regimen continuity. As many a philosopher (Aristotle, 1953/2004), military general (Aurelius, 1862/1997), and religious leader (Confucius, 1993/2000) have posited throughout the millennia, the best course of action is to have a balance between the extremes of using violence as a tool of authority. Transformation of society cannot sway to a position either too far to the right or too far to the left.

American leaders can also recognize authorities outside of Western circles that call for an end to violent extremism (Al-Misri, 1991/1994). Shaykh Saalih bin "Abdul" Azeez Ali-Shaykh (2008), Grand Mufti and Head of the Ministry of Islamic Affairs, in Saudi Arabia has refuted the use of Islam to commit violent acts of extremism. His small book, A Warning Against Extremism Ali-Shaykh, 2008), serves as guidance on denying violence as a way of Islam. Yet, his book draws little attention to his authoritative words on interpreting Islam. This may be because the Grand Mufti, in his earlier days, delivered fatwas on Islam that were viewed as controversial in the West. His warning that extremism will destroy those using it, goes unnoticed by many. Also ignored are warnings by Chomsky (2003/2004; 2007) and Giroux (2014) on the path America is following concerning its actions to ensure regime continuity.

Election years promote extreme ideologies as candidates vie for popular and electoral votes. The 2015 terrorist attacks in France have shed new fears of violent extremism occurring in America—at least from Islamists. Unwarranted in the presidential debate is continuing discussion on the plight of refugees from Syria. Denial of refugees to America based on religion will only feed the aggressive pedagogy of violent extremism (Fantz & Brumfield, 2015). Keeping out family, friends, and fellow compatriots could be the straw that breaks the camel's back; driving otherwise peaceful people to resort to extreme violence against an oppressive hegemonic government. Ideas such as allowing only Syrian Christians (Nuzzi, 2015) into America are a call for a Manzanarian philosophy to resurface (Houston & Houston, 1973/2007), opening old wounds in the culture of America. Even worse is the call for a total prohibition of Muslims entering America (Johnson & Weigel, 2015). Rationalizing America's safety on exclusion is shallow and feeds the fears that become the worst in humanism.

The hegemonically provoked violent extremism theory holds that the choices to the left of balancing the government use of violence are a state of anarchy. If everyone gets to do what he wants as part of exercising his freedom, then no one is in control. Conversely, if the government decides everything a person can do or think, then America will become a police state. Contemporary indications are that America is heading in this direction. Either extreme will result in more violence. Taking the middle road is the best option for creating a society that is responsible to its citizenry while reducing the pedagogy of violent extremism.

References

Ali-Shaykh, S. S. b. A. A. (2008). *A warning against extremism*. Dar Ibn Rajab: Madeenah.

Al-Misri, A. I. N. (1991/1994). *Reliance of the traveler: A classical manual of Islamic sacred law*. Beltsville: Maryland: Amana Publications.

Aristotle. (1953/2004). *The Nicomachean ethics* (J. A. K. Thompson, Trans.). New York: Penguin Classics.

Aurelius, M. (1862/1997). *Meditations* (George Long, Trans.). Chesapeake: Dover Publications.

Chomsky, N. (2003/2004). *Hegemony or survival: America's quest for global dominance*. New York: Henry Holt.

Chomsky, N. (2007). *Interventions*. San Francisco: City Lights Books.

Chomsky, N. (2016, May 10). The US 'war on terror' is playing right into ISIS' hands. *The Nation*. Retrieved from https://www.thenation.com/article/the-us-war-on-terror-is-playing-right-into-isiss-hands/.

Confucius. (1993/2000). *Analects* (Raymond Dawson, Trans.). New York: Oxford University Press.

Crenshaw, R. (1974). *Naval Shiphandling* (4th Ed.) Newport: Naval Institute Press.

Fanon, F. (1952/2008). *Black skin: White masks: Get political*. London: Grove Press.

Fanon, F. (1961/2004). *The wretched of the earth* (R. Philcox, Trans.). New York: Grove Press.

Fantz, A., & Brumfield, B. (2015, November 19). More than half the nation's governors say Syrian refugees not welcome. *CNN*. Retrieved from http://www.cnn.com/2015/11/16/world/paris-attacks-syrian-refugees-backlash/.

Freire, P. (1970/2000). *Pedagogy of the oppressed*. New York: Bloomsbury.

Giroux, H. A. (2014). *The violence of organized forgetting: Thinking beyond America's disimagination machine*. San Francisco: City Lights Books.

Habeck, M. (2012, June 27). Can we declare the war on al Qaeda over? *Foreign Policy*. Retrieved from http://foreignpolicy.com/2012/06/27/can-we-declare-the-war-on-al-qaeda-over/.

Hobbs, F., & Stoops, N. (2002). *Demographic trends in the 20th Century*. Washington, DC: U.S. Census Bureau.

Houston, J. W., & Houston, J. D. (1973/2007). *Farewell to Manzanar*. Boston: Houghton Mifflin Company.

Illich, I. (1968, April 28). *To hell with good intentions*. Address presented to the Conference on Inter American Student Projects (CIASP) in Cuernavaca, Mexico. Retrieved from http://www.swaraj.org/illich_hell.htm.

Johnson, J., & Weigel, D. (2015, December 8). Donald trump calls for 'total' ban on Muslims entering United States. *The Washington Post*. Retrieved from https://www.washingtonpost.com/politics/2015/12/07/e56266f6-9d2b-11e5-8728-1af6af208198_story.html.

Lee-Ashley, M. (2016, March 24). Congress should confront the rise of violent extremism on America's public lands. *Center for American Progress*. Retrieved from https://www.americanprogress.org/issues/green/report/2016/03/24/133730/congress-should-confront-the-rise-of-violent-extremism-on-americas-public-lands/.

Moeller, S. (2004, March 18). Think again: Bush's war on terror. *Center for American Progress*. Retrieved from https://www.americanprogress.org/issues/security/news/2004/03/18/615/think-again-bushs-war-on-terror/.

Nuzzi, O. (2015, November 16). Jeb Bush & Ted Cruz only want to save Christians. *The Daily Beast*. Retrieved from http://www.thedailybeast.com/articles/2015/11/16/jeb-cruz-only-want-to-save-christians.html.

Rice, Z. (2016, January 20). How Fresno, California, became hotspot for anti-Sikh violence in America. *Identities.mic*. Retrieved from https://mic.com/articles/132552/how-fresno-california-became-a-hotspot-for-anti-sikh-violence-in-america#.6gvZgupNA.

Ross, B., & Ferran, L. (2011, September 30). How Anwar al-Awlaki inspired terror from across the globe. *ABC News*. Retrieved from http://abcnews.go.com/Blotter/anwar-al-awlaki-inspired-terror/story?id=14643383.

Stavridis, J., & Girrier, R. (2007). *Watch officer's guide* (15th Ed.). Newport: Naval Institute Press.

REFERENCES

9/11 Commission. (2004). The 9/11 commission report; Final report to the national commission on terrorist attacks upon the United States. Harrisonburg: W.W. Norton & Company.

"A post-colonial France: A chronicle of years of fire, France's relationship with its Arab population is defined by hatred and hurt." (2014, March 1). *The Economist*.

Achenbach, J., Wan, W., Berman, M., & Balingit, M. (2016, July 8). Five Dallas police officers were killed by a lone attacker; authorities say. *The Washington Post*. Retrieved from https://www.washingtonpost.com/news/morning-mix/wp/2016/07/08/like-a-little-war-snipers-shoot-11-police-officers-during-dallas-protest-march-killing-five/.

Adi. (2012, September 19). Characteristics inherent to the Occidental and Oriental races: A comparative study. *Faith & Heritage*. Retrieved from http://faithandheritage.com/2012/09/characteristics-inherent-to-the-occidental-and-oriental-races-a-comparative-study/.

Admin. (2014, November 4). '350 million Muslims secretly live as Christian converts.' *Muslim World Press, Statistics*. Retrieved from https://muslimstatistics.wordpress.com/2014/11/04/350-million-muslims-are-secretly-living-lives-as-christian-converts/comment-page-1/.

Agence France-Presse. (2016, June 17). Brussels bombing suspect Youssef EA formally charged by Belgian authorities. *The Guardian*. Retrieved from https://www.theguardian.com/world/2016/jun/18/brussels-bombing-suspect-youssef-ea-formally-charged-by-belgian-authorities.

Aguila, E., & Godges, J. (2013). *Heavy lift: Truly comprehensive immigration reform would span the migrant labor lifecycle*. Rand Review, pp. 18–26.

Akers, S. (2013, October 2). Muslim man wakes from coma, converts to Christianity. *Charisma News*. Retrieved from http://www.charismanews.com/culture/41212-muslim-man-wakes-from-coma-converts-to-christianity.

Al Jazeera America. (2013, September 12). Somalia's al-Shabaab kills US fighter: Omar Hammami, known as al-Amriki or the American, killed in an ambush after falling out with group's leader. *Al Jazeera America*. Retrieved from http://www.aljazeera.com/news/africa/2 013/09/201391293315761506.html.

Algemeiner. (2014, January 27). Hate-filled protest in France attracts thousands: Crowd chants 'Jew, France is not for you!' *The Algemeiner*. Retrieved from http://www.algemeiner. com/2014/01/27/hate-filled-protest-in-france-attracts-thousands-crowd-chants-jew-france-is-not-for-you-video/.

Ali-Shaykh, S. S. b. A. A. (2008). *A warning against extremism*. Dar Ibn Rajab: Madeenah.

Allen, R. L. (2004). Whiteness and critical pedagogy. *Educational Philosophy and Theory*. Vol. 36/2.

Allen, R. L, & Rossatto, C. A. (2009). Does critical pedagogy work with privileged students? *Teacher Education Quarterly*. Winter, pp. 163–180.

"Almost 100 hate crime killings linked to one website: Report." (2014, April 18). *The Guardian*. Retrieved from the Huffington post at http://www.huffingtonpost.com/2014/04/08/ hate-crimes-linked-to-website_n_5173944.html?icid=maing-grid7 | main5 | dl7 | sec1_ inl2%26pLid%3D466548.

Al-Misri, A. I. N. (1991/1994). *Reliance of the traveler: A classical manual of Islamic sacred law*. Beltsville: Maryland: Amana Publications.

Al Qaeda Terrorist Training Manual (AQTM). (2000). (UK/BM-2 Translation, May) Manchester: UK/BM2.

Alter, C. (2013, September 24). Born in the USA: 5 American terrorists: If Americans were among the Kenya mall attackers as claimed, they'll join a growing list of home-grown terrorism. *Time*. Retrieved from http://world.time.com/2013/09/24/born-in-the-usa-5-american-terrorists/.

Amadeo, K. (2016, February 23). War on terror: Facts, costs, timeline. *About Money*. Retrieved from http://useconomy.about.com/od/usfederalbudget/f/War_on_Terror_Facts.htm.

American-Arab Anti-Discrimination Committee (ADC). (2015). Countering violent extremism (CVE) programs. Retrieved from the ADC website at http://www.adc.org/counter ing-violent-extremism-cve/.

American Civil Liberties Union (ACLU). (2016, February 4) ACLU briefing paper; What is wrong with the government's "Countering Violent Extremism programs. Retrieved from https://theintercept.com/wp-uploads/sites/1/2016/02/CVE-Briefing-Paper-Feb-2016.pdf.

American Civil Liberties Union (ACLU). (2016, December). nationwide ant-Muslim activity. *ACLU Webpage*. Retrieved on July 17, 2016 from https://www.aclu.org/map/nation wide-anti-mosque-activity.

Anonymous. (2012, September 14). Converting to Islam: "I'm a 17-year-old Latin-American girl who switched from Christianity to Islam." *Huffington Post*. Retrieved from http://www. huffingtonpost.com/2012/09/12/converting-to-islam_n_1877655.html.

Ansolabehers, S., Persily, N., & Stewart, C. III. (2010, April). Race, region, and vote choice in the 2008 election: Implications for the future of Voting Rights Act. *Harvard Law Review*, Vol. 123, No. 6, pp. 1386–1436.

"Anti-immigration groups." (2001). *Southern Poverty Law Center.* Retrieved from http://www.splcenter.org/get-informed/intelligence-report/browse-all-issues/2001/spring/blood-on-the-border/anti-immigration-.

Ardizzone, L. (2003). Generating peace: A study of nonformal youth organizations. *Peace & Change.* Vol. 28, No. 3, pp. 420–445.

Aristotle. (1953/2004). *The Nicomachean ethics* (J. A. K. Thompson, Trans.). New York: Penguin Classics.

Artsinger, A., & Roberts, R. (2007, January 2007). But it's Thomas Jefferson's Koran! *The Washington Post.* Retrieved from http://www.washingtonpost.com/wp-dyn/content/article/2007/01/03/AR2007010300075.html.

Aurelius, M. (1862/1997). *Meditations* (George Long, Trans.). Chesapeake: Dover Publications.

Arango, T., & Yeginsu, C. (2016, July 16). Turkey detains thousands in military in bid to regain control. *The New York Times.* Retrieved from http://www.nytimes.com/2016/07/17/world/europe/turkey-attempted-coup-erdogan.html.

Aslan, R. (2009). *How to win a cosmic war: God, globalization and the end of the war on terror.* New York: Random House.

Associated Press. (2012, February 16). Interracial marriages in the U.S. hit all-time high 4.8 million: 1 in 12 involved in interracial union, rise pegged to steadily flow of Asian and Hispanic immigrants. *Daily news.* Retrieved from http://www.nydailynews.com/life-style/interracial-marriages-u-s-hit-all-time-high-4-8-million-article-1.1023643.

Aucoin, J. (2014, October 24). The superhero diversity problem. *Harvard Political Review.* Retrieved from http://harvardpolitics.com/books-arts/superhero-diversity-problem/.

"Authorities say hate motivated Kansa shooting." (2014, April 14). *Associated Press.* Retrieved from http://www.aol.com/article/2014/04/14/suspect-in-killings-at-kansas-jewish-centers-has-hate-filled-his/20868805/?icid=maing-grid7 | main5 | dl6 | sec1_lnk2%26plid%3D464554.

Aydinli, O., & Ersel, U. (2003). Winning a low intensity conflict: Drawing lessons from the Turkish case, pp. 101–118. In Efraim, I. (Ed.) *Democracies and small wars.* Portland: Frank Crass.

Balko, R. (2016, July 6). Alton Sterling's death appears to be another police shooting that was both legal and preventable. *The Washington Post.* Retrieved from https://www.washingtonpost.com/news/the-watch/wp/2016/07/06/alton-sterlings-death-appears-to-be-another-police-shooting-that-was-both-legal-and-preventable/.

Basit, T. N. (2009). White British; dual heritages; British Muslim: young Britons' conceptualization of identity and citizenship. *British Educational Research Journal.* October, Vol. 35/5, pp. 723–743.

Beaubien, J. (2011, July 7). Drug cartels prey on migrants crossing Mexico. *National Public Radio.* Retrieved from http://www.npr.org/2011/07/07/137626383/drug-cartels-prey-on-migrants-crossing-mexico.

Becerra, D., Androff, D. K., Ayon, C., & Castillo, J. T. (2012). Fear vs. facts: Examining the economic impact of undocumented immigrants in the U.S. *Journal of Sociology & Social Welfare,* December, Vol. 39, No. 4, pp. 111–135. Retrieved from http://www.google.com/url?sa=t&rct=j&q=&esrc=s&source=web&cd=2&ved=0CCcQFjAB&url=http%3A%2F%2Fwww.wmich.edu%2Fhhs%2Fnewsletters_journals%2Fjssw_institutional%2Finstitutional_sub

scribers%2F39.4.Becerra.pdf&ei=m2y3U_GXN9TboATn1oKAAQ&usg=AFQjCNH0iex
eGuoXJbQQ7yyVFdYImbOsUQ.

Beck, G. (2015). *It is about Islam: Exploring the truth about ISIS, Al Qaeda, and the Caliphate.*
Mercury Radio Arts: New York.

Beutel, A. J. (2007). Radicalization and homegrown terrorism in western Muslim communities:
lessons learned for America. *Minaret of Freedom Institute: Calling the faithful to Freedom.*
Retrieved from http://www.google.com/url?sa=t&rct=j&q=&esrc=s&source=web&cd=
5&ved=0CDsQFjAE&url=http%3A%2F%2Fwww.minaret.org%2FMPAC%2520Back
grounder.pdf&ei=6mC4U770MoffoAT004CQDA&usg=AFQjCNF1D79j_vew_
HEP3EFDzZYxdzfdqA.

Berrebi, C., & Ostwald, J. (2013, February). *Terrorism and the Labor Force: Evidence of an effect
on female labor force participation and the labor gender gap.* RAND Working Paper, Santa
Monica: RAND.

Blake, A. (2015, January 6). The GOP's major 2016 problem—in 3 maps. *The Washington Post.*
Retrieved from http://www.washingtonpost.com/news/the-fix/wp/2015/01/06/the-gops-
2016-problem-in-3-maps/.

Blake, J. (2011, September 11). Four ways 9/11 changed America's attitude toward religion. *CNN.*
Retrieved from http://religion.blogs.cnn.com/2011/09/03/four-ways-911-changed-ameri
cas-attitude-toward-religion/.

Blinder, A. (2016, May 24). Death penalty is sought for Dylann Roof in Charleston church killings. *The New York Times.* Retrieved from http://www.nytimes.com/2016/05/25/us/dylann-
roof-will-face-federal-death-penalty-in-charleston-church-killings.html.

Bloom, M. (2005). *Dying to kill: The allure of suicide terror.* New York: Columbia University
Press.

Bocanegra, M. (n.d.). Homegrown terrorism in the United States. *Michael Bocanegra: Political
And Social Issues.* Retrieved from http://mikebocanegra.hubpages.com/hub/Homegrown-
Terrorism-in-the-United-States.

Boffey, D. (2013, January 12). Immigration is British society's biggest problem, shows survey to
public. *The Guardian.* Retrieved from http://www.theguardian.com/uk/2013/jan/13/immi
gration-british-society-biggest-problem.

Bonner, R., & Weiser, B. (2006, August 11). Echoes of early design to use chemicals to blow up
airliners – Asia – Pacific – International Herald Tribune. *The New York Times.* Retrieved
from http://www.nytimes.com/2006/08/11/world/asia/11iht-web.0811manila.2447764.html.

Boozeman, J. (2014) Immigration reform & border security. On John Boozman US Senator
for Arkansas website. Retrieved from http://www.boozman.senate.gov/public/index.cfm/
immigration-reform-border-security.

Bothelho, G., & Sciutto, J. (2014, August 27). Slain ISIS jihadi among more than 100
Americans fighting with militants in Syria. *CNN.* Retrieved from http://www.cnn.
com/2014/08/26/world/meast/syria-american-killed/.

Bovsun, M. (2013, June 15). 750 sickened in Oregon restaurants as cult known as the Rajneeshees
spread salmonella in the town of The Dalles. *Daily News.* Retrieved from http://www.nyda
ilynews.com/news/justice-story/guru-poison-bioterrorists-spread-salmonella-oregon-arti
cle-1.1373864.

Braukis, H. (2014, April 14). Europe, U.S. immigration issues are worlds apart. *AZ Central.* Retrieved from http://www.azcentral.com/story/opinion/op-ed/2014/04/13/europe-us-immigration-issues-different/7685611/.

Brooks, R. A. (2011). Muslim 'homegrown' terrorism in the United States: How serious is the threat? *International Security.* Vol. 36, No. 2 (Fall), pp. 7–47.

Brown, M. (2011, December 6). Do American Muslims want to take over our country? *Town Hall.com.* Retrieved from http://townhall.com/columnists/michaelbrown/2011/12/06/do_american_muslims_want_to_take_over_our_country/page/full.

Burch, J. (2011, May 2). Afghans describe bin Laden as al Qaeda's "No 1 Martyr." *Reuters.* Retrieved from http://www.reuters.com/article/us-binladen-afghanistan-reaction-idUS TRE74120A20110502.

Burke, J. How the changing media is changing terrorism. *The Guardian.* Retrieved from https://www.theguardian.com/world/2016/feb/25/how-changing-media-changing-terrorism.

Bush, G. W. (2002, September). *The national security strategy of the United States of America.* Washington, DC: GPO.

Bush, G. W. (2007). *National Strategy for Homeland Security (NSHS).* Washington, DC: Government Printing Office.

Bushnaq, I. (1986). *Arab folktales.* (Inea Bushnaq, Ed. and Trans.). New York: Pantheon Books.

Camarota, S. A. (2004). The high cost of cheap labor: Illegal immigration and the federal budget. *Center for Immigration Studies.* Retrieved from http://cis.org/High-Cost-of-Cheap-Labor.

Camarota, A. A., Poston, D. l. Jr., & Baumle, A. K. (2003, October). Remaking the political landscape: The impact of illegal and legal immigration on Congressional apportionment. *Center for Immigration Studies.* Retrieved from http://cis.org/ImmigrationEffectCongressio nalApportionment.

Canble Network News (CNN). (2010, January 6). Study: Threat of Muslim-American terrorism in U.S. exaggerated. *CNN.* Retrieved from http://edition.cnn.com/2010/US/01/06/muslim.radicalization.study/.

Carafano, J., Bucci, S., & Zukerman, J. (2012, April 25). *Fifty terror plots foiled since 9/11: The homegrown threat and the long war on terrorism.* The Heritage Foundation. Retrieved from http://www.heritage.org/research/reports/2012/04/fifty-terror-plots-foiled-since-9-11-the-homegrown-threat-and-the-long-war-on-terrorism.

Casey, N. (2014, July 30). U.N. blames Israel for shelter attack. *The Wall Street Journal.* Retrieved from http://online.wsj.com/articles/gaza-health-ministry-explosions-at-school-kill-15-1406705906?mod=wsj_india_main.

Castagnera, J. O. (2009, June). America's homegrown terrorists of the 21st Century: The disgruntled, the obsessed, and the mad three types, one challenge? *Homeland Security Review.* Vol. 3, No. 2, p. 75-100.

Carter, S. (2014a, Jun 16). 'They keep coming': The 'rehearsed' answers illegal immigrants are using at the border to gain entry into the U.S. *The Blaze.* Retrieved from http://www.the-blaze.com/stories/2014/06/16/they-keep-coming-the-rehearsed-answers-illegal-immigrants-are-using-at-the-border-to-gain-entry-into-the-u-s/.

Carter, S. (2014b, June 24). 'Potential for a public health disaster': Illegal immigrant surge leaves officials with 'no idea' which diseases are coming across. *The Blaze*. Retrieved from http://www.theblaze.com/stories/2014/06/24/potential-for-a-public-health-disaster-illegal-immigrant-surge-leaves-officials-with-no-idea-which-diseases-are-coming-across/.

Caulderwood, K. (2014, June 17). Different ends same means: Research shows what terrorists and crime syndicates have in common. *International Business Times*. Retrieved from http://www.ibtimes.com/different-ends-same-means-research-shows-what-terrorists-crime-syn dicates-have-common-1603628.

Center for Disease Control (CDC). (2015, February 20). Measles Outbreak—California December 2014–February 2015. *Center for Disease Control*. Retrieved from https://www.cdc.gov/mmwr/preview/mmwrhtml/mm6406a5.htm.

Center for Immigration Studies (CIS). (2015, February, 9). Vaccination rates among immigrants are a legitimate concern. *Center for Immigration Studies*. Retrieved from http://cis.org/cis/vaccination-rates-among-immigrants-are-legitimate-concern.

Chang, A. (2014, July 11). Morning Edition: Administration officials defend funding request to stem border crisis. *National Public Radio*. Sound recording available at http://www.npr.org/2014/07/11/330631664/administration-officials-defend-funding-request-to-stem-bor der-crisis.

Chomsky, N. (2003/2004). *Hegemony or survival: America's quest for global dominance*. New York: Henry Holt.

Chomsky, N. (2007). *Interventions*. San Francisco: City Lights Books.

Chomsky, N. (2016, May 10). The US 'war on terror' is playing right into ISIS' hands. *The Nation*. Retrieved from https://www.thenation.com/article/the-us-war-on-terror-is-play ing-right-into-isiss-hands/.

Confucius. (1993/2000). *Analects* (Raymond Dawson, Trans.). New York: Oxford University Press.

Christian Apologetics & Research Ministry (CARM). (2014). *CARM*. Retrieved on August 3, 2014 from http://carm.org/more-stuff/features/religious-tolerance-america.

Christian Broadcasting Network. (1990). Q & A: Why are so many westerners converting to Islam? Retrieved from http://www.cbn.com/spirituallife/onlinediscipleship/understandin gislam/why_are_westerners_converting.aspx.

Chumley, C. K. (2014, August 29). Fort Hood shooter Nidal Hasan petitions to be 'citizen' of Islamic State. *The Washington Times*. Retrieved from http://www.washingtontimes.com/news/2014/aug/29/fort-hood-shooter-nidal-hasan-petitions-be-citizen/.

Churchill, R. P. (2006). *Human rights and global diversity*. Upper Saddle River: Pearson Education.

Citizenship in the Balance: How anti-immigration activists twist the facts, ignore history, and flout the Constitution. (2011, February). *People for the American Way*. Retrieved on July 5, 2014 from http://www.pfaw.org/rww-in-focus/citizenship-the-balance-how-anti-immi grant-activists-twist-the-facts-ignore-history-and.

Cohen, L. (2013, October 14). Shutdown power play: Stroking racism, fear of culture change to push anti-government agenda. *Forbes*. Retrieved from http://www.forbes.com/sites/rob waters/2013/10/14/shutdown-power-play-stoking-racism-fear-of-culture-change-to-push-anti-government-agenda/.

College Board. (2014). *Major profile, American Indian Studies* webpage at https://bigfuture.col legeboard.org/majors/area-ethnic-cultural-gender-studies-ethnic-cultural-minority-gen der-group-studies-american-indian-studies.

Combs, C. C. (2013). *Terrorism in the twenty-first century* (7th Ed.). Boston: Pearson.

Condon, S. (2011, November 18). Americans split on American exceptionalism, poll shows. *CBS news* Online. Retrieved from http://www.cbsnews.com/news/americans-split-on-amer ican-exceptionalism-poll-shows/.

Considine, C. (2013, May 26). Honoring Muslim American veterans on memorial Day. *The Huffington Post*. Retrieved from http://www.huffingtonpost.com/craig-considine/lets-hon or-muslim-america_b_3339838.html.

Cooper, C., & Block, R. (2006). *Disaster: Hurricane Katrina and the failure of Homeland Security*. New York: Henry Holt and Company, LLC.

Cortes, J. (2014, June 25). Honduran kids flee terror at home, hope for opportunity in U.S. *Reuters*. Retrieved from http://uk.reuters.com/article/2014/06/25/uk-usa-immigration-mexi co-idUKKBN0F00CS20140625.

Coughlin, C. (2014, November 5). How social media is helping Islamic State to spread its poison. *The Telegraph*. Retrieved from http://www.telegraph.co.uk/news/uknews/ defence/11208796/How-social-media-is-helping-Islamic-State-to-spread-its-poison.html.

Corasanti, N., Perez-Pena, R., & Alvarez, L. (2015, June 18). Church massacre suspect held as Charleston grieves. *The New York Times*. Retrieved from http://www.nytimes. com/2015/06/19/us/charleston-church-shooting.html?_r=0.

Corman, L. (2011). Impossible subjects: The figure of the animal in Paulo Freire's *Pedagogy of the Oppressed*. *Canadian Journal of Environmental Education*. Vol. 16, pp. 29–45.

Cox, J. D. (2014, July 10). The unsung heroes in the immigration crises. *National Border Patrol Council Local 2554*. Retrieved from http://www.nbpc2554.org/.

Crenshaw, M. (1998). Logic of terrorism: Terrorist behavior as a product of strategic choice. pp. 7–17. *Origins of terrorism*. (Reich, Walter, Ed.). Baltimore: John Hopkins University.

Crenshaw, R. (1974). *Naval Shiphandling* (4th Ed.). Newport: Naval Institute Press.

Cronin, A. K. (2006, Summer). How al-Qaeda end: the decline and demise of terrorist groups. *International Security*, Vol. 31, No. 1, pp. 7–48.

Cullors, P., Tometi, O., & Garza, A. (2016). Black lives matter. Official Website. Retrieved from http://blacklivesmatter.com/about/.

Currey, C. B. (1997). *Victory at any cost: The genius of Viet Nam's Gen. Vo Nguyen Giap*. Dulles: Potomac Books.

Dade, C. (2012, December 24). Obama administration deported record 1.5 million people. *National Public Radio (NPR)*. Retrieved from http://www.npr.org/blogs/itsallpolitics/2012/12/24/167970002/ obama-administration-deported-record-1-5-million-people.

DAM (Da Arab Mcs.). (2006). *Who's the terrorist?* (Min Erhabi?). Video available at http:// vimeo.com/7163495. Lyrics available at http://www.damrap.com/album/whos-terrorist- %D9%85%D9%8A%D9%86-%D8%A5%D8%B1%D9%87%D8%A7%D8%A8%D9 %8A/116.

DAM (Da Arab Mcs.). (2008). *Born here*. Video available at DAM.com at http://www.damrap. com/media/clip/dam-born-here-hebrewarabic-english-subtitles/35.

Darder, A. (1991/2012). *Culture and power in the classroom*. Boulder: Paradigm Publishers.

Darder, A. (2002). *Reinventing Paulo Freire: A pedagogy of love*. Cambridge: Westview Press.

Dassanayake, D. (2015, February 13). Islamic State: What is IS and why are they so violent? *Express*. Retrieved from http://www.express.co.uk/news/world/558078/Islamic-State-IS-what-is-ISIS-why-are-ISIL-so-violent.

Davidson, A. (2013, February 12). Do illegal immigrants actually hurt the U.S. economy? *The New York Times*. Retrieved from http://www.nytimes.com/2013/02/17/magazine/do-illegal-immigrants-actually-hurt-the-us-economy.html?pagewanted=all&_r=0.

Dawsey, J., Perez, E., & Barrett, D. (2013, May 8). Manhunt ends with capture of Boston bombing suspect. *The Wall Street Journal*. Retrieved from http://online.wsj.com/news/articles/SB10001424127887324493704578432030609754740.

Desilver, D. (2015, February 2). U.S. students improving—slowly—in math and science, but still lagging internationally. *Pew Research Center*. Retrieved from http://www.pewresearch.org/fact-tank/2015/02/02/u-s-students-improving-slowly-in-math-and-science-but-still-lagging-internationally/.

De Vries, H. (2002). *Religion and violence: Philosophical perspectives from Kant to Derrida*. Baltimore: The John Hopkins University Press.

Dickson, C. (2014, June 23). How Mexico's cartels are behind the border kid crises. *The Daily Beast*. Retrieved from http://www.thedailybeast.com/articles/2014/06/23/how-mexico-s-cartels-are-behind-the-border-kid-crisis.html.

Didymus, J. (2015, December 4). San Bernardino shooter Syed Farook clashed with Jewish co-worker Nicholas Thalasinos over religion, was teased about his long Islamic beard. *Inquisitor*. Retrieved from http://www.inquisitr.com/2608967/san-bernardino-shooter-syed-farook-clashed-with-jewish-co-worker-nicholas-thalasinos-over-religion-was-teased-about-his-long-islamic-beard/.

Dienst, J., Valiquette, J., Nious, K., & Millman, J. (2015, April 3). 2 Queens women accused of plotting to plant bombs in U.S. talked suicide attacks, had propane tanks: Complaint. *NBC New York*. Retrieved from http://www.nbcnewyork.com/news/local/Terror-Arrest-New-York-FBI-NYPD-Police-297422441.html.

Dinan, S. (2013a, February 5). Top democrat warns against using the term 'illegal immigrants.' *The Washington Times*. Retrieved from http://www.washingtontimes.com/blog/inside-politics/2013/feb/5/top-democrat-warns-against-using-term-illegal-immi/.

Dinan, S. (2013b, August 23). Obama adds to list of illegal immigrants not to deport: Parents. *The Washington Times*. Retrieved from http://www.washingtontimes.com/news/2013/aug/23/new-obama-policy-warns-agents-not-detain-illegal-i/?page=all.

Dowling, T. (2015, November 27). One month later, what's next for the University of Missouri protesters? *USA Today*. Retrieved from http://college.usatoday.com/2015/11/27/whats-next-university-of-missouri/.

Dumalaon, J., Korolyov, A., & Jones-berry, S. (2014, March 31). Immigration backlash is on the rise in Europe. *USA Today*. Retrieved from http://www.usatoday.com/story/news/world/2014/03/31/europe-anti-immigration/5706575/.

Dyloco, P. (2012, January 6). What are Japanese averse to immigration? *Japan Today*. Retrieved from http://www.japantoday.com/category/opinions/view/why-are-japanese-averse-to-im migration.

Dynon, N. (2014, March 5). Kunming: A new phase of terrorism in China. *The Diplomat*. Retrieved from http://thediplomat.com/2014/03/kunming-a-new-phase-of-terrorism-in-china/.

Epstein, R. (2014, March 4). National council of La Raza leader calls Barak Obama 'deporter-in-chief.' *Politico*. Retrieved from http://www.politico.com/story/2014/03/national-coun cil-of-la-raza-janet-murguia-barack-obama-deporter-in-chief-immigration-104217.html.

Esposito, J. L. (2010). *The future of Islam*. New York: Oxford Press.

Executive Office of the President. (2013). *The economic benefits of fixing our broken immigration system*. Washington, DC: Government Printing Office.

Fanon, F. (1952/2008). *Black skin: white masks: Get political*. London: Grove Press.

Fanon, F. (1961/2004). *The wretched of the earth* (R. Philcox, Trans.). New York: Grove Press.

Fantz, A., & Brumfield, B. (2015, November 19). More than half the nation's governors say Syrian refugees not welcome. *CNN*. Retrieved from http://www.cnn.com/2015/11/16/ world/paris-attacks-syrian-refugees-backlash/.

Fernandez, M., Perez-Pena, R., & Bromwich, J. (2016, July 8). Five Dallas officers were killed as payback, police chief says. *The New York Times*. Retrieved from http://www.nytimes. com/2016/07/09/us/dallas-police-shooting.html.

Ferran, L. (2014, July 31). 'Troubling': Suicide bomber hung out in US after terror training. *ABC News*. Retrieved from http://abcnews.go.com/Blotter/troubling-suicide-bomber-hung-us-ter ror-training/story?id=24790407.

Ferrechio, S. (2014, February 6). House republicans hit wall on immigration reform. *Washington Examiner*, as linked to "GOP leaders face wave of Opposition on immigration reform" on the Tea Party website at http://www.teaparty.org/gop-leaders-face-wave-opposition-immi gration-reform-34247/.

Fife, G. (2004). *The terror: The shadow of the guillotine: France 1792–1794*. New York: St. Martin's Press.

Fischer, A. (2007, January 3). News from the Library of Congress. *Library of Congress*. Retrieved from http://www.loc.gov/today/pr/2007/07-001.html.

Fontanella-Khan, A. (2016, July 16). Fetullah Gulen: Turkey coup may have been 'staged' by Erdogan regime. *The Guardian*. Retrieved from https://www.theguardian.com/world/2016/ jul/16/fethullah-gulen-turkey-coup-erdogan.

Fraley, M. (2015, October, 6). Accused Oikos University massacre shooter declared competent to stand trial. *The Mercury News*. Retrieved from http://www.mercurynews.com/crime-courts/ci_28924738/oakland-accused-oikos-massacre-shooter-declared-competent-stand.

Freeman, K. D. (2012). *Secret weapon: How economic terrorism brought down the U.S. stock market and why it can happen again*. Washington, DC: Regnery Publishing.

Freire, P. (1970/2000). *Pedagogy of the oppressed*. New York: Bloomsbury.

Freire, P. (1985). *The politics of education: Culture power and liberation* (D. Macedo, Trans.). Westport: Bergin & Garvey.

Freire, P. (1988). *Pedagogy of freedom: Ethics, democracy, and civic courage* (P. Clarke, Trans.). Lanham: Rowman & Littlefield Publishers.

Freire, P., & Macedo, D. (1987). *Literacy: Reading the word and the world.* Westport: Bergin & Garvey.

Freudenrich, C. (2015). How IEDs work. *How Stuff works.* Retrieved from http://science.howstuffworks.com/ied1.htm.

Friedersdorf, C. (2012, August 8). Why the reaction is different when the terrorist is white. *The Atlantic.* Retrieved from http://www.theatlantic.com/politics/archive/2012/08/why-the-reaction-is-different-when-the-terrorist-is-white/260849/.

Fuchs, P. (1995, June). Jumping to Conclusions in Oklahoma City? *American Journalism Review.* Retrieved from http://ajrarchive.org/article.asp?id=1980.

Fukuyama, F. (2014, March 10). American power is waning because Washington won't stop quarreling. *New Republic.* Retrieved from https://newrepublic.com/article/116953/american-power-decline-due-partisanship-washington.

Galula, D. (1964/2006). *Counterinsurgency warfare: Theory and practice.* Westport: Praeger Security International.

German, M. (2007). *Thinking like a terrorist: Insights of a former FBI undercover agent.* Washington, DC: Potomac Books.

Giap, V. N. (1976). *How we won the war.* Philadelphia: Recon Publishers.

Gibbons-Neff, T. (2015, December 4). The striking militarization of the San Bernardino shooters. *The Washington Post.* Retrieved from https://www.washingtonpost.com/news/checkpoint/wp/2015/12/04/the-weapons-used-by-the-san-bernardino-shooters-were-strikingly-militarized/.

Gibson, G. (2013, July 24). Steve King doubles down on 'drug mules' comment. *Politico.* Retrieved from http://www.kfiam640.com/media/podcast-handel-on-demand-BillHandel/immigration-crisis-7a-0703-24985857/.

Gimpel, J. G. (2014, April 24). Immigration's impact on republican prospects, 1980 to 2012. *Center for Immigration Studies.* Retrieved from http://cis.org/immigration-impacts-on-republican-prospects-1980-2012.

Giroux, H. A. (2014). *The violence of organized forgetting: Thinking beyond America's disimagination machine.* San Francisco: City Lights Books.

Glanz, J. Rotella, S., & Sanger, D. E. (2014, December 21). In 2008 Mumbai attacks, piles of spy data, but an uncompleted puzzle. *The New York Times.* Retrieved from http://www.nytimes.com/2014/12/22/world/asia/in-2008-mumbai-attacks-piles-of-spy-data-but-an-uncompleted-puzzle.html?_r=0.

Gohmert: US will become 'third world nation' if feds cont. enforce immigration laws. (2014, July 1). *CBS, DC.* Retrieved from http://washington.cbslocal.com/2014/07/01/gohmert-us-will-become-third-world-nation-if-feds-dont-enforce-immigration-laws/.

Goldberg, D., & Griffey, T. (Eds.). (2010). *Black power at work: Community control, affirmative action, and the construction industry.* Ithaca: Cornell University Press.

Goldfarb, Z. (2006, December 21). Va. Lawmaker's remarks on Muslims criticized. *The Washington Post.* Retrieved from http://www.washingtonpost.com/wp-dyn/content/article/2006/12/20/AR2006122001318.html.

Goldschmidt, A. Jr., & Davidson, L. (2009). *A concise history of the middle east* (9th Ed.). Boulder: Westview Press.

Gonzalez, M. (2013, August 28). The new American divide. Opinion. *New York Post*. Retrieved from http://nypost.com/2013/08/28/the-new-great-american-divide/.

Greenman, E., & Xie, Y. (2008, March). Is assimilation theory dead? The effect of assimilation on adolescent well-being. *Social Science Research*, Vol. 31, No. 1, pp. 100–113. Retrieved from http://www.ncbi.nlm.nih.gov/pmc/articles/PMC2390825/.

Grimes, W. (2005, September 2). Legion of the lost: The true experience of an American in the French Foreign Legion. *The New York Times*. Retrieved from http://www.nytimes.com/2005/09/01/arts/01iht-bookfri.html?_r=0.

Griswold, D. (2002, February 8). Immigrants have enriched American culture and enhanced our influence in the world. CATO Institute, originally appeared in *Insight* magazine. Retrieved from http://www.cato.org/publications/commentary/immigrants-have-enriched-american-culture-enhanced-our-influence-world.

Guevara, E. C. (1995/2003). *The motorcycle diaries: Notes on a Latin American Journey*. Melbourne: Ocean Press.

Guevara, E. C. (1961/2012). *Guerrilla warfare*. Melbourne: Ocean Press.

Habeck, M. (2012, June 27). Can we declare the war on al Qaeda over? *Foreign Policy*. Retrieved from http://foreignpolicy.com/2012/06/27/can-we-declare-the-war-on-al-qaeda-over/.

Hagerty, B. B. (2010, March 18). Is the Bible more violent than the Quran? *National Public Radio, All things Considered*. Retrieved from http://www.npr.org/templates/story/story.php?storyId=124494788.

Handel, B. (2014, July 3). Immigration crises 7A. *KFI AM Radio*, podcast available at http://www.kfiam640.com/media/podcast-handel-on-demand-BillHandel/immigration-crisis-7a-0703-24985857/.

Haughney, C. (2013, April 23). The Times shifts on "illegal immigrant," but doesn't ban the use. *The New York Times*. Retrieved from http://www.nytimes.com/2013/04/24/business/media/the-times-shifts-on-illegal-immigrant-but-doesnt-ban-the-use.html?pagewanted=all.

Healy, J., & Lovett, I. (2015, October 2). Oregon killer described as man of few words, except on topic of guns. *The New York Times*. Retrieved from http://www.nytimes.com/2015/10/03/us/chris-harper-mercer-umpqua-community-college-shooting.html.

Hennessy-Fiske, M., Bennett, B., & Carcamo, C. (2014, June 20). Obama administration acts to ease immigration legal crunch at border. *Los Angeles Times*. Retrieved from http://www.latimes.com/nation/nationnow/la-na-nn-border-migrants-white-house-20140620-story.html#page=1.

Hermann, P., & Marimow, A. E. (2013, September, 25). Navy yard shooter Aaron Alexis driven by delusions. *The Washington Post*. Retrieved from https://www.washingtonpost.com/local/crime/fbi-police-detail-shooting-navy-yard-shooting/2013/09/25/ee321abe-2600-11e3-b3e9-d97fb087acd6_story.html.

Heyes, J. D. (2014, July 2). Mexican drug cartels using illegal immigration flood as cover to smuggle operatives and hard drugs into the U.S. *Natural News*. Retrieved from http://www.naturalnews.com/045822_illegal_immigration_Mexican_cartels_drug_smuggling.html.

Hill, R. C., Griffiths, W. E., & Lim, G C. (2011). *Principles of econometrics* (4th Ed.). Hoboken: John Wiley & Sons.

Hobbs, F., & Stoops, N. (2002). *Demographic trends in the 20th Century.* Washington, DC: U.S. Census Bureau.

Hoffman, B. (2006). *Inside terrorism.* New York: Columbia University Press.

Hoffman, B. (2013, April 27). Answers to why people become terrorists. *The Daily Beast.* Retrieved from http://www.thedailybeast.com/articles/2013/04/27/answers-to-why-people-become-terrorists.html.

Hoffman, B., Rosenau, W., Curiel, A., & Zimmermann, D. (2007). *The radicalization of Diasporas and terrorism: A joint conference by RAND corporation and the Center for Security Studies, ETH Zurich.* Santa Monica: RAND.

Holmes, D. L. (2006). The faiths of the Founding Fathers. New York: Oxford University Press.

Homeland Secretary: Agency that removes immigrants will be out of money by mid-September at 'current burn rate.' (2014, July 11). *CBS Local.* Retrieved from http://washington.cbslocal.com/2014/07/11/homeland-secretary-agency-that-removes-immigrants-will-be-out-of-money-by-mid-september-at-current-burn-rate/.

Hopkirk, P. (1990/1994). *The great game: The struggle for Empire in Central Asia.* New York: Kodansha.

House of Commons. (2005). *Report of the official account of the bombings in London on 7th July 2005.* London: The Stationary Office.

Houston, J. W., & Houston, J. D. (1973/2007). *Farwell to Manzanar.* Boston: Houghton Mifflin Company.

"How cartels use tunnels to send drugs into US." *New York Post,* Associated Press. Retrieved from http://nypost.com/2014/01/14/how-smuggling-tunnels-are-built-used-along-us-border/.

Hsu, H. (2009, January 1). The end of white America? The Atlantic. Retrieved from http://www.theatlantic.com/magazine/archive/2009/01/the-end-of-white-america/307208/.

Huffman, A. O. (2011). *Homegrown terrorism in the United States: Comparing radicalization trajectories in Britain and America* (Master's thesis). Retrieved from http://respository.library.georgetown.edu/bitstream/handle/10822/553516/huffmanAlexia.pdf?sequence=1.

Hughes, D. M., Chon, K. Y., & Ellerman, D. P. (2007, September. Modern-day comfort women: The U.S. military, transnational crime, and the trafficking of women. *The University of Rhode Island.* Retrieved from http://www.google.com/url?sa=t&rct=j&q=&esrc=s&source=web&cd=8&ved=0CFIQFjAH&url=http%3A%2F%2Fwww.cops.usdoj.gov%2Fhtml%2Fcd_rom%2Fsolution_gang_crime%2Fpubs%2FDreamsGangsandGunsTheInterplayBetweenAdolescent.pdf&ei=DJ24U4mMCJCgogTmz4LYBg&usg=AFQjCNHLNY5ET9OFEDvqEBMFl48J90EJAg&bvm=bv.70138588,d.cGU.

Hughes, S. (2005). Theorizing oppressed family pedagogy: Critical lessons from rural family in the post-Brown south. *Educational Foundations.* Summer-Fall, pp. 45–72.

Human Rights Watch (HRW). (1999, October 1). Anti-Christian violence on the rise in India: New report details behind extremist Hindu attacks. *Human Rights Watch.* Retrieved from http://www.hrw.org/en/news/1999/09/29/anti-christian-violence-rise-india.

Huntington, S. P. (1996). *The clash of civilizations and the remaking of world order*. New York: Touchstone.

Huxley, A. (2013, January 25). It's official: "Terrorist" is the most inappropriately over-used word in American English. *Forming the Thread*. Retrieved http://formingthethread.wordpress.com/2013/01/25/its-official-terrorist-is-the-most-inappropriately-over-used-word-in-american-english/.

Husain, E. (2013, September). A global venture to counter violent extremism. *Council on Foreign Relations*. Retrieved from http://www.cfr.org/radicalization-and-extremism/global-venture-counter-violent-extremism/p30494.

Ibrahim, R. (2012, May 15). Mexican jihad. *Front Page Mag*. Retrieved from http://www.frontpagemag.com/2012/raymond-ibrahim/mexican-jihad/.

"Illegal immigrants cause public school crisis." (2008, March 11). *The Judicial Watch*. Retrieved fromhttp://www.judicialwatch.org/blog/2008/03/illegal-immigrants-cause-public-school-crisis/.

Illich, I. (1968, April 28). *To hell with good intentions*. Address presented to the Conference on Inter American Student Projects (CIASP) in Cuernavaca, Mexico. Retrieved from http://www.swaraj.org/illich_hell.htm.

Illiach, I. (2000). *Deschooling society*. London: Marion Boyers Publishers.

"Immigration facts: Immigration and terrorism polls." (2009). *Federation for American Immigration Reform*, retrieved from http://www.fairus.org/facts/immigration-and-terrorism-polls.

Immigration Watch Canada. (2014). Homepage at http://www.immigrationwatchcanada.org/.

Inserra, D. (2015, June 8). 69th Islamist Terrorist Plot: Ongoing Spike in Terrorism Should Force Congress to Finally Confront the Terrorist Threat. *The Heritage Foundation*. Retrieved from http://www.heritage.org/research/reports/2015/06/69th-islamist-terrorist-plot-ongoing-spike-in-terrorism-should-force-congress-to-finally-confront-the-terrorist-threat.

Jackson, S. (2007). Freire re-viewed. *Educational Theory*. Vol. 57/2.

Jansen, B. (2016, July 17). 3 police officers shot dead in Baton Rouge. *USA Today*. Retrieved from http://www.usatoday.com/story/news/2016/07/17/reports-baton-rouge-police-officers-shot/87218884/.

Jansen, J. J. G. (1986/2013). *The neglected duty: The creed of Sadat's assassins*. New York: RVP Publishers, pp. 199–213.

Jeffers, G. Jr., Scoggin, A., & Solis, D. (2014, June 28). Clay Jenkins wants Dallas County to house children. *Dallas News*. Retrieved from http://www.desertsun.com/story/news/local/2014/07/04/murrieta-california-border-patrol-immigration-protests-undocumented-immigrants-july-fourth/12217279/.

Jenkins, B. M. (2010). *Would-be warriors: Incidents of jihadist terrorist radicalization in the United States since September 11, 2001*. Santa Monica: RAND.

Jenkins, B. M. (2011). *Stray dogs and virtual armies: Radicalization and recruitment to jihadist terrorism in the United States since 9/11*. Santa Monica: RAND.

Jenkins, B. M., Liepman, A., & Willis, H. (2014). *Identifying enemies among us: Evolving terrorist threats and the continuing challenges of domestic intelligence collection and information sharing*. Santa Monica: RAND.

Jenkins, B. M. (2014, July 30). An evil wind. *The RAND Blog* at http://www.rand.org/blog/2014/07/an-evil-wind.html.

Jillson, C. (2009). *American Government: Political development and institutional change* (5th Ed.). New York: Taylor & Francis.

Jimenez, T. R. (2010). *Replenished ethnicity: Mexican Americans, immigration, and identity.* Berkley: University of California Press.

Johnson, J. (2014). *Quadrennial Homeland Security Review Report (QHSR).* Washington, DC: Government Printing Office.

Johnson, T. (2011, September 30). *Threat of homegrown Islamist terrorism.* Council on Foreign Relations. Retrieved from http://www.cfr.org/terrorism/threat-homegrown-islamist-terrorism/p11509.

Johnson, J., & Weigel, D. (2015, December 8). Donald trump calls for 'total' ban on Muslims entering United States. *The Washington Post.* Retrieved from https://www.washingtonpost.com/politics/2015/12/07/e56266f6-9d2b-11e5-8728-1af6af208198_story.html.

Johnston, D., & Shane, S. (2009, November 9). U.S. knew of suspect's tie to radical cleric. *The New York Times.* Retrieved from http://www.nytimes.com/2009/11/10/us/10inquire.html.

Jomini, A.-H. (1862/2011). *The art of war* (G. H. Mendell, & W. P. Craighill, Trans.). Memphis: Bottom of the Hill Publishing.

Jones, A. (2011, May 11). 18 facts prove illegal immigration is absolute nightmare for U.S. economy. *Infowars.* Retrieved from http://www.infowars.com/18-facts-prove-illegal-immigration-is-absolute-nightmare-for-u-s-economy/.

Jones, L. (2014, February 28). Too many celebrities, not enough heroes. *The Washington Post.* Retrieved from https://www.washingtonpost.com/opinions/too-many-celebrities-not-enough-heroes/2014/02/28/dbfc3f5c-98e0-11e3-80ac-63a8ba7f7942_story.html.

Jurgensmeyer, M. (2000). *The global rise of religious violence.* Berkeley: University of California Press.

Juergensmeyer, M. (2003). *Terror in the mind of god* (3rd Ed.). New York: University of California Press.

Kaleem, J. (2014, October 6). Here's why these Muslims are refusing to criticize ISIS. *Huffington Post.* Retrieved from http://www.huffingtonpost.com/2014/10/06/muslims-condemn-isis-debate_n_5927772.html.

Kaplan, A., & Phillip, A. (2015, September 16). They thought it was a bomb: 9th grader arrested after bringing a home-built clock to school. *The Washington Post.* Retrieved from http://www.washingtonpost.com/news/morning-mix/wp/2015/09/16/they-thought-it-was-a-bomb-ahmed-mohamed-texas-9th-grader-arrested-after-bringing-a-home-built-clock-to-school/.

Kaplan, E. (2009, January 8). Terrorists and the internet. *Council on Foreign Relations.* Retrieved from http://www.cfr.org/terrorism-and-technology/terrorists-internet/p10005.

Kettl, D. (2014). *System under stress: The challenge to 21st century governance.* Los Angeles: Sage.

Kenber, B. (2013, August 28). Nidal Hassan sentenced to death for Fort Hood shooting rampage. *The Washington Post.* Retrieved from http://www.washingtonpost.com/world/national-security/nidal-hasan-sentenced-to-death-for-fort-hood-shooting-rampage/2013/08/28/aad28de2-0ffa-11e3-bdf6-e4fc677d94a1_story.html.

Kilner, J. (2003). The pedagogy of terrorism. *Education Links*, Vol 66/67, pp. 5–11.

Khaled, L. (1973/2008). *My people shall live: The autobiography of a revolutionary*. O. Sandberg, Digital Edition. Retrieved from https://archive.org/stream/MyPeopleShallLive/My%20 People%20Shall%20Live%20by%20Leila%20Khaled#page/n1/mode/2up.

Khan, Y. (2008). *The great partition: The making of India and Pakistan*. New Haven: Yale University Press.

Kifner, J. (1995, December 31). McVeigh's mind: A special report; Oklahoma bombing suspect: Unraveling of a frayed life. *The New York Times*. Retrieved from http://www.nytimes. com/1995/12/31/us/mcveigh-s-mind-special-report-oklahoma-bombing-suspect-unravel ing-frayed-life.html.

Killerman, S. (2014). 30+ examples of Christian privilege. Its Pronounced Metrosexual. Retrieved from http://itspronouncedmetrosexual.com/2012/05/list-of-examples-of-chris tian-privileg/.

Kirby, S. M. (2015, April 19). Congressman Ellison and Jefferson's Koran: What does Ellison know about the Koran he used for his ceremonial swearing-in? *Front Page Magazine*. Retrieved from http://www.frontpagemag.com/fpm/255250/congressman-ellison-and-jef fersons-koran-dr-stephen-m-kirby.

Kotkin, J. (2010, August). The changing demographics of America: The United States population will expand by 100 million over the next 40 years. Is this a reason to worry? *Smithsonian Magazine*. Retrieved from http://www.smithsonianmag.com/40th-anniversary/ the-changing-demographics-of-america-538284/.

Kumamoto, R. (2006). *The historical origins of terrorism in America: 1644–1880*. New York: Rutledge.

Krukenberg, K. A. (2008, April). *Multi-hued America: The case for the civil rights movement's embrace of multiethnic identity*. From the selected works of Kamaria A. Kruckenberg, retrieved from http://works.bepress.com/cgi/viewcontent.cgi?article=1000&context=ka maria_kruckenberg.

Lake, E. (2013, September 12). Americans join Syrian jihad, sparking U.S. intelligence fears. *The Daily Beast*. Retrieved from http://www.thedailybeast.com/articles/2013/09/12/ameri cans-join-syrian-jihad-sparking-u-s-intelligence-fears.html.

Lampen, C. (2016, July 18). Can you spot the reason people are upset about Paul Ryan's latest Instagram post? *AOL News*. Retrieved from http://www.aol.com/article/2016/07/18/can-you-spot-the-reason-people-are-upset-about-paul-ryans-lates/21433945/.

Lance, P. (2013, February 26). The blind sheikh: A flashpoint for terror 20 years after the World Trade Center bombing: Just how dangerous is the blind sheikh? *Alternet*. Retrieved from http://www.alternet.org/blind-sheikh-flashpoint-terror-20-years-after-world-trade-center-bombing.

Lawrence, B. (Ed.) (2005). *Messages to the world: The statements of Osama bin laden*. New York: Verso.

Lawrence, T. E. (2011). *Seven pillars of wisdom: A triumph*. Blacksburg: Wilder Publications.

Lazear, E. P. (2005, March). *Mexican assimilation in the United States*. Research report for the Hoover Institute and Graduate School of Business, Stanford University.

LeBaron, G. Jr. (1995). Mormon fundamentalism and violence: A historical analysis. *ExMormon*. Retrieved from http://www.exmormon.org/violence.htm.

Lee-Ashley, M. (2016, March 24). Congress should confront the rise of violent extremism on America's public lands. *Center for American Progress*. Retrieved from https://www.amer icanprogress.org/issues/green/report/2016/03/24/133730/congress-should-confront-the-rise-of-violent-extremism-on-americas-public-lands/.

Lehrer, J. (2007, June 18). Churches providing sanctuary for illegal immigrants. *Public Broadcasting System*, podcast transcript available at http://www.pbs.org/newshour/bb/social_ issues-jan-june07-sanctuary_06-18/.

Leistyna, P. (2004). Presence of mind in the process of learning and knowing: A dialogue with Paulo Freire. *Teacher Education Quarterly*. Winter, pp. 17–29.

Lengall, S. (2014, February 12). Supreme Court Justice Clarence Thomas: Racism worse now than era segregated South. *Washington Examiner*. Retrieved from http://washingtonexam iner.com/supreme-court-justice-clarence-thomas-racism-worse-now-than-era-of-segregat ed-south/article/2543918#null.

Leon, M. (2015, October 31). 'Captain America' writer slams Fox News for sympathizing with his xenophobic villains. *The Daily Beast*. Retrieved from http://www.thedailybeast. com/articles/2015/11/01/captain-america-writer-slams-fox-news-for-calling-his-xenopho-bic-villains-ordinary-americans.html.

Leong, N. (2013, June). Racial capitalism. *Harvard Law Review*, Vol. 126, No. 8, pp. 2152–2226.

Lerche, C. O. III. (1998). The conflicts of globalization. *The International Journal of Peace Studies*. Vol. 3, No. 1. Retrieved from http://www.gmu.edu/programs/icar/ijps/vol3_1/learch. htm.

Levy, G. (2016, March 10). Immigration dominates democratic debate. *U.S. News & World Report*. Retrieved from http://www.usnews.com/news/articles/2016-03-10/immigra tion-dominates-democratic-debate.

Lewis, T. E. (2009). Education in the realm of the senses: Understanding Paulo Freire's aesthetic unconscious through Jacques Ranciere. *Journal of Philosophy of Education*. Vol. 43/2, pp. 285–299.

Lewis, T. E. (2010). Paulo Freire's last laugh: Rethinking critical pedagogy's funny bone through Jacques Ranciere. *Educational Philosophy & Theory*, Vol. 42/5-6, pp. 635–648.

Lewis, T. E. (2012). Exopedagogy: On pirates, shorelines, and the educational commonwealth. *Educational Philosophy & Theory*, Vol. 44, No. 8, pp. 845–861.

Lewiston mayor reacts to immigrants' protest. (2014, July 2). *Lewiston-Auburn Sun Journal*. Retrieved from http://www.sunjournal.com/news/lewiston-auburn/2014/07/02/lewiston-may or-reacts-immigrants-protest/1556623#.

Lind, D. (2014, May 9). What do pro-enforcement groups want out of the deportation review? *Vox*. Retrieved from http://www.vox.com/2014/5/9/5699288/what-do-pro-enforcement-groups-want-out-of-the-deportation-review.

Lipovsky, I. P. (2012). *Early Israelites: Two peoples, one history: Rediscovery of the origins of Biblical Israel*. Igor P. Lipovsky.

Lister, T. (2014, June 13). ISIS: The first terror group to build an Islamic state? *CNN*. Retrieved from http://edition.cnn.com/2014/06/12/world/meast/who-is-the-isis/.

Lovett, I., & Montgomery, D. (2014, July 21). For two slain Americans, commitment came early. *The New York Times*. Retrieved from http://www.nytimes.com/2014/07/22/world/middleeast/2-americans-among-israeli-soldiers-killed-in-gaza.html?_r=0.

Lowe, L. (1996). *Immigrant Acts: On Asian American cultural politics*. Durham: Duke University Press.

Lublin, J. S. (2014, January 9). Bringing hidden biases into light: Big businesses teach staffers how 'unconscious bias' impacts decisions. *The Wall Street Journal*. Retrieved from http://online.wsj.com/news/articles/SB10001424052702303754404579308562690896896.

Lucassen, J. (2009). The mobility transition revisited, 1500–1900: What the case of Europe can offer to global history. *Journal of Global History*, 4, Issue 3, p. 347-377.

Lyles, M. C. (2012). *The man of wiles in popular Arabic literature: A study of a medieval Arab Hero*. Edinburgh: Edinburgh University Press.

Macdonald, A. (1978/1996). *The Turner diaries*. Fort Lee: Barricade Books.

Mapping Police Violence. (2017, January 1). Unarmed black people were killed by police at 5X the rate of unarmed whites in 2015. *Mapping Police Violence*. Retrieved from http://mappingpoliceviolence.org/unarmed/.

Mardrus, J. C., & Mathers, P. (1964/1987). *The book of the thousand nights and one night* (J. C. Mardrus & Powys Mathers, Trans.). New York: Dorset Press.

Machiavelli, N. (2008). The Prince: And other writings (W. K. Marriott, Trans.). New York: Fall River Press.

Mansfield, L. (2006). *His own words: Translation and analysis of the writings of Dr. Ayman Al Zawahiri*. San Bernardino: TLG Publications.

Marighella, C. (1969/2008). *Minimanual of the urban guerrilla*. St. Petersburg: Red and Black Publishers.

Martinelli, T. (2006, October 10). Unconstitutional policing: The ethical challenges in dealing with noble cause corruption. *The Police Chief*, Vol. 73, No. 10. Retrieved from http://www.policechiefmagazine.org/magazine/index.cfm?fuseaction=display&article_id=1025&issue_id=102006.

Marszal, A. (2014, June 6). Sword fight at India's Golden temple on raid anniversary. *The Telegraph*. Retrieved from http://www.telegraph.co.uk/news/worldnews/asia/india/10880015/Sword-fight-at-Indias-Golden-Temple-on-raid-anniversary.html.

Marx, K., & Engles, F. (1948). *Manifesto of the communist party*. New York: International Publishers.

Marx, K. (1983). *The portable Karl Marx* (Eugene Kamenka, Ed.). New York: Penguin Books.

Marzulli, J. (2013, May 27). Adis medunjanin, terrorist foiled in 2009 bomb plot on New York subway, to serve life sentence in notorious Colo. Prison: 'Cleaner version of hell.' *Daily News*. Retrieved from http://www.nydailynews.com/news/national/foiled-terrorist-serve-life-notorious-colo-prison-article-1.1355289.

Mascaro, L., & Bennett, B. (2014, June 29). Obama's bid to deport children complicates immigration reform effort. *Los Angeles Times*. Retrieved from http://www.latimes.com/nation/la-na-obama-immigration-reform-20140630-story.html#page=1.

Mateu-Gelabert, P. (2002). Dreams, gangs, and guns: The interplay between adolescent violence and immigration in a New York City neighborhood. *Vera Institute of Justice*.

Retrieved from http://www.google.com/url?sa=t&rct=j&q=&esrc=s&source=web&cd=
8&ved=0CFIQFjAH&url=http%3A%2F%2Fwww.cops.usdoj.gov%2Fhtml%2Fcd_
rom%2Fsolution_gang_crime%2Fpubs%2FDreamsGangsandGunsTheInterplayBe
tweenAdolescent.pdf&ei=DJ24U4mMCJCgogTmz4LYBg&usg=AFQjCNHLNY5E
T9OFEDvqEBMFl48J90EJAg&bvm=bv.70138588,d.cGU.

Matthews, C. (2015, June 5). Edward Snowden: Privacy remains 'under threat.' *Fortune*.
Retrieved from http://fortune.com/2015/06/05/edward-snowden-privacy-oped/.

McCartney, C. (2013, August 26). Mob of 1,000 Buddhists burns down Muslim homes and
shops in Myanmar. *The Global Post*. Retrieved from http://www.globalpost.com/dispatches/
globalpost-blogs/belief/mob-1000-buddhist-burn-down-muslim-homes-and-shops-myan-
mar.

McIntyre, A. (2000). Constructing meaning about violence, school, and community: Participatory action research with urban youth. *The Urban Review*, Vol. 32, No. 2, pp. 123–154.

McKinley, J. C. Jr., (2005, January 6). A Mexican manual for illegal migrants upsets some
in U.S. *The New York Times*. Retrieved from http://www.nytimes.com/2005/01/06/interna
tional/americas/06mexico.html?_r=0.

Mears, B. (2014, February 12). Analysis: Justice Thomas comments spark fresh debate on race.
CNN Politics. Retrieved from http://www.cnn.com/2014/02/12/politics/clarence-thom-
as-racism/.

"Measuring America: The decennial census from 1790 to 2000." (2015). *U.S. Census Bureau*.
Decennial Census data. Retrieved from https://www.census.gov/history/www/programs/
demographic/decennial_census.html.

"Medal of Honor Recipients: African American World War II Medal of Honor Recipients."
(2015). *U.S. Army*. Retrieved from http://www.history.army.mil/moh/mohb.html.

Mehta, J. (2013, May/June). Why American education fails: And how lessons from abroad
could improve it. *Foreign Affairs*. Vol. 92, No. 3, p. 105-116.

Menon, R., & Fuller, G. E. (2000, March/April). Russia's ruinous Chechen war. *Foreign Affairs*.
Retrieved from http://www.foreignaffairs.com/articles/55844/rajan-menon-and-graham-e-
fuller/russias-ruinous-chechen-war.

"Mobility measured: America is no less socially mobile than it was a generation ago." (2014,
February 1). *The Economist*.

Moeller, S. (2004, March 18). Think again: Bush's war on terror. *Center for American Progress*.
Retrieved from https://www.americanprogress.org/issues/security/news/2004/03/18/615/
think-again-bushs-war-on-terror/.

Moran, S. (2015). Kant's conception of pedagogy. *South African Journal of Philosophy*. Vol. 34/1,
pp. 29–37.

Myers, D., & Pitkin, J. (2010). *Assimilation today: Evidence shows the latest immigrants to America
are following in our history's footsteps*. Washington, DC: Center for American Progress.

Myre, G. (2013, April 20). Boston bombings point to growing threat of homegrown terrorism. *National
Public Radio*. Retrieved from http://www.npr.org/blogs/thetwo-way/2013/04/20/177958045/
boston-bombings-point-to-growing-threat-of-homegrown-terrorism.

Nakamura, D., & Harris, H. R. (2015, October 10). 20 years after the Million Man March, a
fresh call for justice on the Mall. *The Washington Post*. Retrieved from https://www.wash

ingtonpost.com/politics/20-years-after-the-million-man-march-a-fresh-call-for-justice-on-the-mall/2015/10/10/b3d8ffca-6f66-11e5-b31c-d80d62b53e28_story.html.

Napolitano, J. (2010). *Quadrennial Homeland Security Review Report (QHSR)*. Washington, DC: Government Printing Office.

Napolitano, J. (2012). *Department of Homeland Security Strategic Plan: Fiscal years 2012–2016*. Washington, DC: US Government Printing Office.

"Native Americans say US violated human rights: A Native American group is asking the international community to charge the United States with human rights violations in hopes of getting help with a land claim." (2014, April 14). *Associated Press*. Retrieved from AOL News at http://www.aol.com/article/2014/04/14/native-americans-say-us-violated-human-rights/20868905/?icid=maing-grid7 | main5 | dl19 | sec1_lnk2%26pLid%3D464622.

Nebraska Studies. The missionary spirit: The conversion struggle. *Nebraska Studies*. Retrieved from http://www.nebraskastudies.org/0400/frameset_reset.html?http://www.nebraskas tudies.org/0400/stories/0401_0129.html.

Nelson, R. (2010). *A growing terrorist threat? Assessing "Homegrown" extremism in the United States*. Center for Strategic & International Studies A report of the CSIS homeland security and counterterrorism program. Washington, DC: CSIS.

Nelson, R., & Bodurian, B. (2010, March). A growing terrorist threat? Assessing "Homegrown" extremism in the United States. *Center for Strategic & International Studies A report of the CSIS homeland security and counterterrorism program*. Washington, DC. Retrieved from http://csis.org/files/publication/100304_Nelson_GrowingTerroristThreat_Web.pdf.

Nelson, S. S. (2013, September 16). German nationalists protest against Muslim immigration. *National Public Radio*. Retrieved from http://www.dailystormer.com/german-nation alists-protest-against-muslim-immigration/.

NewsOne. (2013, April 19). Muslim woman attacked after Boston Marathon bombings. *NewsOne*. Retrieved from http://newsone.com/2396424/heba-abolaban-boston-mara thon-bombings-terrorist/.

Nimmo, K. (2011, July 6). Russian FSB Boss: Internet a Haven for Terrorists. *InfoWars.com*. Retrieved from http://www.infowars.com/russian-fsb-boss-internet-a-haven-for-terrorists/.

Nuzzi, O. (2015, November 16). Jeb Bush & Ted Cruz only want to save Christians. *The Daily Beast*. Retrieved from http://www.thedailybeast.com/articles/2015/11/16/jeb-cruz-only-want-to-save-christians.html.

Oakes, E. T. (2008, January 29). Atheism and violence. *First Things*. Retrieved from http://www.firstthings.com/web-exclusives/2008/01/atheism-and-violence.

Obama, B. (2011a). *Presidential Policy directive – 8: National Preparedness*. Washington, DC: Government Printing Office.

Obama, B. (2011b). *Empowering local partners to prevent violent extremism in the United States*. Washington, DC: Government Printing Office.

Obama, B. (2015, February). *National security strategy*. Washington, DC: GPO.

Obeidallah, D. (2015, May 18). America snores when Christian terrorist threatens to massacre Muslims. *The Daily Beast*. Retrieved from http://www.thedailybeast.com/arti cles/2015/05/18/guess-why-this-christian-terrorist-plot-against-muslims-isn-t-getting-any-press.html.

O'Connor, A. (2011, July 27). Mexican cartels move into human trafficking. *The Washington Post.* Retrieved from http://www.washingtonpost.com/world/americas/mexican-car tels-move-into-human-trafficking/2011/07/22/gIQArmPVcI_story.html.

Office of the Inspector General. (2004, April). *A review of the federal bureau of prisons' selection of Muslim religious services providers.* Washington, DC: U.S. Department of Justice.

Oliker, O. (2013, May 6). Searching for clues on the brothers Tsarnarev. *Rand.* Retrieved from http://www.rand.org/blog/2013/05/searching-for-clues-on-the-brotherstsarnarev.html.

O'Reilly, B. (2014, July 2). Talking points: America growing angrier at the federal government. *Fox News,* video available at http://www.foxnews.com/on-air/oreilly/index.html.

Owens, E. (2012, November 26). Texas school teach Boston tea party as act of terrorism. *The Daily Caller.* Retrieved from http://dailycaller.com/2012/11/26/texas-schools-teach-bos ton-tea-party-as-act-of-terrorism/.

Page, J., & Levin, N. (2014, June 24). Web Preaches Jihad to China's Muslim Uighurs: China Says Internet, Social Media Incite Terrorism Among Uighur Minority. *The Wall Street Journal.* Retrieved from http://www.wsj.com/articles/web-preaches-jihad-to-chinas-mus lim-uighurs-1403663568.

Panza, S. (2014, July 2). Furious California citizens block buses carrying illegal immigrants, force them to turn around. *IJReview.* Retrieved from http://www.ijreview.com/2014/07/152958- even-california-citizens-are-angrily-protesting-against-obamas-plan-to-bus-illegal-aliens- all-over-america/.

Papademetriou, D. (2005, September 1). The global struggle with illegal migration: No end in sight. *Migration Information* Source, Migration Policy Institute. Retrieved from http:// www.migrationpolicy.org/article/global-struggle-illegal-migration-no-end-sight.

Parikh, R. (2006). White males, racism and Christian fundamentalism in American politics. *Sulekha.com.* Retrieved from http://creative.sulekha.com/white-males-racism-and-chris tian-fundamentalism-in-american-politics_190267_blog.

Patten, E., & Lopez, M. H. (2013, July 22). Are unauthorized immigrants overwhelmingly democrats? *Pew Research Center.* Retrieved from http://www.pewresearch.org/fact- tank/2013/07/22/are-unauthorized-immigrants-overwhelmingly-democrats/.

Peck, M. (2013, August 20). Russia Says Cyberspace is New 'Theater of War.' *Forbes.* Retrieved from http://www.forbes.com/sites/michaelpeck/2013/08/20/russia-says-cyberspace-is-new- theater-of-war/.

Post, J. (2005, August). When hatred is bred in the bone: Psycho-cultural foundations of con temporary terrorism. *Political Psychology,* Vol. 26, No. 4, pp. 615–636.

Powell, W. (1971). *The anarchist cookbook.* Fort Lee: Barricade Books.

Preston, J. (2013, September 23). Number of illegal immigrants in U.S. may be on rise again, estimates say. *The New York Times.* Retrieved from http://www.nytimes.com/2013/09/24/ us/immigrant-population-shows-signs-of-growth-estimates-show.html?_r=0.

Public Enemy. (1991). *By the time I get to Arizona.* Written by Ridenhour, C., Rinaldo, G., & Shocklee, H. Produced by Island Def Jam Group. Video available on YouTube at http:// www.youtube.com/watch?v=zrFOb_f7ubw; lyrics available at http://www.publicenemy. com/album/10/34/by-the-time-i-get-to-arizona.html.

Qutb. S. (1953/2000). *Social justice in Islam* (J. B. Hardie, & H. Algar, Trans.). Oneonta: Islamic Publications International.

Qutb, S. (1991). *The Islamic concept and its characteristics.* (Mohammed Moinuddin Siddiqui Trans.). Plainfield: American Trust Publications.

Qutb, S. (2005) *Milestones.* (2nd Ed). Damascus: Dar al-Ilm.

"Race and Higher education: Not black and white. Asians object to affirmative action." (2014, March 22–28). *The Economist.*

Rasley, G. (2014, July 3). Murrieta shows citizens can strike back against illegal alien invasion. *Conservative HQ.* Retrieved from http://www.conservativehq.com/article/17653-murrie ta-shows-citizens-can-strike-back-against-illegal-alien-invasion.

Religion Statistics. (2014). U.S. Census Bureau. Retrieved from http://www.census.gov/com pendia/statab/cats/population/religion.html.

"Reports 1: Religious affiliation" and "Report 2: Religious beliefs & practices/social & political views." (2014). *Pew Forum.* Retrieved from http://religions.pewforum.org/reports.

Resnick, G. (2015, September 29). Seven times the Taliban was supposedly defeated. *The Daily Beast.* Retrieved from http://www.thedailybeast.com/articles/2015/09/29/sev en-times-the-taliban-was-supposedly-defeated.html.

Rice, C. (2007). *Trafficking in persons reports.* Washington, DC: US Government Printing Office.

Rice, Z. (2016, January 20). How Fresno, California, became hotspot for anti-Sikh violence in America. *Identities.mic.* Retrieved from https://mic.com/articles/132552/how-fresno-cali fornia-became-a-hotspot-for-anti-sikh-violence-in-america#.6gvZgupNA.

Riddell, K. (2014, April 9). Sheriffs warn of violence from Mexican cartels deep into interior of U.S. *The Washington Times.* Retrieved from http://www.washingtontimes.com/news/2014/ apr/9/sheriffs-warn-of-violence-from-mexican-cartels-dee/?page=all.

Robbins, L., & Hamill, S. D. (2009, April 4). Gunman kills 3 police officers in Pittsburgh. *The New York Times.* Retrieved from http://www.nytimes.com/2009/04/05/us/05pittsburgh. html.

Roberts, P. (2007). The years on: Engaging the work of Paulo Freire in the 21st Century. *Studies in Philosophy & Education,* Vol. 26, pp. 505–508.

Robertz, F. J. (2007, July 30). Deadly dreams: what motivates school shootings? [Preview]. *Scientific American.* [Excerpt from *The science of gun violence and gun control in the U.S.*] Retrieved from http://www.scientificamerican.com/article/deadly-dreams/?page=3.

Rockwell, N. (1958, September 20). *Runaway.* Retrieved from http://www.art.com/products/ p9388040471-sa-i5446828/norman-rockwell-runaway-september-20-1958.htm.

Rodgers, E. (2015, August 12). The insiders: The Black Lives Matter movement is bad for Democrats. *The Washington Post.* Retrieved from https://www.washingtonpost.com/blogs/ post-partisan/wp/2015/08/12/the-insiders-the-black-lives-matter-movement-is-bad-for-democrats/.

Roediger, D. (2005). *Working toward whiteness: How America's immigrants became white: The strange journey from Ellis Island to the suburbs.* New York: The Perseus Books Group.

Romano, J. (2015, June 20). Romano: Killer's crusade for white America defies logic. *Tampa Bay Times*. Retrieved from http://moms.tampabay.com/news/courts/criminal/romano-kill ers-crusade-for-white-america-defies-logic/2234485.

Rose, S. (2014, October 7). The Isis propaganda war: A hi-tech media jihad. *The Guardian*. Retrieved from http://www.theguardian.com/world/2014/oct/07/isis-media-machine-pro paganda-war.

Ross, B., & Ferran, L. (2011, September 30). How Anwar al-Awlaki inspired terror from across the globe. *ABC News*. Retrieved from http://abcnews.go.com/Blotter/anwar-al-awlaki-in spired-terror/story?id=14643383.

Rubin, A. J., Blaise, L., Nossiter, A., & Breeden, A. (2016, July 15). France says truck attacker was Tunisia native with record of petty crime. *The New York Times*. Retrieved from http:// www.nytimes.com/2016/07/16/world/europe/attack-nice-bastille-day.html.

Rudolph, E. (2013, April 24). Are Christians more violent than Muslims? *Abagond*. Retrieved from http://abagond.wordpress.com/2013/04/24/are-christians-more-violent-than-muslims/.

Rustom, R. (2012, September 15). Why most terrorists are Muslims. *Islam Watch*. Retrieved from http://www.islam-watch.org/authors/142-rami/1145-why-most-terrorists-are-mus lims.html.

Saad, L. (2013, October 31). U.S. crime is up, but Americans don't seem to have noticed. *Gallup*. Retrieved from http://www.theatlantic.com/magazine/archive/2009/01/the-end-of-white-america/307208/.

Said, E. W. (1978/1994). *Orientalism*. New York: Vintage Books.

Said, E. W. (1993). *Cultural imperialism*. New York: Vintage Books.

Said, E. W. (1994). *Representations of the intellectual: The Reith lectures*. New York: Vintage Books.

Said, E. W. (2004). *Humanism and democratic criticism*. New York: Columbia University Press.

Sanchez, T, & Cano, R. (2014, July 5). Dueling immigration rallies in Calif. Town: 6 arrested. *The Desert Sun*. Retrieved from http://www.desertsun.com/story/news/local/2014/07/04/ murrieta-california-border-patrol-immigration-protests-undocumented-immigrants-ju ly-fourth/12217279/.

Sakuma, A. (2015, August 6). Immigration issues dominate opening of GOP presidential debate. *MSNBC*. Retrieved from http://www.msnbc.com/msnbc/immigration-issues-dom inate-opening-gop-presidential-debate.

Sankaran, K. (2003). Indian way in counterinsurgency. In Efraim, I. (Ed.) *Democracies and small wars*, pp. 85–97. Portland: Frank Crass.

Savage, C. (2014, June 23). Court releases large parts of memo approving killing of American in Yemen. *The New York Times*. Retrieved from http://www.nytimes.com/2014/06/24/us/ justice-department-found-it-lawful-to-target-anwar-al-awlaki.html?_r=0.

Seibert, T. (2013, February 27). Ocalan negotiations bring Turkey a step closer to peace with Kurds. *The National*. Retrieved from http://www.thenational.ae/news/world/europe/oca lan-negotiations-bring-turkey-a-step-closer-to-peace-with-kurds.

Serrano, R. Blankstein, A., & Gerber, M. (2013, June 8). Santa Monica shooting suspect, possible motive identified, officials say. *Los Angeles Times*. Retrieved from http://arti

cles.latimes.com/2013/jun/08/local/la-me-ln-santa-monica-gunman-identified-john-za wahri-20130608.

Sewall, S. (2016, March 30). Our common struggle against violent extremism. *US Department of State.* Retrieved from http://www.state.gov/j/remarks/255314.htm.

Schanzer, D., Kurzman, C., & Moosa, E. (2010). Anti-terror lessons of Muslim-Americans. *Duke University.* Retrieved from http://www.google.com/url?sa=t&rct=j&q=&esrc=s&source=web&cd=1&ved=0CB0QFjAA&url=http%3A%2F%2Fsites.duke.edu%2Ftcths%2Ffiles%2F2013%2F06%2FSchanzer_Kurzman_Moosa_Anti-Terror_Lessons1.pdf&ei=ZqneU6uTL9PooATEiIHQBA&usg=AFQjCNETb-hEGBweLfZYZMkmPkqYfv_xpw&bvm=bv.72197243,d.cGU.

Schubert, W. H. (2008). Perspectives on the pedagogy of democracy. *Curriculum and Training Dialogue,* Vol. 10/1-2, pp. 157–164.

Schladen, M. (2014, July 2). DPS: Cartels helping immigrant children enter US illegally. *El Paso Times.* Retrieved from http://www.kfiam640.com/media/podcast-handel-on-demand-BillHandel/immigration-crisis-7a-0703-24985857/.

Schoch, J. (2012, November 9). 20 athletes we wish were better role models. *Bleacher Report.* Retrieved from http://bleacherreport.com/articles/1394702-20-athletes-we-wish-were-better-role-models.

Schroeter, S. (2013). "The way it works" doesn't: Theatre of the oppressed as critical pedagogy and counternarrative. *Canadian Journal of Education,* Vol. 36/4, pp. 394–415.

Schmidt, M. S., & Perez-Pena, R. (2015, December 4). F.B.I. treating San Bernardino attack as terrorism case. *The New York Times.* Retrieved from http://www.nytimes.com/2015/12/05/us/tashfeen-malik-islamic-state.html.

Sergie, M. A., & Johnson, T. (2015, March 5). Boko Haram. *Council on Foreign Relations.* Retrieved from http://www.cfr.org/nigeria/boko-haram/p25739.

Shapira, I. (2010, March 7). Pentagon shooter's spiral from early promise to madness. *The Washington Post.* Retrieved from http://www.washingtonpost.com/wp-dyn/content/article/2010/03/06/AR2010030602537.html.

Shrestha, N. (2010, September 29). Explore other cultures to understand your own. *Collegiate Times.* Retrieved from http://www.collegiatetimes.com/opinion/columnists/article_8c7d4da2-8ff9-548f-857e-03b9384e2193.html.

Silsby, G. (2013, August 7). Why people take the risk of illegal immigration. *Futurity:* University of Southern California Study. Retrieved from http://www.futurity.org/why-people-take-the-risk-of-illegal-immigration/.

Singh, J. (2014, June 16). Robert Bergdhal's beard is not the threat. *Huffington Post.* Retrieved from http://www.huffingtonpost.com/jasjit-singh/robert-bergdahls-beard-is_b_5500749.html.

Sizgorich, T. (2008). *Violence and belief in late antiquity: Militant devotion in Christianity and Islam (Divinations: Rereading late ancient religion).* Philadelphia: University of Pennsylvania Press.

Sloan, A. A. A., & Al-Ashanti, A. (2011). *A critique of the methodology of Anwar Al-Awlaki and his errors in the Fiqh of Jihad.* Leyton: Jamiah Media.

Snowden, P. (2014). The revolution will be uploaded: Vernacular video and the Arab Spring. *Culture Unbound.* Vol. 6, pp. 401–429.

Snyder, M. (2013, August 10). 19 very disturbing facts on illegal immigration every American should know. *Right Side News*. Retrieved from http://www.rightsidenews. com/2013081033026/us/homeland-security/19-very-disturbing-facts-on-illegal-immi gration-every-american-should-know.html.

Soergel, A. (2015, February 3). Better test scores could mean trillions of dollars for the U.S. economy. *US News & World Report*. Retrieved from http://www.usnews.com/news/arti cles/2015/02/03/better-test-scores-could-mean-trillions-of-dollars-for-the-us-economy.

Southern Poverty Law Center (SPLC). (2009, February 26). Hate group numbers up by 54% since 2000. *Southern Poverty Law Center*. Retrieved from http://www.splcenter.org/get-in formed/news/hate-group-numbers-up.

Sonner, S. (2014, July 10). Report shows how Cliven Bundy has emboldened right-wing extremists. *Huffington Post*. Retrieved from http://www.huffingtonpost.com/2014/07/10/ cliven-bundy-report_n_5574512.html.

Squires, N. (2008, October 5). Protests in Italy against escalating racism. *The Telegraph*. Retrieved from http://www.telegraph.co.uk/news/worldnews/europe/italy/3141066/Pro tests-in-Italy-against-escalating-racism.html.

Stern, J. (2000). *The ultimate terrorists*. Boston: Harvard University Press.

Stavridis, J., & Girrier, R. (2007). *Watch officer's guide* (15th Ed.). Newport: Naval Institute Press.

Straziuso, J., Forliti, A., & Watson, J. (2012, January 14). Al Shabaab's American recruits in Somalia. *Huffington Post*. Retrieved from http://www.huffingtonpost.com/2012/01/14/ americans-al-shabaab_n_1206279.html.

Takeda, A. (2015, July 16). Colorado theater shooter James Holmes found guilty of first-degree murder. *US Weekly*. Retrieved from http://www.usmagazine.com/celebrity-news/news/col orado-theater-shooting-verdict-james-holmes-found-guilty-of-murder-2015167.

Taraby, J. (2013, August 14). A rare meeting with reclusive Turkish spiritual leader Fethul-lah Gulen. *The Atlantic*. Retrieved from http://www.theatlantic.com/international/ archive/2013/08/a-rare-meeting-with-reclusive-turkish-spiritual-leader-fethullah-gu len/278662/.

Tashman, B. (2011, March 29). Tea party group warns of white "extinction" in America. *Right Wing Watch*. Retrieved from http://www.rightwingwatch.org/content/tea-party-group-warns-white-extinction-america.

Thaler, D., Brown, R. Gonzalez, G., Mobley, B, & Roshan, P. (2013). *Improving the U.S. mil-itary's understanding of unstable environments vulnerable to violent extremist groups: Insights from social science*. Santa Monica: RAND.

"The church and racism: Toward a more fraternal society." (1997). *Political Commission Jus-tice and Peace*, Eternal World Television Network (EWTN), Global Catholic Network. Retrieved from http://www.ewtn.com/library/curia/pcjpraci.htm.

"The path of least resistance: The republicans may be groping their way to compromise." (2014, February 8). *The Economist*.

"The Dish: Biased and Balanced." (2014). Retrieved from http://dish.andrewsullivan. com/2014/04/28/the-pernicious-poison-of-palin-ctd.

The White House. (2015, February 18). Fact sheet: The White House Summit on countering violent extremism. *Office of the White House Press Secretary*. Retrieved from https://www.whitehouse.gov/the-press-office/2015/02/18/fact-sheet-white-house-summit-countering-violent-extremism.

Thompson, P. (2010, May 16). Autistic child charged with terrorism over school drawing. *The Telegraph*. Retrieved from http://www.telegraph.co.uk/news/worldnews/northamerica/usa/7731513/Autistic-boy-charged-with-terrorist-offence.html.

Tiger, C. (1999). *The classic treasury of Aesop's fables*. (Caroline E. Tiger, Ed.). Philadelphia: Running Press.

Toews, V. (2013). *2013 public report on the terrorist threat to Canada*. Canada; Ministry of Public Safety.

Tone, H., & Uwimana, S. (2013, February 1). 10 myths conservative media will use against immigration reform. *Media Matters for America*. Retrieved from http://mediamatters.org/research/2013/02/01/10-myths-conservative-media-will-use-against-im/192494.

Tse-tung, M. (2012). On guerrilla warfare. San Bernardino: Import Books.

Tures, J. (2009). Do terrorists win elections? *Homeland Security Affairs*, September. Vol. V, No. 3, p. 1-10. Retrieved from http://www.hsaj.org/?fullarticle=5.3.5.

Tzu, S. (1994). *The art of war* (R. D. Sawyer, Trans.). New York: Fall River Press.

U.S. Census Bureau. (2012). Statistical abstract of the United States: 2012. U.S. Census Bureau. Retrieved from http://www.google.com/url?sa=t&rct=j&q=&esrc=s&source=web&cd=1&ved=0CB0QFjAA&url=http%3A%2F%2Fwww.census.gov%2Fprod%2F2011pubs%2F12statab%2Fpop.pdf&ei=UHDeU8n9F8XaoATLr4D4DQ&usg=AFQjCNHabHgDXuO-kS1UMDIUFyYAbw8CSQ&bvm=bv.72197243,d.cGU.

U.S. Department of Health and Human Services (USDHHS). (2016, June 23.). Community immunity. Retrieved from http://www.vaccines.gov/basics/protection/.

Utley, R. M., & Washburn, W. E. (2002). *Indian wars*. New York: American Heritage Press.

Vadum, M. (2015, October 9). The Million Man March comes to Washington: Violence on the Horizon? *Front Page magazine*. Retrieved from http://www.frontpagemag.com/fpm/260399/million-man-fraud-comes-washington-matthew-vadum.

Venugopal, A. (2011, May 24). Immigrants assimilate more successfully in the U.S. than in Europe: Report. *WNYC*. Retrieved from http://www.wnyc.org/story/136690-immigrants-assimilate-more-successfully-us-europe-according-report/.

Vetter, R. (2013, August 5). Border security costs taxpayers $12 Billion. *IVN*. Retrieved from http://ivn.us/2013/08/05/border-security-costs-taxpayers-12-billion-2/.

Vigdor, J. (2008). *Measuring immigrant assimilation in the United States*. Manhattan: Center for Civic Innovation.

Vinzant, J. H. (2006). *Supreme Court interpretation and policy making in American Indian Policy*. Dissertation, Southern Illinois University, UMI Number: 3229889

Von Clausewitz, C. (1976/2008). On war. (M. Howard, & P. Paret, Trans. & Eds.). Princeton: Princeton University Press.

Voorhees, J. (2013, April 23). Slatest PM: How the Tsarnaev Brothers learned to make their bombs. *The Slate*. Retrieved from http://www.slate.com/blogs/the_slatest/2013/04/23/inspire_magazine_tsarnaev_brothers_used_al_qaida_magazine_for_directions.html.

Walser, R., McNeill, J. B., & Zuckerman. (2011). The human tragedy of illegal immigration: Greater efforts needed to combat smuggling and violence. *The Heritage Foundation.* Retrieved from http://www.heritage.org/research/reports/2011/06/the-human-trage dy-of-illegal-immigration-greater-efforts-needed-to-combat-smuggling-and-violence.

Warrick, J. (2015). *Black flags: The rise of ISIS.* New York: Doubleday.

Watanabe, T. (2015, November 20). Occidental College protesters to end sit-in, vow to keep fighting bias. *The Los Angeles Times.* Retrieved from http://www.latimes.com/local/lanow/ la-me-ln-oxy-protest-ends-20151120-story.html.

Watson, J. (2014, July 2). Buses with migrant families rerouted amid protest. *Associated Press.* Retrieved from http://talkingpointsmemo.com/news/buses-with-migrant-families-rerout ed-protests.

Weathers, C. (2014, June 4). Jon Stewart chides Fox news: You'd like Bob Bergdahl's beard if Hewas on 'Duck Dynasty.' *Alternet.* Retrieved from http://www.alternet.org/news-amp-pol itics/jon-stewart-chides-fox-news-youd-bob-bergdahls-beard-if-he-was-duck-dynasty.

Wellman, J. (2013, July 7). Should Christians have non Christian friends? *What Christians Want to Know.* Retrieved from http://www.whatchristianswanttoknow.com/should-chris tians-have-non-christian-friends/.

Werner, E., & Caldwell, A. A. (2014, July 14). Possible compromise emerges on border security. *Associated Press.* Retrieved from http://www.aol.com/article/2014/07/10/possible-com promise-emerges-on-border-request/20928845/?icid=maing-grid7 | main5 | dl17 | sec1_ lnk2%26pLid%3D500053.

Wilber, D. Q. (2010, January 7). Von Brunn, white supremacist Holocaust museum shooter, dies. *The Washington Post.* Retrieved from http://www.washingtonpost.com/wp-dyn/con tent/article/2010/01/06/AR2010010604095.html.

Williams, P. (2007). *The day of Islam; The annihilation of America and the western world.* New York: Prometheus Books.

Williams, P. (2014, May 30). Florida Man Identified as Syria Suicide Bomber. NBC News. Retrieved from http://www.nbcnews.com/news/investigations/florida-man-identified-syr ia-suicide-bomber-n118926.

Wolf, N. (2015, February 20). Chilling report details how Elliot Rodger executed murderous rampage. *The Guardian.* Retrieved from https://www.theguardian.com/us-news/2015/ feb/20/mass-shooter-elliot-rodger-isla-vista-killings-report.

Woodyard, C., & Heath, B. (2015, December 3). San Bernardino shooters lived a double life. *USA Today.* Retrieved from http://www.usatoday.com/story/news/2015/12/03/san-ber nardino-shooter/76710658/.

Woodsome, K. (2013, April 26). Immigration shapes US political parties as much as demographics. *Voice of America.* Retrieved from http://www.voanews.com/content/immigra tion-shapes-us-parties-as-much-as-demographics/1649600.html.

Wright, B. (1916). *The real Mother Goose* (Blanche F. Wright, Illus.). New York: Scholastic, Inc.

Zakaria, F. (2013, January/February). Can America be fixed? The new crisis of democracy. *Foreign Affairs.*

Zalikind, S. (2015, June 22). How ISIS's 'Attack America' Plan Is Working. *The Daily Beast*. Retrieved from http://www.thedailybeast.com/articles/2015/06/22/how-isis-s-attack-amer ica-plan-is-working.html.

Zein, Q. (2007, May 14). The list: The world's fastest growing religions. *Foreign Policy*. Retrieved from http://www.foreignpolicy.com/articles/2007/05/13/the_list_the_worlds_ fastest_growing_religions.

Ziv, S. (2014, November 25). Report details Adam Lanza's life before Sandy Hook. US *Newsweek*. Retrieved from http://www.newsweek.com/report-details-adam-lanzas-life-sandy-hook-shootings-286867.

Zorn, J. (2001). Henry Giroux's pedagogy of the oppressed. *Academic Questions*. Fall.

INDEX

A

'AbdurRahman Sloan, Abu Ameenah, 34
Abusalha, Moner Mohammad, 110
Acculturation, 95–97
Advance and transfer, 131–133
Afghanistan, 8, 18, 26
African Americans and police, 108–109
Al-Amriki, Omar Hammami, 109–110
Al-Ashanti, 'AbdulHaq, 34
Al-Awlaki, Anwar, 18–19, 27, 28,
    109–110
  death of, 81
  success as global spokesperson for Al
    Qaeda, 34–35
Al-Baghdadi, Abu Bakr, 4, 18, 27
Ali-Shaykh, Shaykh Saalih bin "Abdul"
    Azeez, 136
Al Qaeda, 13, 18, 109–110, 132
  Al-Awlaki as spokesperson for, 34–35
  model of terrorism, 77
  plans to break American will, 19
Al Qaeda Training Manual, 31–35
Al-Rashid, Harun, 27
Al Shabaab, 109–110
Al Zawahiri, Ayman, 18, 19, 27, 34
  as student of history, 19
America. See United States, the
American-Arab Anti-Discrimination Com-
    mittee (ADC), 14
American Civil Liberties Union (ACLU),
    14
Anti-immigration attitudes, 94, 100
  on the right, 101–102
Anti-immigrationism, 101–102
Art of War, The, 33
Assimilation of immigrants, 94
  failure in, 97–98
Atheism, 112, 113
Athletes as heroes, 25

B

Baldwin, Brooke, 21
Banking education, 1–2
Banking hegemony, 134–135
    analysis of American strategy on
        preventing violent extremism, 12–14
    domestic area and American, 20–22
    faces of American civilization and, 69
    global area and American, 16–20
Beck, Glenn, 21
Becoming, 11
Bergdhal, Bob, 110–111
Bergdhal, Bowe, 110–111
Bias, unconscious, 69
Bin Laden, Usama, 4, 18, 27, 28, 34
    death of, 77
    as student of history, 19, 20
    use of the Internet, 34
Black Lives Matter movement, 109
Blitzer, Wolf, 21
Book of One Thousand and One Nights, The, 27
Born Here, 29
Boston Marathon bombings, 81, 97, 99,
    110, 114
Brussels, Belgium, attacks of 2016, 19
Buddhism, 112
Bundy, Clive, 110, 111
Bushnaq, Inea, 27
By the Time I get to Arizona, 29, 30

C

Caliphate, Islamic, 19, 27
Captain America character, 24
Cavuto, Neil, 21
Census Bureau, U. S., 64–65, 72
Chomsky, Noam, 2, 13, 21, 135, 136
Christianity, American
    extremism in, 110–112
    faces of American civilization and, 68–70
    faith, conversion, and fundamentalism
        and, 70–72

Civilization, faces of American, 68–70
Civil liberties, 14
CNN, 21
Colonialism, 18, 21
Communism, 3
Critical pedagogy, 2–3, 11
Critical thinking and social justice, 2
Crusading, 23
Culture and Power in the Classroom, 22

D

Da Arabian MC, 29–30
Darder, Antonia, 2, 21, 22
Deism, 111
Demographic shift, United States', 63–66
    decay of religious tolerance and, 113–114
    diaspora and tribalism and, 72–75
    enriching America's third civilization
        and, 79–80
    fear of change and, 112–113
    future of violent extremism and, 114–115
    violent extremism in response to, 66–68
Department of Homeland Security, U. S.,
    91, 95, 105
Department of Justice, U. S., 76
Diaspora and tribalism, 72–75
Discovery, 15–16, 35
Disneyland, 101
Doggart, Robert, 81
Duck Dynasty, 111

E

Education, banking, 1–2
Elite, hegemonic, 18, 20–21, 69
Ellison, Keith, 70–71, 112
Emanuel African Methodist Episcopal
    Church, 67
Empathy, 20–21
Empowering Local Partners to Prevent Violent
    Extremism in the United States, 13–14

Extremists
    Christian, 110–112
    Islamic, 109–110

F

Failure to assimilate, 97–98
Faith and power, 70–72, 83
Faith & Heritage Newsletter, 68
Faiths of the Founding Fathers, The, 111
Fanon, Frantz, 3, 11, 18, 21, 134
Faraj, Muhammad abd-al-Salam, 18, 19
Farook, Syed, 10, 106
Farook, Tashfeen, 10
Fear of change, 112–113
Fire triangle, 5, 6
Folktales, 24–28
Fort Hood shootings, 34
Fox network, 21, 24
Franklin, Ben, 25
Freire, Paulo, 1–2, 3, 18, 134
Fundamentalism, Christian, 70–72

G

Gangs, street, 76
Giap, Vo Nguyen, 19
Giroux, Henry, 2, 13, 21, 136
Golden Age of Islam, 27
Goode, Virgil, 112
Guevara, Che, 3
Gulen, Fethullah, 109

H

Hasan, Nidal, 34, 110
Hate, discovering how to, 15–16, 21
Hegemonically provoked violent extremism, 4–10
Hegemonic dyadic relations (HDR), 7–8
Hegemonic elite, 18, 20–21, 69

Hegemonic oppression, 10–12
Heroes, childhood, 24–28
Hinduism, 112, 113
Hitler, Adolph, 82
Holmes, David, 111
Homegrown violent extremism in the U. S., 76–78, 107–109
    calculus of convergent variables in creating, 82–83
Human trafficking, 105–106
Huntington, Samuel, 113
Hurricane Katrina, 75, 82

I

Iceberg of violent extremism, 9–10
Illegal aliens, 104
Illegal immigrants, 102–103, 104
Illich, Ivan, 2, 134
Immigrants, 67–68
    acculturation of, 95–97
    analysis of threats now and in the future regarding, 105–106
    diaspora and tribalism among, 72–75
    effects of, 94–95
    illegal, 102–103, 104
    and immigration as IED components, 92–94
    inferences of policies towards, 106–107
    the left and proimmigrationism towards, 103–105
    power, 98–100
    refugee, 65, 136
    the right and antiimmigrationism towards, 94
    strengthening America, 80
India, 73, 81
Intelligentsia, 80
Internet, the, 33, 80–81
Iraq, 8, 26
Islam, 108, 112–113
    caliphate, 19, 27
    decay of religious tolerance towards, 114

extremists, 109–110
growth in America, 72
heroes of, 26–28
the Quran and, 70–71, 112
Islamic State, 4, 8, 13, 16, 26
training curriculum, 33–34
use of the Internet, 80–81
Islamophobia, 13–14, 22
Israel, 19
It IS about Islam, 21

J

Jefferson, Thomas, 71, 112
Jihad, 18
pedagogical methodology in spreading,
35
social media and, 34
Johnson, Micah, 108–109
Jomini, Antoine-Henri, 33
Judaism, 112, 113
Jurgensmeyer, Mark, 23

K

Khaled, Leila, 4
King, Martin Luther, Jr., 29

L

Lanza, Adam, 15–16
Lawrence, T. E., 17
Leong, Nancy, 20
Lincoln, Abraham, 25

M

Macdonald, Andrew, 21, 23, 34
Macedo, Donaldo, 2, 21
Mao Tse Tung, 20

Marighella, Carlos, 31–32
Marxist theory, 3, 5
McNeil, Terrence, 13
McVeigh, Timothy, 21, 22–24, 71, 99, 108,
110, 111
Media pundits, 21, 24
Milestones, 16, 21
Min erhabi-Who is the Terrorist?, 28–30
Minimanual of the Urban Guerrilla, 31–35
Mixed-race persons, 75
Mormonism, 72, 112
Muhammad, Prophet, 27
Murrah building bombing. See Oklahoma
City bombing
Music videos, 29–30

N

National Council of La Raza, 94–95
National Public Radio, 111
Native Americans, 74, 79, 111–112
Naval shiphandling and violent extremism,
131–133
Neglected Duty, The, 18
Neo-plantationist attitudes, 69
Normalcy, hegemonic, 11

O

Obama, Barack, 13, 75, 94, 101–102
Ocalan, Abdullah, 82
Occidental College, 25
Occidentals vs Orientals, 68
Office of the Inspector General, 76
Oklahoma City bombing, 21, 22–24, 71, 99
On War, 33
Operation Bojinka, 16
Oppression
banking education and, 1–2
banking of hegemony and, 16, 134–135
changes through the last 100 years, 3–4
hegemonic, 10–12

hegemonically provoked violent extremism and, 4–10
learning how to hate and, 15–16, 21
meaning in Marxist and socialist theory, 5
portrayed in music videos, 29–30
power of, 1, 3
O'Reilly, Bill, 21
Orientalism, 17

P

Palestinian-Israeli conflict, 4
Pan-Islamic heroes, 26–27
Paris, France, attacks of 2015, 19, 136
Paternalism, 18
Pedagogy of Freedom, 2
Pedagogy of the Oppressed, 1, 2
Phenomenology of violent extremism, 3–4
Politics of Education, The, 2
Power, immigrant, 98–100
Prison time, 32
Proimmigrationism, 103–105
Public Enemy, 29–30
Pundits, media, 21, 24

Q

Quran, the, 70–71, 112
Qutb, Seyyid, 16, 18, 19, 21, 23, 31, 34

R

Racial Capitalism, 20
Refugees, 65, 136
Regime continuity, violent extremism supporting, 22–24
Religion. *See also* Christianity, American; Islam
  Christian extremism and, 110–112
  decay of tolerance toward, 113–114

fear of change and, 112–113
  Islamic extremism and, 109–110
Resignation, levels of, 7–8
Robertz, Frank, 6
Roediger, David, 20
Roof, Dylan, 22–24, 67, 81
Runaway, 66
Ryan, Paul, 70

S

Said, Edward, 17
San Bernardino, California, attacks of 2015, 10, 97
Sandy Hook Elementary School, 15–16
School shootings, 6, 15–16
Scientific American, 6
September 11, 2001, attacks, 12, 19, 27, 33, 97, 108
Seven Pillars of Wisdom, 17
Shiphandling and violent extremism, 131–133
Siddiqui, Asia, 81
Sikhism, 112
Snowden, Edward, 81
Socialism, 5
Social justice and critical thinking, 2
Social media, 33, 80–81
Stewart, Jon, 110–111
Street gangs, 76
Sun Tzu, 19, 20, 33
Sykes-Picot Agreement, 34
Syria, 136

T

Tale within a Tale, A, 27
Taliban, the, 26, 110–111
Tea Party movement, 94
Terror in the Mind of God, 23
Terrorism. *See* Extremists; Violent extremism

Theory of hegemonically provoked violent extremism, 4–10
Thomas, Clarence, 69
Tokenism, 96–97
Training, terrorist, 31–35
Tribalism and diaspora, 72–75
Tsarnarev brothers, 81, 93, 99, 110, 111
Turkey, 73, 109
Turner Diaries, The, 21, 22–23, 34, 99

U

Unconscious bias, 69
Undocumented aliens, 104
United States, the. *See also* Immigrants
   American hegemony, 10–11
   analysis of strategy on preventing violent extremism by, 12–14
   anti-immigration attitudes in, 94
   banking American hegemony in the domestic area, 20–22
   banking American hegemony in the global arena, 16–20
   citizens turned jihadi terrorists, 109–110
   civil liberties in, 14
   demographic shift in, 63–66
   diaspora and tribalism in, 72–75
   enriching America's third civilization in, 79–80
   ethnic struggles in, 29–30
   faces of American civilizations and, 68–70
   hegemonic authority, 10–11
   immigration policies and agencies, 91–94
   Islamophobia in, 13–14
   mixed-race persons in, 75
   Native Americans and, 74, 79, 111–112
   refugees in, 65, 136
   rise of homegrown violent extremism in, 76–78, 82–83, 107–109
   terrorist attacks in, 10, 12, 16, 19, 27, 33
   welcoming of Immigrants in, 14

USA Freedom Act, 77
USA PATRIOT Act, 5, 77
USS Cole, 27
USS Sullivans, 16

V

Velentzas, Noelle, 81
Violent extremism
   American border security and protection against, 105–106
   analysis of American strategy on preventing, 12–14
   collective interpretation of what is right and defining, 4
   complexities in ending, 135–137
   critical pedagogy of, 2–3
   discovering how to hate and, 15–16
   evolution of terrorist training curriculum and, 31–35
   folktales, heroes and, 24–28
   future of, 114–115
   iceberg of, 9–10
   the Internet and, 33, 80–81
   lessons of Sun Tzu and, 20
   music videos and, 29–30
   naval shiphandling and, 131–133
   phenomenology of, 3–4
   in response to demographic shift, 66–68
   rise of homegrown American, 76–78, 82–83, 107–109
   supporting regime continuity, 22–24
   theory of hegemonically provoked, 4–10
Von Clausewitz, Carl, 33

W

Warning Against Extremism, A, 136
Washington, George, 25
Whiteness, 96, 97
White supremacy movements, 24
Working Toward Whiteness, 20

World Trade Center bombing, 1993, 16, 19,
    20, 109
World War I, 98
Wretched of the Earth, The, 17

X

Xenophobia, 29

Violence Studies

Felix Ó Murchadha, *General Editor*

The Violence Studies series aims to publish work that explores violence in the diverse areas of human life from the bedroom to the battlefield and in its different modes of appearance from language to social and economic structures to the infliction of physical harm. This series is particularly, though not exclusively, directed toward scholars in the areas of philosophy, literature, sociology, and cultural studies. It seeks to encompass a wide range of theoretical approaches and disciplinary orientations investigating the phenomena of violence and how they are expressed and codified in literature, cultural and political practice, and in the forms of human society. It also welcomes works that explore the ways in which violence is inflicted on the non-human world of animals and the environment. We are especially interested in books exploring the intersections of violence and religion, violence in language and rhetoric, as well as studies on the issues of gender, power and ideology as they relate to questions of violence. This series welcomes both individually authored and collaboratively authored books and monographs as well as edited collections of essays and conference proceedings.

For additional information about this series or for the submission of manuscripts, please contact:

Peter Lang Publishing
Acquisitions Department
29 Broadway, 18th Floor
New York, New York 10006

To order other books in this series, please contact our Customer Service Department:

800-770-LANG (within the U.S.)
(212) 647-7706 (outside the U.S.)
(212) 647-7707 FAX

Or browse online by series at:

www.peterlang.com